CW00969633

The GOLDWYN *Touch*

ALSO BY MICHAEL FREEDLAND

Jolie — The Story of Al Jolson
Salute to Irving Berlin
James Cagney
Fred Astaire
Sophie — The Story of Sophie Tucker
Jerome Kern
Errol Flynn (In USA, The Two Lives of Errol Flynn)
Gregory Peck
Maurice Chevalier
Peter O'Toole
The Warner Brothers
Dino — The Dean Martin Story
Jack Lemmon
Katharine Hepburn
So Let's Hear the Applause — The Story of the Jewish Entertainer
The Secret Life of Danny Kaye
Shirley MacLaine

(*And with Morecambe and Wise*)
There's No Answer To That

The GOLDWYN *Touch*

A Biography of Sam Goldwyn

MICHAEL FREEDLAND

HARRAP
LONDON

TO
YEHUDIT

First published in Great Britain 1986
by HARRAP Ltd
19–23 Ludgate Hill, London EC4M 7PD

ISBN 0 245–54262–0

Designed by Roger King Graphic Studios

Printed and bound in Great Britain
by Biddles Ltd, Guildford

CONTENTS

ILLUSTRATIONS

All photographs are reproduced by courtesy of the Kobal Collection

Frances and Sam at the time of *Porgy and Bess,* his last film
Bette Davis in *The Little Foxes*
Mabel Normand – a Sam protégé
The Goldwyn Girls in *Whoopee*
Danny Kay and Dinah Shore in *Up In Arms*

ACKNOWLEDGMENTS

Sam Goldwyn was much more than a collection of mispronounced words and sentences used in ways that would make lexicographers spin in uncontrollable circles.

That he was became very clear to me in my interviews with people who knew him well and recounted his story for me freely.

To them, my profound thanks. Among them were: Sammy Cahn, Saul Chaplin, Jack Cummings, the late Howard Dietz, Irene Dunne, George 'Bullets' Durgom, Julius Epstein, Irving Fein, Mel Frank, Mike Frankovich, John Green, Abby Greshler, Bob Hope, Michael Kidd, Mervyn LeRoy, Rouben Mamoulian, Virginia Mayo, the late Lewis Milestone, Bill Orr, Norman Panama, David Raksin, two gentlemen unrelated by the name of David Rose, Jack Rose, Walter Scharf, Melville Shavelson, Milton Sperling, Hal Wallis, Jack Warner Junior, Billy Wilder and Loretta Young.

Also for their great help my thanks to the librarians of the Academy of Motion Picture Arts and Sciences, Beverly Hills, the British Film Institute and the British Library, and my son Jonathan who helped with research.

And I know only too well that nothing would have been written without the help of my dearest, devoted wife Sara.

Michael Freedland
London, January 1986

INTRODUCTION
Wonder Man

He was the archetypal Hollywood mogul—an immaculate suit on his back, and a command of the English language that wasn't exactly learnt at Harvard, at Oxford or even at a neighbourhood elementary school. Except that what Sam Goldwyn did was in a different class from the other studio bosses.

For one thing he wasn't really a mogul at all; perhaps just a few stars and writers on the books at any one time, with another company distributing the sometimes one or two films he made in a year. And as for that command of the language—he commanded it the way a tailor or a cook in uniform commands an army. The language commanded him—with the frequently humorous, disasterous results that have become part of Hollywood folklore. As he might, or might not, have said: we've, most of us, passed a lot of water since we heard our first Goldwynism.

They were, of course, a minor part of the Goldwyn story—and they tend to minimize the innate sense of superiority that his name also represented.

Like most Hollywood stories, much of what has been written about Goldwyn is shrouded in myths. This book will, I hope, remove some of those shrouds. If myths remain, they will be explained—for there is much to explain about the man most people think of when that altogether deceptive word 'mogul' is used.

Not only was Sam (few called him Samuel—it was a name left for legal documents and the opening card on his movie credits) not a studio boss in the usually accepted sense of the term; he was not even a partner in MGM. How the name Goldwyn got enmeshed between Metro and Mayer is part of the story that follows.

What also follows is a distinctly human tale; a variation surely on the rags to riches story, but rags to riches in not just monetary terms.

It is in some ways a reassessment. People who knew Sam Goldwyn and were frightened of him now see that the velvet glove was a lot thicker—and warmer—than the iron fist they previously imagined it covered.

The rags of bitterness have given way to the richness of shared experiences many of these people would give a great deal to be part of today.

Few holds are going to be barred—or, as Sam might have put it, few bars are going to be held—in telling this story. To do otherwise would make it very incomplete and Sam Goldwyn was a very complete man. But neither am I in the business of trying to destroy the reputation of a man who, even in his toughest most uncompromising phases, was always recognized as inserting a degree of quality into his products that was unknown to his rivals and contemporaries.

'I don't want 'em good,' Harry Warner was reputed to have said to his brothers, 'I want 'em Tuesday.'

Well, if they weren't good for Sam Goldwyn, Tuesday would never come.

Send Sam Goldwyn a poor script, then he was likely to instruct his producers to include him out. This book intends to very much include him in.

1
Palmy Days

Hollywood is the land of the bigger-than-life story, the myth that fiction is always a great deal more fun than fact. So let's start by killing of a myth. Sam Goldwyn was not born Sam Goldfish—or even Goldfisch.

The film town which made a modern art out of changing the nomenclature of prosperity-making actors with strange-sounding names somehow or other never sought to pretend that Sam Goldwyn was born with that gold name in his mouth. Strangely, it also never attempted to point out that calling Mr G. 'Goldfish' was the joke of some perverted immigration clerk at Ellis Island.

It was actually in Warsaw that at the brief ceremony of circumcision—the *brit mila*—in 1882 (give or take a year: there were no birth certificates or other documentation to prove it) he was welcomed into the Jewish fold as Shmuel ben Avraham, Samuel the son of Abraham—Abraham Gelbfisz, a scholar in a city of scholars, a learned man who, had he only had a rouble for every clever thing he had worked out, would have been a millionaire at thirty.

The story is that he probably worked as a tailor, although his head was in the clouds—a *luftmensch*—but his wife Hannah was different. Usually, while he studied, she worked as the local money-lender—which may not have been the most respected profession thereabouts (certainly nothing could have been as respected as being a scholar), but brought in a certain amount of income, since the other clever people in their district were usually not clever enough to earn their own livings in regular instalments, and her services were frequently required. Shmuel plainly picked up his business sense from his mother.

He picked up one other thing from her—a superficial knowledge of the United States. Hannah earned a little money on the side from writing letters to what they all knew as the Goldena Medina—the golden country—for illiterate neighbours. As a woman who could read and write, she was a notable person in their parts.

Warsaw was an unusual city in that last quarter of the nineteenth century. Like today, it was the capital of Poland—except that Poland was a mere province of the Tsarist empire and encouraging the populace to think of it as a capital city was to encourage the risk of insurrection or worse.

It was unusual, particularly in pre-Revolutionary Russia—because about a third of the population was Jewish. Jewish population of the Russia of Alexander II and Alexander III were confined to an area to the West known as the Pale of Settlement. Only in rare cases were they permitted to study outside, let alone carry on busineses. Consequently, they were confined to the agrarian villages and hamlets that have gone down in both history and folklore as the *shtetl*, *Fiddler on the Roof* territory. The exceptions were the Jews who thronged the centres of Jewish learning, like Vilna and Kovna in Lithuania—and Warsaw.

Warsaw was a city of pious families for whom say, working on the Sabbath, eating bread on the Passover or daring to consume meat from an animal which had not been killed in the strictly kosher ritual, was virtually unthinkable.

The 306,000 Jews in the capital had, by 1882, when Shmuel was born, formed the largest community in Europe.

There were distinctly Jewish areas of the city—as there still are in other districts with large Jewish populations; it made it easier to set up their synagogues, kosher butchers—and restaurants and communal institutions. But there was no ghetto. An enforced Jewish residential area had been abolished twenty years earlier and it was left to Hitler to re-establish it, albeit in a fiendishly murderous way which even the endemically anti-Semitic Poles had never considered.

There had been pogroms, but it wasn't until a huge anti-Jewish riot of 1881 that people there started seriously thinking about packing up and leaving. For the most part, even so, they were too busy consolidating what they had.

Most of the bankers and publishers in Warsaw were Jews. Many of the businesses in the city were Jewish owned and, before long, most of the lawyers and doctors there were Jews, too. But they were the exceptions. On the whole, the people were poor, unlettered and with little ambition. If they had aspirations, it was to follow the example of some of Mrs Gelbfisz's customers and aim for the Goldena Medina.

Shmuel also had two sisters, Sally and Manya—who was known as Nettie. They were among those who thought about going to America, but when they talked about it to their parents they might just have easily have been talking about suddenly and miraculously being whisked away into the pages of a fairy story.

But they thought about it even more. Whether they knew much about the way their mother earned her living isn't on record. But what is sure is that they grew to hate and find ever more oppressive the strict religious ways enforced on his family by Abraham, a young man who to them always seemed old—doubtless because he stayed indoors even in bright sunlight and the only exercise he took was to remove and then replace holy books on his shelves.

But his health was still better than Hannah's. She was constantly sick, a factor which, as in the best of those fairy stories, only made her son Shmuel yearn to earn enough to take her away from the daily drudgery and make something of her life and his.

He was, he already determined, an important man. The fact that he was only ten years old was not allowed to curb his ambitions.

At eleven he had left what served as school—like most boys of his age and kind education consisted mainly of daily religious instruction at the local 'cheder', where the lessons were centred around books printed in Hebrew given by tired, bearded and skull-capped men who spoke only in Yiddish.

The eleventh birthday—two years away from that most significant and important event in a Jewish boy's life, his barmitzvah—was agreed as his Day of Freedom. He could leave school and start earning his living—and helping the family earn theirs. He took a job as an office boy. The trouble was that Shmuel was busy thinking every time he picked up the few copecks that made up his week's wages—thinking of the time those copecks would become roubles, and more relevant, when those roubles became dollars, the mysterious currency which his mother had told him about after reading one of those letters to which she was replying.

Now, other boys dutifully presented their pay packets to their mothers and poured their contents into their aprons while they swayed back and forth in rocking-chairs. The women may not have been more than in their thirties or forties but to the children of this generation they were already old and spent.

That fact, together with Hannah's constant illness, should have convinced Shmuel to be a good boy and help at home. In truth, he probably would have wanted to. He loved his mother and, in any case, she was already teaching him about courage and the need to face the problems of the world. But his own intuition of being an important man somehow seemed more urgent.

It was especially so when on his way home one day he was beaten up by an anti-Semitic policeman who, not content with the bruising he had inflicted, robbed the 'Jew boy', as he called him, of his week's earnings.

There was no stopping him now. An important man called Shmuel Gelbfisz was not to be held back.

Shmuel was still only eleven years old when he took it upon himself to pack up and seek that new life. In so doing, he was not only saying goodbye to the way he had been living, but also to the people who had guided that life, his parents.

It was perhaps the first time that the future Samuel Goldwyn showed he was not like other men. Small boys running away from home usually—or so the stories told us—did so wearing the clothes in which they were standing and with their worldly goods wrapped in a handkerchief carried aloft at the end of a large stick.

Shmuel was more complicated. He had taken a suit of his father's to a nearby tailor—he knew the boy in the shop—and ordered it to be cut down to his size. When the suit was ready, he filled its pockets with savings made from the pocket-money he had been earning doing odd jobs and with a little bit more he had borrowed from his mother's interest takings.

With these aids at his disposal, Shmuel Gelbfisz set off for the German border, the inevitable, the only exit gate for Polish Jews wanting to move out.

There were, of course, certain formalities—the purchase of a ticket, which he presumed his assembled riches would cover; and a passport—which he also hoped his money would provide.

Passports were supplied in Warsaw, but not the kind Shmuel could get. He had to just hope that he would be able to hand over a few notes with a handshake to an only-a-little-bit corrupt official who would turn a blind eye in exchange.

His petty official was waiting at thecustoms-point on the banks of the River Oder—with eye averted and hand held out. The required number of roubles were placed in the eager palm . . . and the immigration man immediately handed Shmuel over to the police and accused him of attempted bribery. He was told he would be sent back with a flea in both his ear and his knapsack.

The boy thought quickly—his father's Talmudic mind had not been totally lost on him—and asked to be allowed to go to the lavatory. For a reason not readily understood, the police let him go to relieve himself. Inside the toilet was an open window overlooking the river. Shmuel climbed, took a look at the sight in front of his eyes and without bothering to think too deeply—for the greater the thought the less likely the deed—held his nose and jumped. Within a few minutes he had swum to the German border, which could have represented quite a feat in itself; as it was, in later years, he claimed that until that moment he had never been able to swim a stroke.

The instant bravery paid off and Shmuel found his way to Hamburg, the golden gate to the golden land—for anyone with money to make it happen. On this occasion, Shmuel was less lucky. What with the bribe to the border official—which, needless to say, was not returned with the call to the police—and dropping some of the notes into the icy waters of the Oder, there was virtually nothing at all left of either his money or his mother's when he finally walked down the streets of the German city.

It was a sobering experience. An eleven-year-old boy's stomach feels particularly uncomfortable with no food to put in it. Suddenly all thoughts of adventure and excitement go and in their place a desperate longing for the familiar—to say nothing of parents.

It was wandering through the streets of the Hamburg docklands that he saw a name above a shop doorway that instantly brought back memories and set his heart thumping with a degree of hope he thought he had long before abandoned.

The shop sold gloves, nothing else, just gloves; but inside was the chance that the proprietor would be a 'landsman', an exile from '*der heim*', the old country.

The proprietor was out, but Jacob Libglid was in and the two struck up an immediate rapport. Libglid was the shop-owner's apprentice and before long was plainly thinking that there but for the grace of the God he had been brought up to believe watched everything he did went he.

The boy heard every sentence of Shmuel's story and related to it. He gave him some of his own food supply for the day and then disappeared. What his boss thought about that disappearing act isn't on the record, but what is known is that young Jacob came back with a hat full of coins which he immediately handed over to Shmuel. He had been out collecting enough money to pay for a ticket on a steamship to England.

England? The stories of how people set out for the new world are full of tales of Russian immigrants walking the streets of London's Whitechapel or the Gorbals in Glasgow convinced that they were in New York. That wasn't Shmuel's problem. The ticket money collected by Jacob wouldn't stretch any further. Besides he was planning to go to England because he had relatives in Birmingham, which as far as he was concerned was just a suburb of London. Or was it? It didn't really matter: 'anywhere' might just have easily have been the other side of the moon. But he was an important man and that would carry him wherever he decided to go.

Birmingham was not one of the places that Jewish immigrants made for, on the whole. It was the second biggest city in Britain, created by the Industrial Revolution as a sprawling mass of smoke-belching factories. But it held little attraction for the Jewish newcomers. There were no stories spread by imaginative former residents of Warsaw of its streets being paved with gold. More prosaically, no one had heard of its being famous for its clothing sweat-shops where Jews could work on an assembly line making cheap suits or dresses or blouses (and grab ten minutes to recite their afternoon and evening prayers—and in winter, the morning service too as soon as it got light).

Leeds was the centre of the textile industry and the Jews moved there or to Manchester, the rainwear centre. But London was where it all seemed to happen and it was in the teeming tenements of the East End, just a stone's-throw from the docks where they arrived and so like the Lower East Side of New York, that most of the Jews seemed to settle.

For every Jew who settled in the provinces, two came to London and most of them through that same route. Shmuel came with the others. He hated the slums and the degradation that seemed to be part of the very fabric of Spitalfields and Whitechapel, but found it difficult to get away. He got a night or two's accommodation from the Jews Temporary Shelter. It was an organization set up to provide a roof and a little food for indigent newcomers with the hope and expectation that they would soon move on, leaving room for those who were to arrive on the next boat.

Shmuel wanted to move on even more than the Shelter wanted to get rid of him. He wandered westwards and spent a night or two in Hyde Park—opposite the smart hotels which before very long would be his accepted residence every time he visited the British capital. For the moment, however, all he could do was dream.

That instinctive business sense in him was as present as ever. A hunch told him to pop into a West End pawnbroker—just as that earlier hunch had taken him into the Hamburg glove shop.

He thought that possibly the man who stood under the sign of the three brass balls might speak Polish. Why he thought that is not readily explainable. But he did better than that. He spoke Yiddish. To Shmuel it was no more than an omen, the kind of luck he had a right to expect.

In exchange for two days work, the businessman gave the boy enough money to cover a hitch-hiking trek up the old Roman road to Birmingham, the city where Hannah Gelbfisz's sister had settled when her husband got a job working in a factory that was making irons for fireplaces—pokers and shovels and ashpans—now all relics of a bygone age, but then as essential a part of British life as the mess left on the streets by the horses or the streaky bacon which all his father's teaching had put at the top of his prohibitions list.

To say that Shmuel was warmly welcomed by his aunt and uncle was as much an overstatement as claiming that the Tsar was the best friend the Jews ever had.

It wasn't that they were bad to the puny, under-fed boy who had never learned how to use a handkerchief, let alone to sit down at a table with its own cloth and cutlery. They had children of their own whom they were trying to bring up as young Englishmen, no easy job in a city where the only melting-pot was the kind used for metals in the local foundries.

Before long, he had a job with some more relatives, the Salbergs: Dora and Isaac.

For a time, he was working as a blacksmith's apprentice which, roughly translated into Yiddish, was not much of a job to a Jewish boy—particularly one who found it difficult to pick up his aunt's coal-scuttle, let alone handle and shape red-hot iron.

He then became a sponge salesman, a job that seemed to have a lot of holes in it. At the age of fourteen, he had to make a choice: be a seller of sponges all his life or really try for the Goldena Medina. There really was no contest. Shmuel Gelbfisz had to get to America. The main difficulty was that he didn't have enough money. Was that really a problem to an important man? Shmuel thought about it and decided it wasn't. So he stole the money.

Exactly what he did steal and how he did it was not one of the stories the later Mr Goldwyn was prepared to reveal, but there seems little doubt that that was how he earned his steerage passage on one of those ocean-going tramp-steamers which should have been condemned at about the time America was fighting its Civil War or Britain was engaged in the Crimea.

It was a journey no immigrant would ever forget. Hundreds of people huddled in the lowest deck of the ship, eating, sleeping, excreting, making love, praying, stealing, hoping . . . always hoping.

For eight or nine days they journeyed, tossed about, just as Emma Lazarus had written in her inscription on the plinth of the Statue of Liberty not all were certain they would be spared to see. Young Mr Gelbfisz did see it, although not as Mr Gelbfisz. At Ellis Island that unknown immigration official was poised to have his little joke and the boy who had entered the hall as Shmuel Gelbfisz left it as Samuel Goldfish, although there is some evidence that he spelled it—once he had learned to spell, that is—Goldfisch. The facts thereafter speak for themselves. The 'c' in the name didn't stay there for very long and the young immigrant lad who didn't speak a word of English had no idea how funny it sounded. By the time he could spell it, the name was so much a part of him that it didn't seem important—for the time being at least.

The fact was that Sam Goldfisch or Goldfish was now determined to be an American, which was never really all that difficult in the land of the immigrants.

In years to come there would be plenty of manifestations of latent anti-Semitism in the Golden Land, but none of them made the American Jew feel a stranger. He was no more strange than the German American, the Scandinavian American, the Italian American, the Spanish . . . .

Just as instinctively as in London he had made for the East End, so in New York he found his way to the Bronx and one of its boarding houses. The first rule of business, especially for an important man, was to start by adopting existing practices and then move on. Now, just as instinctively, he was determined to make enough money to make that move.

He found a job as a telegraph boy, which may have seemed the height of chutzpah for a lad who couldn't read or write English. But he was going to evening classes and was picking up a word here and there. He never discovered what a noun was or how to use an adjective and there isn't much doubt that his gift for becoming the biggest slayer of the English language since Mrs Malaprop, began here, but it did get him going. And he was learning to read the newspapers—some two or three days old, but new enough for his purposes. The New York *Sun* and the *Daily News* were proving a better education than anything he was able to pick up at night school.

At first, he scoured the papers picking out the words he had learned to recognize. As he got more and more proficient, he began to devour them. He read about the world's crises and the World Series. He read the advertisements with the dedication of a student of Shakespeare who had just discovered a previously unknown Folio edition.

One of those ads struck home. There was a notice that a glove factory was looking for a cutter. Now Sam knew no more about cutting gloves than he did about circumcising babies. But that wasn't going to stop him. He was going to show himself to be the best glove cutter in America. Incredibly, he was to be almost precisely that.

The factory run by the Lehr family was in Gloversville—which might sound like a weird coincidence until you realize that the trade made the town and the town took the name, the way that a dozen other trades changed a dozen other towns in various parts of the United States.

Gloversville in upstate New York had originally been called Stump City, which anyone with a sense of poetry must appreciate didn't have the ring of Gloversville about it. When a number of other glove factories set up business in the town—it made sense to be together; employees going from one firm to another knew the trade, raw materials were delivered in bulk to one station, customers had only one journey to make on buying expeditions—the name was changed.

The Lehr family believed they had made an economic success by going to Gloversville. What they had not bargained for was Mr Sam Goldfish, who was to put the same devoted attention into cutting hides for gloves as he had in running away from Warsaw.

Not that he was put to work cutting gloves straight away. That was a skilled man's job and not even an important man like Sam Goldfish—the 'c' had gone for ever by then—could convince his boss that he was yet that. So he made do with sweeping floors, in what he later identified as a sweat-shop, going to more English classes—where the chances are he provided a great deal of entertainment both to his teachers and fellow-students—and being very happy indeed to be promoted to the sewing machines.

Gloversville was about forty miles from Albany, a sleepy town that resembled New York City not in the least. There was little that was luxurious about Albany and what there was he regarded as out of his social reach, even though he had the money.

For instance, there was the Kingsborough Hotel where the local élite gathered. He heard it had marble floors and walls of polished mahogany. The girls in the Lehr factory used to joke about the brass spittoons near the potted palms.

When he decided he was rich enough to go there, its principal attraction was the big plate-glass window through which he could watch the beautiful girls of Gloversville—and there were a few, daughters of the bosses and workers at the glove factories—pass by on Saturday nights. Other workers in the factory talked about the vacation when they had used their entire savings on a visit to the State capital as though it had been a trip in a gondola on the Venice canals or a ride on a camel through the Sahara Desert. Sam was bored by such talk. He knew there were bigger, more exciting places to see, more thrilling ways of spending a great deal more money. At fifteen he already knew he was going to be bigger than everybody else. He was, after all, an important man. Soon everybody would know that.

The first step along the way to that happening was when Mr Albert Lehr, the boss, promoted young Sam to being one of his cutters, the very job the boy had gone after in the first place.

His progress was remarkable—as much because of his business acumen as because of his skill with the shears and leather.

Many years later he said: 'It was a revelation to me to find a place where work was rewarded, and where the more a man worked, the more he was paid.'

At 6.50 a.m. the morning whistle blew, but Sam always got there before that. Lunch was a quick perfunctory thing. He worked late at night.

Within two years he was making $20 a week. His boss was so intrigued by this one-man production line that he invited him home to lunch.

The man asked what he intended to do with his life. It surprised him. Sam answered in the traditional Jewish way—with another question.

'How can you get ahead except by working harder than everyone else?' he replied.

Before long he had struck up a close friendship—so close that it would last for life—with the boss's son Abe, who wasn't nearly as enthusiastic for the art of cutting a glove as was the greenhorn Sam, who believed it an article of faith (in himself) that he exceed the output generally considered reasonable for a normal man.

Between them, Sam and Abe cooked up a scheme which seemed to suit them both very well—in fact, it was to suit Sam a great deal more. The idea was that Sam would work an extra hour each day, while Abe worked an hour less. Abe was happy with this arrangement. He knew his father would get the same amount of output, while he wouldn't be put to all the inconvenience of so much sheer unadulterated hard work. Sam knew better. By working an extra hour a day, his own piecework would show astonishingly better results—not just because of what could be done in an hour but because he was doing more than any of his fellow-workers; the foreman was passing him the best skins—and the better a skin, the easier it was to cut.

The arrangement seemed to suit everyone very well indeed. Not least of all the senior Mr Lehr who saw the output figures and happily paid out the piecetime rates which—had he been able to advertise them—would have meant a queue outside his doors a hundred yards long, job or no job.

When he discovered the root cause of young Mr Goldfish's evident prosperity—he had taken to wearing suits that didn't have patches in them, clean white shirts and a Homburg hat—the ploy that excited his newest employee so much, he sacked both Sam and his own son. And then took them back again—on condition they didn't work together. Not even that could dissipate the Goldfish ambition or the friendship for Abe. Sam continued to make money as though he were printing dollar bills instead of cutting gloves.

He was not just making money—but spending it, wasting it, gambling it in denominations that wouldn't have seemed feasible just months earlier. It wasn't unusual for him to have $100 in his pocket—a vast, unimaginable sum for most sixteen-year-olds; for immigrants and the families they had left behind, these were riches that did not come easily.

Possibly because business success had a great deal of the gamble about it, he was drawn irretrievably to the lure of a pack of cards. He worried himself about the way gambling took him. One night he took from his pockets all the dollars he was carrying—all 120 of them. He put $20 in another pocket and handed the remaining $100 to Abe Lehr. 'Keep it for me', he said, 'Under no circumstance give it back to me until tomorrow.'

Lehr agreed—until Sam came calling. He demanded another $20. Soon there was nothing left. He lost every cent of the $120.

Then he turned on Lehr. What sort of friend was he to do a thing like that? He was not to be trusted. He was not faithful. He was treacherous. He was wicked. It was a lesson Lehr would learn. Doing what Sam asked him to do was not always doing what Sam was asking him to do!

Old man Lehr saw the potential of a man like Goldfish. He wasn't sure he liked it when Sam asked to change his job. No, he wasn't dissatisfied. There weren't many people who could cut gloves as well as he could, but there weren't many who were quite so obviously cut out as businessmen, he assured Lehr. He wanted to become a glove salesman.

He sold the idea, as he would be selling the actual gloves. They gave him what was generally known as the 'graveyard territory', Pittsfield, Mass, best known to the industry as not prime ground for glove salesmen.

Sam changed all that. He started selling gloves like a barker in a fairground. Suddenly, and unknowingly, he had discovered show business. He went to see buyers and told them about the favours he was doing *them* in agreeing to grant them the privilege of buying his gloves. 'You shouldn't turn me down', he told his potential customers, 'without seeing what I've got to sell. You may be missing a bargain.' His first order was worth a fortune—$300.

It was as though he were selling them a magic garment sewn with silk woven specially for the Lehr company by fairies who flew in each morning in specially reserved air-lanes.

He opened his mouth and his voice, a particularly high voice with an accent he wasn't able to control, told a story every customer wanted to hear. His hands told a similar story—as they always would. When he wanted to convince, Sam Goldfish used those hands to help him do the convincing. There were other inducements he drew up—bigger discounts for bigger orders and not an occasional gift of a packet of dollar bills for store-buyers who could produce the biggest demands for gloves.

The story is that, before his eighteenth birthday, Sam was regarded as the most successful glove salesman in the whole of the United States.

He became sales manager for another glove manufacturer with an office on Fifth Avenue in New York.

Certainly, he had enough money in his pocket—and had long before more than covered the deposit he had to pay his boss for his initial supply of gloves—to take a two-month holiday. It wasn't simply that he wanted a rest, although the amount of energy Goldfish was burning up meant he needed a break as soon as he could arrange it. No, much more important was that he wanted to go to Europe—to see his mother.

Going to Poland didn't seem a good idea. The atmosphere at the turn of the century was no more happy than it was when he left and there was that little matter of having escaped over the river Oder. Besides, he was now a rich man and he wanted to enjoy his wealth. So he sent his mother a ticket to Karlsbad and himself took off for the spa resort. It was an enjoyable experience and a very rewarding one. He was indeed an important man.

His mother enjoyed admiring her successful son and was happy that he could restore not just the money he had borrowed from her, but sufficient 'interest'—and the promise of a great deal more to come—to enable both her and her husband never to have to worry about the future again.

By 1909, Sam was earning up to $15,000 a week. Perhaps those figures ought to be repeated—$15,000 a week in *1909*. The output of Mr Samuel Goldfish was phenomenal and so were the results for both company and salesman. They hadn't made them like Sam before. Other salesmen had been prepared to work hard but Goldfish was putting in eighteen hours a day. It wasn't that he had a Midas touch. It was work, work, work—and that gift for showmanship and salesmanship which, when combined, was prodigious indeed.

One would think that with all this money flooding in—sums that were equivalent of monies which today would be counted in six figures—he would be on very friendly terms indeed with his bank manager. Porbably he would have been—except that he didn't have a bank manager.

Sam Goldfish may have been a very unusual man, but in one respect he would be like many another young fellow who had come over steerage from the old country—he had a profound dislike (it bordered on a distrust) of banks. Why need a bank when he had a good mattress under which to keep his dollar bills? Or perhaps a decent safe.

Sometimes, he spread his assets out a bit. A good friend was the station-master at New York's Grand Central Station, who quite literally played the Goldfish banker, even paying some interest on his investment.

There were other investments that young Sam was after. He stayed with the glove firm, being held up as a paragon wherever glove salesmen met over a glass of beer to talk shop—which they always did when they did get together. By the time he was thirty, in 1912, he was after realizing his assets.

Did he want to be in gloves all his life? And if he did, did he want to do so all alone?

He used to pass a nickelodeon—the earliest kind of cinema—in Herald Square on his way to work each morning.

The films lasted only about five minutes each and weren't anything to write home to Warsaw about.

One day he ventured inside—but only after looking left and right to make sure no one saw him go in. The film being projected was a *Bronco Billy* adventure. He thought it was so daring, they could have been showing *Ladies Night in a Turkish Bath* for all he knew.

But he considered that a well-off man had to broaden his horizons. And there had for a long time been a woman he had in mind with whom to share his now firmly established prosperity.

Her name was Bessie Ginzburg, niece of his boss. Now, whether or not he fell in love with the plump young lady at first sight cannot now be said with any degree of certainty. What is sure is that by the time he decided to propose to her—three years after their first meeting—she had accepted the proposal of a New York theatre man called Jesse Lasky. Lasky was busy in vaudeville.

He also played in vaudeville, in a so-so act with his sister Blanche. It was the time when families went to vaudeville performances virtually as part of one of the necessities of life.

Vaudeville was the respectable side of the variety business. A few years earlier, no man would have dreamed of taking his wife or children to a vaudeville show. They were vulgar entertainments at which beer was swilled and waiters with twirly moustaches sang songs no decent gentleman would have wanted his ladies to hear. The comedians were even rougher and the dancing girls . . . well, rumour had it they sometimes showed their ankles.

It had all been cleaned up. The more raucous elements had gone to burlesque—'the old burlecue' as the professionals knew it—where more than shapely lower legs were on view. Vaudeville itself was something rather different.

Comedians, musicians and dancers would work for a series of circuits who controlled theatres from one end of America to the other, and the artists would take their same material from New York to Los Angeles, going from town to town, some big, some small, travelling by train, staying in theatrical boarding-houses. It could take sometimes two to three years to cover the whole circuit, by which time the same act—now all but forgotten even by the regular patrons—would wend its way back in the opposite direction.

The Laskys had a music act—or so the colourful sign that went up on the easel at the side of the stage said. He played the violin, she the piano, and in between their musical numbers, they had a song and dance act too.

They were Jewish, but far from the mainstream of Jewish life, as indeed could only be expected of a couple of vaudeville troupers whose home was in San Francisco, not known for its superb examples of Jewish culture.

Sam had first met them when they were playing one of the small theatres in the Catskill Mountains—yet to earn the name Borscht Belt, but already something of a nursery for good showmen. Jesse couldn't claim that either he or his sister were exactly 'good' but Sam, taking a rare evening off from the sales pitch in the midst of his territory, enjoyed them.

Sam started taking an interest in Blanche. His own fame had spread pretty far and quite wide by that time. Jesse Lasky is reputed to have had a warning from a friend of his to have nothing to do with 'that momzer Goldfish' ('Momzer' is a less than delightful Yiddish word which quite literally means 'Bastard'). The friend's name was Mayer, Louis B Mayer.

Lasky, of course, at that time had no reason to harbour any hard feeling against the man who was then paying court to his sister. Sam could have bought and sold the Lasky household two or three times over by then and a solid income was one of the principal requirements for an approved match in any Jewish family. Besides, he liked Sam's 'chutzpah' quite as much as Goldfish admired his own.

It was well known in the glove business that the best gloves came from Europe, not Gloversville. Not only were the skins finer and the workmanship better, they were also a lot cheaper. If it weren't for the import duty imposed by the customs authorities, it wouldn't have been worth anyone's while making a single pair of gloves in the United States. As it was, the duty system was sufficiently protectionist to keep America's own industry in business.

Sam, though, set out to beat it—and that word 'single' now takes on a totally different kind of meaning. Sam bought gloves in France, and then told the manufacturers to separate every single pair. Then he ordered all the left gloves to be sent to a fictitious man in New York and all the right gloves to another dealer in New Orleans—he didn't exist either.

His plan worked beautifully. Sure enough, no one came forward to claim the consignments and, as always happened, Sam looked out for the notices in the local paper. The law said they had to be auctioned off, but the smiles on the faces of the people at the sale hardly compared with that of the auctioneer as he had to admit that he was only selling left-hand gloves. No, there were no right gloves on offer. Sam bid $5—and collected the lot. At another sale in New Orleans he did the same thing with a collection of right-hand gloves. For $10 he had beaten the entire duty system imposed by the United States Government and cleared a fortune.

Jesse laughed when he heard that. His sister wasn't going to be poor, married to Mr Goldfish. He gave his blessing and their mother did, too. (Meanwhile Sam was sending off regular amounts to his now widowed mother. She decided to stay in Poland. America, gloves . . . it was no life for a Yiddisher mama.)

Jesse was now also a vaudeville manager, although not too successfully. He had recently had an enormous flop called *Folies Bergère*, which he had dared to take to Broadway if not to his bank manager.

The show had lost a vast amount of money borrowed from friends and family, but none of his enthusiasm or 'chutzpah', the principal ingredient, it appeared, required for doing well—certainly a lot more than mere talent.

Bessie seemed to approve of that. Sam Goldfish's continued pressing of hints of love and marriage were as nothing compared to Jesse Lasky's firm proposals. Together, they eloped to Atlantic City and set up home in Brooklyn with Blanche and their mother.

When Sam met him again and saw how happy he was, he proposed to Blanche, married her and joined the Lasky family in the same house. Sam was still making a veritable fortune, but saw that as no reason to squander all his resources on a new house of his own. Besides, there was a lot of attraction in the way his new brother-in-law was making his living and he was glad to be close where it all seemed to be happening.

That was when they moved into the movie business.

The idea of going into movies had been with Jesse for quite some time. A year earlier, it had been put to him by a man whose name deserves to be honoured in some kind of Hollywood Hall of fame, but is, alas, virtually forgotten—Arthur S. Friend.

Friend, a young lawyer, could see films as the entertainment medium of the future; a peep behind the peep show. But Lasky's endeavours with his Broadway *Folies Bergère* were putting him in no mood for brilliant new notions. Not only were the Broadway patrons not ready for bare-breasted girls dancing around their tables; they weren't ready for the idea of sitting at tables either.

Sam was brought into the discussions, but at that time he still wasn't sure about leaving the glove business. He might have mused that that was like biting the hand that he fed, or at least clothed. Perhaps Goldfish gloves had a nice ring about it. His boss might not like it but was that any reason not to open up on his own?

By the end of 1913, he was in a more receptive frame of mind.

As much as anything, it was due to politics that his attitude changed. A few years before, politics simply was a question whether a thing was good or bad for the Jews—would there be more pogroms or the same (rarely less)? Now, though, he was a fully-fledged American with a citizenship certificate on his wall to prove it. With Woodrow Wilson in power it seemed nothing less than the dawn of socialism. Wilson was going to abandon import tariffs. Now there would be no point in bringing in left-handed gloves. Besides, if America was going to be governed by people like that, who would be around to wear gloves? Whole political systems have tottered on questions of such moment. With Sam Goldfish it was the event that made him think again about being a man of the movies.

Sam went often now to the movies, more often than he had been prepared to let on. The screen flickered alarmingly—which was one reason why the trusts who between them controlled who could and who could not make films and show them were against the idea of full-length movies: they were frightened that they represented a health hazard, and they would find themselves sued.

For a time his idea was to 'coin' it in by operating a theatre himself. Then he had second thoughts. Rents at buildings which could be adapted to showing these 'flickers' were nothing less than astronomical, even for the country's top glove salesman. If he could have found a way to sell one set of tickets for people's right buttock and another for their left, it might have been easier. The only way to make money at it was to *make* movies—which is an indication of how long ago this was.

He didn't just engage everyone he saw in conversation on this one obsessive subject—he hijacked them. He spoke to other glove salesmen and to owners of huge industrial concerns—his way of getting to people was almost as polished then as it was to be in years to come—he talked to small-town bank managers and to heads of Wall Street firms. Broadway producers were encouraged to consider such ventures and so were the operators of little theatres.

To them all he had the same message: the peep-show is over. Movies are not just the medium of tomorrow; they are a whole new growth industry. He wasn't interested in making two-reelers that got people excited simply because they saw things move on a white screen. He talked of spectaculars, of entrance tickets that might one day cost as much as 25 cents. And then they laughed. Twenty-five cents! That was carrying things too far. Goldfish was off his head. No one actually told him to go and swim in another bowl, but that was the general impression.

Jesse Lasky was waylaid more often than most. Sam, of course, knew that he was highly susceptible, but he was still nursing wounds that seemed constantly open and raw from his *Folies Bergère* experience.

But now Jesse was coming round to Sam's madness. Was it such a terrible idea after all? If he fancied himself as a showman, he realized he had to be willing to take risks like this.

Finally Sam found the last lot of money he was looking for. He arranged to meet Arthur Friend to tell him about it. He couldn't have been more excited had he done yet another deal, perhaps for left-footed shoes. 'I've found a backer,' the ecstatic Goldfish told Lasky, panting like a prize spaniel (if he had had a tail he would, assuredly, have been wagging that, too). 'He wants us to met him with a prospectus . . . . What's a prospectus?'

It was difficult to feel cool to a man like that. Friend himself was begged to join in the consortium, but the young man had to decide whether he was a lawyer or a putative movie mogul. He chose to remember all the examinations and other early steps he had to get through to become a lawyer and stuck with it.

So their part of the business was going to stay within the family.

Sam was busy working things out, almost as though there was no glove company to worry about—except that his touch was evident even when he was only half-hearted about it. His takings were still bigger than anyone else's, even when his mind was on that flickering movie screen.

He had meanwhile been doing his homework. Who was the top man in movies, he asked friends who still knew more about the movie industry than he did? The answer was a Southern gentleman called David Wark Griffith, who by then had already turned out films ranging from *Edgar Allan Poe* to *The Song of the Shirt*. Sometimes, eighty of them in a year.

By that time Griffith himself had demonstrated that he saw more to moving pictures than babies laughing or trains appearing to come right out over the heads of the audience. But if he sought a kind of reality in the cinema, he wasn't finding it in Mr Sam Goldfish, whom he considered an upstart who didn't have a great deal going for him in what he regarded a modern art form. 'We want you with us,' Goldfish told him, ignoring the clear, pained expression on the face of the director who had already invented the close-up and had just completed his four-reeler *Judith of Bethulia*.

He wanted an insurance policy and wasn't afraid to say so. 'Show me $250,000 in the bank', he said, 'and we'll talk about it.' Sam couldn't show anything at all in the bank—he still didn't have a bank—and went looking for more help.

By this time, it had become apparent that Samuel Goldfish was going to be the senior partner in the enterprise—or at least the one who was doing all the work, which was precisely the way he wanted it, once he had made up his mind to give this new industry a try.

Meanwhile Jesse Lasky had been busy trying to put on a stage spectacle based on his home state—which, imaginatively, he was calling *California*. The show never got off the ground, but it did result in a meeting between Lasky and a young, balding writer called Cecil B. DeMille. Lasky had tried to employ Cecil's older brother William to write *California* for him. But William DeMille was too successful and too busy to even entertain the idea. So Cecil was suggested. Once they saw that *California* was beyond their collective pockets and imaginations to get going, they toyed with other projects.

It was DeMille's idea to switch everything from stage spectacles to movies. Crazy, Lasky thought. He was trying desperately to pull himself up in the world, to put his 'two-a-day' vaudeville (two performances a day; and sometimes there were three or even four) behind him. Now this idiot DeMille was suggesting investing the hard-earned cash of people, who might be even more foolish enough to lend to them, into a mere peep-show, DeMille, though, had just been to see *The Great Train Robbery*, one of the first pictures that attempted to tell a story.

DeMille's idea was that he would direct a picture like that—no, *better* than that—if Lasky would drum up the necessary cash and set everything in motion. Doing what the youthful aspiring director told him, was called being a producer.

The producer liked the idea, too—except that he worked out he might need as much as $20,000 to get going. He succumbed to DeMille's entreaties and went along to see *The Great Train Robbery* for himself. His conclusion was that it would be even more of a robbery to take people's money if he couldn't do better than that himself. If only given half a chance.

He was lucky that his brother-in-law was equally smitten. *He* had fallen in love with the screen Mary Pickford—much more, in fact than he ever had with the real Blanche. She was already complaining that he was enjoying himself a lot more with fellow glove salesmen than he was with her.

In fact, Goldfish, now in his early thirties, wasn't enjoying gloves very much at all. When Jesse suggested that he join him and his friend Cecil in an entirely new venture, Sam announced he was giving up gloves for good.

The best glove salesman in America was going into a new business. And it was going to fit him . . . like a glove.

2
These Three

On the surface, it seemed to offer everything—a man who was convinced he knew show business like the back of his hand (there would be times when Sam doubted whether Jesse knew much about the back of his hand either, but that is jumping to a totally different conclusion, if not metaphor, altogether), another with a brilliant commercial mind who had more money than his wife knew what to do with, and a third with an artistic bent and an aristocratic name (who had succeeded well enough in hiding his own Jewish birth to beat the anti-Semitism they expected on the way).

The only trouble was that Lasky hadn't really succeeded at anything very much before, Sam was beginning to thrash around like a Goldfish out of water, and DeMille had never handled a movie camera in his life.

There was a third problem—even when the Grand Central stationmaster had handed over at least $10,000 of Sam's money—what sort of film did they want to make? What is certain is that both Jesse and Cecil had a common interest—to make names for themselves doing something that no one had yet done before. As for Sam, he wanted to be sure that there would be a decent profit to hand over at Grand Central next time he went there, and that he would have a little more fun making it than he had had recently selling gloves.

Lasky and De Mille decided they wanted to make a story film, but not a 'short' like the *The Great Train Robbery*. It was going to be a grand movie with a grand cast, directed by a grand director, although that was a job very few people had really had before. It sounded good though, and Cecil was going to be the one to do it.

'We've never produced a picture,' said Sam to Jesse in a line that deserves to be inlaid in gold alongside the stars on the pavements of Hollywood Boulevard, 'and DeMille has never directed one. We should be great.'

Prophetic words. But with nothing, apart from the irony, to base them upon. They hadn't even got a story, any actors, a studio . . . .

But they were ready to set precedents, the kind that would stay the norm for as long as there would be people making what had not yet been called motion pictures. If they were going to do anything they had to do it big, and making big meant paying big money. If something came cheap it wasn't worth having.

It is interesting to speculate whether this philosophy would have developed had the Lasky-DeMille-Goldfish partnership not got under way and taken it for itself. As we shall see, it was but the first of a number of other firsts.

Another was the search for capital. For the last eighty years film men have undertaken a quest for cash which, in return for a hefty share of whatever profits came their way, they would borrow to get a picture rolling. The three partners managed to get together from friends and an assortment of Jesse Lasky's relatives, a thousand dollars here, another thousand there. Together with Sam's $10,000, they collected $25,000—not a tiny sum for 1913. What they paid for their story, however, ought to rank with the selling of Margaret Mitchell's rights in *Gone With The Wind* (and in terms of sheer inflation far outgrossed it). For a stage play Western, they forked out *ten thousand dollars*. It was called *The Squaw Man*.

And with that under their collective gun belts—they were getting a little shell-shocked at the realization of what they had done—they set about getting a star. They chose a youngster called Dustin Farnum.

That being achieved, they set out to see how a film was made. It really was that simple, that basic. They had decided to go into the movie business. They had their own tame director. They had bought both a story and an actor, but they hadn't any idea how anyone else was making films.

It was Sam who first came to the conclusion that it might not be a bad idea to do a bit of studying before they allowed their own shiny new camera and the film they had purchased from an enthusiastic New York laboratory to start doing their work. DeMille went to see a film being shot a short distance away from their own New York base, in what was known as the film capital of the world, Fort Lee in New Jersey. He watched the director's technique for a few minutes, decided he was bored with what he saw and came back to his partners telling them he knew exactly how things were done.

The only difference with the way he was going to make his movie from the way films had been shot before was that he had the idea to shoot it on what would eventually be called location. *The Squaw Man* was about the West, so should be shot out West. In Arizona. In a place called Flagstaff.

Flagstaff sounded right. It was in the heart of what would a little later be called Western country (the term Western would really come to the fore with the cinema; since *The Squaw Man* would, in effect, be the first Western as well as the first full-length film, it wasn't yet used much) and had enough atmosphere to put these aspiring film-makers in the right mood. A team of real Indians met them on their arrival.

What they had not bargained for was that when they were ready to set up their camera it was snowing furiously. Faced with a blizzard on one side and the anger of his business partners on the other, Cecil B. DeMille had to work out which was the more dangerous. He decided that, even if Lasky and

Goldfish were to complain vociferously, there was no way he could afford to stick around and wait for the snow to stop.

Where wouldn't it be snowing? And, more to the point, where would there be a guarantee of perfect sunshine? Only one place—Southern California. And where in Southern California could they reach easily on the next train out of their part of Arizona? Only Los Angeles.

So Cecil B. DeMille took the next train for Los Angeles and was soon sending telegrams to his two partners saying that he had found a barn that would fit his need for a studio perfectly—in a tiny, virtually uninhabited suburb called Hollywood.

His telegram said: FLAGSTAFF NO GOOD STOP HAVE PROCEEDED TO CALIFORNIA STOP WANT AUTHORITY TO RENT BARN IN HOLLYWOOD FOR SEVENTY-FIVE DOLLARS A MONTH

Since nobody had even heard of Hollywood or anywhere else near where his train had stopped, they gave their permission.

There was one main street—Hollywood Boulevard they called it then (they call it Hollywood Boulevard today, too, but that's like saying Fifth Avenue was the same before they put up all the stores there or that Oxford Street was no different before Selfridges and Marks and Spencer moved in). Crossing the Boulevard was Vine Street and a barn they called their studio.

They also had a name for their firm, the Jesse L. Lasky Feature Play Company. (How Sam would allow his name to be omitted from the organization's title is another of the mysteries of the early days of Hollywood; chances are he weighed up the pros and cons and decided that Lasky was the one known in the business and if they needed to be considered a professional organization, using a pro's name was probably no bad thing.) Jesse had previously suggested combining movie-making with selling one of the favourite local foods, the Mexican tamales. Jesse thought their fortune would be assured if they could tie up the tamale concession in New York. Sam said No. It was to be films and only films. Besides The Jesse L. Lasky Feature Play Company sounded better than Lasky's Hot Tamales.

It was, Sam later confessed, an old trick he had learned in the glove business—showing the other fellow how a thing would be to his advantage.

Sam himself wasn't so sure about the other details of setting up a business like this. Later, he confessed that was probably his 'strongest weak point'. He wasn't a man to be bogged down by bureaucratic detail.

People got to know about them. The publisher of the *Los Angeles Times* was so pleased, he asked them to include the credit 'Made in Hollywood' after the titles of their films, to get the area better known.

The really big problem about *The Squaw Man* wasn't the location. In fact, Hollywood seemed a good place to make movies—not, perhaps, a town that would last. Apart from the sunshine, it didn't have a great deal to offer and the Goldfish-Lasky-DeMille partnership realized that the big names in the business, on principle, would want to stay in New Jersey—after all, how could a little hick village like Hollywood compete with the class and glamour of being so close to Manhattan? But for their purposes, the barn at Hollywood and Vine suited them perfectly. Their star wasn't quite such an easy option.

Mr Farnum suddenly realized that he might have bought himself a pup. The Jesse L. Lasky Feature Play Company had offered him a share of the profits. Farnum was disturbed that his present employers in Hollywood couldn't even drum up a real-life Indian for the film. He demanded hard cash—to the tune of $5,000—which was already $5,000 more than they had in accumulated capital.

That was when the glove salesman became the movie salesman—which Sam at that time saw as his principal role, even if it also involved preparing the product he was about to sell.

Goldfish never actually claimed to be a prophet, but he had an inkling that he was on to a very good thing indeed. He wouldn't have attempted an entirely new venture like this had he not been fairly sure he was likely to reap reasonably impressive dividends. Now he was totally convinced that Dustin Farnum, a fair actor but no businessman, had done himself out of millions of dollars—millions that would now be shared among the three partners.

The $5,000 would be a fee not a royalty, he decided. Farnum was delighted with that decision. But once having established that in his mind, how was Sam going to raise that litle bit of extra money? He had no doubts about the answer. As though walking around with a suitcase full of the finest kid gloves that Paris had ever made (newly joined into pairs, of course), Goldfish toured the country and sold rights to *The Squaw Man* to exhibitors from coast to coast. He made speeches. One man paid $4,000 at once. Another $46,000 was raised within weeks.

'The films you have seen so far', he told them 'are just rehearsals for what we're going to do.' Rights for a film that hadn't even yet been shot? Goldfish did more than that. He realized that the showmen—few of whom had really yet come to terms with the fact that movies were finally about to leave the fairground era—might want more than this in exchange for their money. Sam offered them rights to the eleven pictures they would make to follow. Naturally, all the money came up front—with the signatures.

That had the stamp of the Goldfish chutzpah about it—perhaps the first time such methods had been employed in the film industry, an assortment of individuals who on various occasions in the years that followed would have little else to offer. Twenty-five years on, Hollywood salesmen would hold conventions all over the United States at which they would sell wares that were not even yet made, had not even been typed into scripts.

Back in early 1913 it would be a technique that would pay off—and do so handsomely. Farnum would spend the rest of his days cursing both his lack of faith and vision and his impetuous desire to see money in his hand. He literally did himself out of millions—but that was for the future.

For the moment Jesse Lasky was beginning to think that his star had the right idea. Having been burnt once on the cigars of the bankers who demanded the return of the money they had already lent him for the *Folies*, he was coming out in a ready assortment of cold sweats by the time the movie was finished.

The first preview of the film (shot on the highly inflammable nitrate stock) bore all the stamps of that word which before long would be one of the standard 'trade' terms of the business—the rushes; except that these rushes Lasky wished had been left where they found Moses's basket. None of the partners realized that the people who had mastered the notion of threading a spool of film through a camera didn't always get it right when printing up what they had, or when it came to cranking it by hand through one of those new-fangled projectors of which they had just taken delivery—the kind that had no take-up spool (because no one had yet thought of having such a complicated mechanism) and which, as a result, spewed this dangerous and sensitive material alarmingly on to the floor while the frames flickered on to the screen ahead.

On this occasion, the flickering pictures were just the kind none of the people wanted to see. The speeds were all wrong—the ceiling of a room looked as if it were below the floor. No one at the time realized that these were easily adjustable problems, Jesse Lasky, in particular, was distraught. 'We're ruined,' he kept saying, over and over again.

In truth, Lasky had more reason to complain than Goldfish wanted to admit. It wasn't only the fault of the projectionist and his bulky new machine. Much more, it was simply that no one had reckoned with the vagaries of a business which none of them, in truth, really knew anything about.

Cecil B. DeMille wasn't yet a name to conjure with when it came to film direction, and although he had ideas which reflected his attitude to this magic new art form, they also betrayed a total, uninhibited ignorance about the technicalities involved in it all. For instance, it didn't seem a bad idea to hire a series of different cameramen on a day-by-day business—theirs might be the first big film to be made in Hollywood, but it appeared that there were a number of other people with similar ideas working on the still traditional peep show 'short' out there. Laboratories were springing up around them and once the world—or rather that little bit of it engaged in making films—had got to hear about the Lasky Feature Play Company's activities, via a series of carefully planted hints to newsmen (it suited the partners to be seen as working very seriously and very prosperously in the new medium) others flocked to join them.

It was cheap to hire camermen by the day. It seemed even better to let them use their own cameras—just think of all the savings they would make in wear and tear? Let the poor cameramen, the suckers, worry about that.

The weakness of that argument was that no one said anything about them all using the same *type* of camera. The fact that one man was using a Lumière and another an Edison, while there was a good chance another would have his favourite Pathé, wasn't calculated to please. They all used different kinds of film, with differently arranged sprocket holes. Join them together and the result was the kind of chaos they were seeing in front of them now. How no one spotted all this before the newly printed film left the laboratory has never been easily explained.

What actually happened was that when the projector's sprockets fell into place with the holes in the film at one moment, as soon as the type of stock changed—as it inevitably would do with the kind of editing in which they were priding themselves—so the film slipped, got caught and did all sorts of dreadful things to the image on the screen.

The only one who didn't know about this was Sam Goldfish, who, flush with the exhilaration of having made what seemed like some very good money from selling rights in advance, was still capitalizing on his idea.

'Jesse L. Lasky presents . . .' said the credits on the film. But the present he was handing to his partner Mr Goldfish was not one to be shouted about. Sam had to be told. It was time for a series of what had not yet been called even Goldfishisms, which alas were not recorded for posterity. However, he had found out enough about the film business to realize that there were experts who had answers for most things.

In Philadelphia Sig Lubin's film laboratory offered the help they required—once, that is, Lubin had adjusted to what he assumed were the get-rich-quick techniques of his new customers—and had the longest laugh he had allowed himself since opening up shop.

Lubin had read the finally produced Goldfish prospectus—professionally drawn up by a firm of business consultants with the aim of impressing those in the industry who might think it a good idea for this group of unknowns to revolutionize the way they were all making their livings.

'Gentlemen,' said Lubin with a gravity that seemed to indicate the need for an immediate call to the nearest bankruptcy lawyers, 'gentlemen, this is serious.'

They could tell as much. Goldfish was ready to admit that even he didn't have an optimistic word in his head, neither a joke nor a clever bit of salesmanship to counter the gloom. 'Serious,' repeated Lubin, 'but it can be fixed.'

It *was* fixed. By the next day—by pasting a new set of sprockets on to the films. The exhibitors got their film and the coins that piled up at the box-offices now made those that Sam had seen at the Herald Square theatre playing *Bronco Billy* seem as nothing.

That out of the way, the Jesse L. Lasky Feature Play Company was set to honour the rest of the agreement they had with their exhibitors—to let them have exclusive rights to the next eleven films they made. The first of those was *Brewster's Millions*, a story that was to be made umpteen times afterwards, most recently in 1985.

An heir to a fortune can only get his money if he spends another fortune in the month prior to the legacy coming into force. That could have been the story of Sam Goldfish and his partners.

In years to come Sam would tell people: 'I have a rule'. He hadn't established it for himself in those early years, but if he had, he might have said 'I have a rule. Never preview a film without an audience—or with the wrong audience.' For that is precisely what he did with *Brewster's Millions*. It was intended to be a fast-moving farce—and in those days of hand-turned projectors, farces, could be very, very fast indeed—except that when the partners saw it, they didn't even titter among themselves.

No one had pointed out that to enjoy a comedy like this you needed to be surrounded by lots of other people who were enjoying it, too. Instead, the moguls sat there on their wooden seats, biting their nails and watching each other's stomachs churning. They were new fathers watching the birth of their own baby and they were entirely anaethetized by the experience.

'Comedy doesn't work on the screen,' said Sam, and the way he said it sounded rather like one of those pronouncements that seemed to be inscribed on a framed piece of film if not engraved on pillars of stone.

He would be the first to realize that these were words meant for swallowing. But, for the moment, he was desperate. And he would doubtless have remained that way had he not previously scheduled a further showing of the film for all those exhibitors he was now sure he had 'conned' into showing his movie.

This time, Sam was like the expectant father who refused to see his baby being born—or rather reborn, for this turned into a totally new life for his *Brewster's Millions*. The exhibitors sat in the dark while Mr Goldfish went for a walk—to return only when he thought he heard laughter coming from out of the makeshift projection room installed at the Vine Street barn. His ears pricked and he moved closer just to check. He was glad he did. By the time he got to the barn's doors, the laughter was almost overpowering. He might have wished he had never said that about comedy not working on the screen.

It was working very well. People weren't yet talking about Goldfish's millions, but it looked as if it would soon be a very appropriate title. More important, the three partners semed to be getting on very well together—with Sam appearing to run most of the show, while no one seemed to complain about his doing so.

If there were now a movie business to speak about, it was speaking about the Jesse L. Lasky Feature Play Company and what it had done.

The team really had created a new kind of business. The Patents Trust who had thought they had tied up the industry very neatly into their own hands were defeated at their own game—just as the vaudeville syndicates would be beaten in years to come. More significantly, they were proving that full-length films were what the public wanted. And while they were about it, weren't there great advantages about filming in Hollywood?

No need to worry about changing light—just perhaps the occasional low-flying hawk or some other big bird casting unwanted shadows. Apart from that, the word was spread: Hollywood was the place to come; and come they did.

Adolph Zukor, the former fur salesman, who ran the Famous Players outfit, saw that Hollywood was where he ought to be, too.

In 1912 he imported the Sarah Bernhardt film, a four-reeler called *Queen Elizabeth*. He was so pleased with himself he took as his slogan 'Famous Players in Famous Plays'.

He even congratulated the Feature Play Company on their ingenuity. Before long, he was talking of merger—another Hollywood game that would be growing in popularity very soon. But it made a lot of sense. Zukor was doing very well and already had a stable of top stars at this time, particularly those whom he persuaded to come to Hollywood from Broadway, like James K. Hackett, Minnie Maddern Fiske and James O'Neill. But even *he* deferred to Goldfish and his partners when it came to running a movie outfit—after all, those laughs at that exhibitors' preview were not to be sniffed at.

Apart from that, there were other reasons for mutual admiration. At about this time Jesse Lasky was concerned about one asset that his rival had but which neither he nor his partners did. 'Zukor and all the other big fellows in the pictures smoke big cigars,' he told Sam. 'So should we.' It was a reasonable enough suggestion, come to think of it. It wasn't enough to be big, you had to be seen to be big, too.

If there were still rumours buzzing around that perhaps the Feature Play Company wasn't doing as well as it liked to say, being the only ones who didn't smoke large Havanas was not a good thing to be.

They tried. Lasky found the passion of a lifetime. Almost never again was he to be seen in public without a cigar clenched between his teeth. Sam wasn't quite so lucky. He tried the cigar and found the cigar tried him—it made him violently sick.

He had to find other ways of exerting his strength. He thought for a time that he ought to have been satisfied with just running the firm. Except that now Jesse L. Lasky was himself finding the movie business so satisfying that he didn't want to know about Sam being left behind to mind the store. It was his store, too, and he wanted to do his own minding.

He had previously been nurturing his share of the vaudeville business—a reasonable insurance, he decided, if the bottom should suddenly fall out of the film industry, which, with all their success, always seemed a possibility.

Now, though, they were talking of merging with Adolph Zukor's company, and dollar signs seemed the best logo for their firm. He wanted a greater slice of the working action. Goldfish didn't want to give it to him, and the peace that had reigned along with all the prosperity was relegated to the past, where it was going to stay.

Along with that was Sam's appetite for work. If he could work eighteen hours a day selling gloves, doing the same thing with the fascinating business of the movies wasn't asking a great deal. Or so it seemed. He didn't see very much of his wife, even now that she had given birth to a daughter whom they named Ruth. He didn't see much of the baby either. In his own way, that was nothing to feel guilty about. The old Jewish work ethic was that one struggled for all the hours one possibly could to keep wife and child away from the fear of hunger. Now that starvation figured nowhere on the Goldfish agenda, he was completely unable to accept that fact—which might have been all right for him, but was hard not just on his family but also on his business associates.

He had promised to make one new film a month and that was not a time scale they found very easy to implement. When Sam wanted to know why, the rows started again.

Lasky took great exception, needless to say, when a series of advertisements appeared in the trade press, leaving no doubt where he saw himself in the business.

One in the *Motion Picture Herald* read:

SAMUEL GOLDFISH
HEAD OF JESSE L. LASKY FEATURE PLAY COMPANY

Now, the firm still bore Jesse L. Lasky's name, but if this seemed self-effacing on Sam's part, the advertisements put paid to that notion. When Lasky protested about the publicity, Sam said he knew nothing about the advertisements. But he couldn't resist adding: 'Well, I *am* the head of the company.'

He said it as though he knew he were also claiming to be head of America. Possibly in his heart he thought he could be that, too. His dreams of grandeur were certainly of running an empire.

His big inspiration, he would always say, was not another film or business mogul, but the former President of the United States, Theodore Roosevelt. Now Sam Goldfish never had any ambition to lead charges up San Juan Hill or to shout 'Bully'. (Can you imagine the still Polish-accented Samuel Goldfish with his high thin voice, crying 'Bully'?)

But Roosevelt was a fighter, and he appreciated that. 'Roosevelt teaches that the only things worth having are what you fight for,' he told his old buddy Arthur Friend, who while still carrying on a very successful practice as a lawyer kept up both his friendship and his own fascination with the movie business.

The way Sam said it sounded rather as if he were talking about a deity. In a way he was. This young immigrant was already developing a philosophy that was characteristic of all the foreign-built movie magnates: that America was God's own country which had offered them a safe haven and should be appreciated and honoured for ever more for doing so.

He was now editing his films. At the same time, he was in charge of diffusing office/studio politics. It was his job, as he saw it, to keep women away from his directors. They needed to spend their time making movies not love.

The rows between Sam and Lasky, and with Cecil B. DeMille taking Jesse's part most of the time, grew ever more heated. Friend finally joined the company, in the hope he could smooth things out. He couldn't. He was asked to back the move of the other partners to oust Sam from the company.

Could they do it? Friend didn't think so. He knew there was still too much good feeling, a very definite innate sense of loyalty if not affection in Lasky and DeMille to allow it to happen.

He knew how difficult Goldfish could be. He told them: 'I'm willing to vote Sam out if you promise to stick to it. But I won't vote him out today and vote him back in tomorrow. I know he'll break your heart and you'll vote him back in again.'

It was a particularly astute prophecy. That very night the partners met, took a vote and decided that there was no place in the Feature Play Company for a man who was causing so much trouble. Sam Goldfish was out.

The next day they thought again. They had told him of their decision and he had broken down. How could they do it to a man who had created everything they had? Where would they be had he not sold the company's merchandise the way he had his previous products? The way salesmen worked in the Lower East Side of New York from their pushcarts and barrows?

They thought about it, worried about it and brought Sam back.

Sam saw his independence being threatened whenever anyone looked as though he were moving into territory he considered his own. He took whatever opportunity came his way to be seen to be the important man—not just in his own studio, but in Hollywood.

In 1915 he joyfully accepted an invitation to become the chairman of a committee set up to interest film people in a $1 million endowment that would help out-of-work or aged actors. It was a tremendously far-sighted project. Hollywood was a new community. Its actors were mostly young, but Sam, still only thirty-three himself, guessed the time would come when a number of them would be ready for the scrap heap unless something was done.

It was just one of his prescient decisions, and there would be many other examples of trails he would blaze before anyone else imagined there were any sparks. He also knew it wouldn't do his own image any harm.

Above all else, he considered himself a salesman. When he first started, selling movies which his own company made was just an extension of selling gloves. It was more fun, but merely another project.

Now he was getting himself involved in every aspect of film-making. He was noticing the way his pictures were made. The Lothario of the studio was becoming aware of what his directors were getting up to—inserting close-ups of girl friends where they were not intended to be. He put a stop to that, using many a choice epithet that would also have found difficulty being fitted into a film-script. But selling pictures was never as easy as knowing how to go into a store with a suitcase of fine kid gloves. There were always other people involved to hinder what he was beginning to think was his unique ability to make movies.

Some of those professional rivals were also enemies. Others wore a cloak of friendship. Among them was Abe Lincoln Erlanger, one of the country's vaudeville Tsars whose circuit, run in conjunction with Mark Klaw, was known as the Syndicate. A powerful man. A dangerous man. To other theatre-owners, operating houses in towns where his syndicate wasn't represented, he ran a virtual protection outfit—either pay commission to use our artists or be squeezed out of the business altogether.

Every week Goldfish and Lasky lunched with Erlanger and every week he ridiculed them. 'Films', he said, 'are only good as chasers—between vaudeville shows. They are not shows themselves.' 'Chasers' meant films that were intended to 'chase' people out of the theatres to make way for those in the next house. Both Lasky and Goldfish set their target as chasing people *into* their theatres.

In years to come Sam would remember Erlanger's words. They represented a lesson—never to ignore the new developments in the world of show biz.

As a sub-plot to this story is that of another motion picture company that was to earn its place in Hollywood lore. Making the films had always been one thing, distributing them another: if they were the authors of what they were doing, the distributors were, in a way, the publishers—they had access to the theatres and consequently took not just their cut, but also had their say in what went into those theatres.

The distributors were small, unwieldy outfits, which suited people like Goldfish and Lasky well enough. But then one of the distributors, a certain Mr William Hodkinson, decided to do something about it—to his own benefit. He formed a new company that was both much bigger and very much better organized which would distribute the films of all their previous clients, who included not only Jesse L. Lasky Feature Play Company but also Zukor's Famous Players.

Neither of them liked what the new company was planning to do. It had a grand name—Paramount—and grand new ideas, like paying a rock-bottom advance of $35,000.

Considering that the Geraldine Farrar picture *Carmen* which they had just made had cost precisely that figure, that wasn't very tempting. (Farrar was a top American opera singer. That didn't worry Sam. He thought she looked beautiful and was convinced that the prestige of the opera house would rub off on him. He was right. The film was a tremendous hit.)

But the whole Paramount idea was so clever there was just nothing anyone could do about it. If they wanted their products to play in the Paramount theatres—and they did—they had to go along with Paramount's ideas. Unless, that is, Lasky and Zukor merged. If they did, they would control about 80 per cent of the market. A united front meant they would be able to call the shots, not Paramount.

The idea stuck in Goldfish's craw. Zukor wasn't like Lasky. He knew the film business as well as Sam did. He wasn't his brother-in-law, but he could be much firmer in getting his will across then ever Jesse managed to be. Sam saw trouble ahead, but had to agree that beating Paramount was even more important than battling it out with Zukor, whom he hated as much out of respect for his abilities as for dislike of his personality.

Zukor was much more keen on joining forces. His firm was bigger than Sam's, but he gave the other partners half his stock and allowed Goldfish to be chairman of the board, which he knew would be much more than a mere sinecure. He knew it was the only way either of them could survive.

Sam was put in charge of negotiations with Paramount. In three months he had bought the company, and his operation and Zukor's were now one. Sam was less than happy. He knew at once that Zukor would try to curb what other people saw as his excesses—the way he interfered in other people's departments, his own womanizing which, as he approached his mid-thirties, began to take on all the signs of an addiction.

Zukor didn't like his business methods either—like paying the famous Broadway impressario David Belasco $100,000, plus a share in the profits, for ten of his top stage successes. When Zukor heard about this he offered Sam his congratulations and called him a 'momzer' to his face. It wasn't the sort of greeting calculated to inspire affection and confidence, although it did convince the older man that Sam Goldfish was the kind of person who was better on his side than against him.

He also smiled at some of Sam's less intelligent decisions—like his constant battle with Cecil B. DeMille, whom he thought was getting too clever by half. He couldn't understand his director's decision to become 'arty'—like photographing some of his actors half in a shadow; a technique DeMille shamelessly admitted he had got from an Old Master. Sam sent a telegram saying that if the exhibitors only saw half an actor, they would pay only half the price. 'CECIL,' he charged, 'YOU HAVE RUINED ME'.

DeMille's reply is now enshrined in Hollywood tradition.

'SAM,' he cabled, 'IF YOU AND THE EXHIBITORS DON'T KNOW

REMBRANDT LIGHTING WHEN THEY SEE IT, DON'T BLAME ME'. To which Goldfish answered 'REMBRANDT LIGHTING WONDERFUL IDEA. FOR THAT THE EXHIBITORS WILL PAY DOUBLE.'

The story is that they did.

Partnerships of any kind are gambles likely to result in disaster. In Hollywood, they had all the hallmarks of a super-colossal epic that was about to end up in the ashcan. The only question was whether Sam and Zukor could bury the hatchet they had been lovingly crafting for each other for long enough to beat their opposition, however weak it might be. Both should have been intelligent enough to realize that it made sense, but only Zukor was desperate to go ahead.

Sam wanted to take his time—and as he waited, so did his partners. They didn't have Sam's devotion to a baby that bore Jesse's name, but over which he didn't have anything like the same control. Now was their chance to flex their muscles and tell Sam he wasn't the only one in the firm. They had dismissed him once, and they could do it again—and Sam knew it, though he was gambling on their needing him a lot more than they were prepared to say.

He wasn't back with his partners long before they were regretting it. While DeMille and Lasky were playing an ever bigger role in producing more and more films, Goldfish could see his total control of the enterprise slipping away.

Now the company was to be called the Famous Players-Lasky company—it was too late to incorporate Goldfish's name. In a way, they were forming their own monopoly, to follow the original Paramount one; the trust to beat any further trusts. Increased rivalry between studios meant a war to win stars—and executives—away from rivals and a consequent increase in salaries. Merging the two firms meant these tiresome employees would virtually have nowhere else to go.

Zukor wasn't any happier working with Goldfish than Goldfish was in working with him. It seemed that one of them was going to have to go. It was fairly obvious that one would be Sam.

3
Up In Arms

The world was at war, although America had not really come to terms with the fact and was saying—before Sam said it—include me out.

It was also precisely what Zukor was saying about his Famous Partner, if not about any of his Famous Players. Certainly it was hard being Sam Goldfish's partner, but it wasn't easy being Adolph Zukor's either, and the older man should have realized it. Except that his idea of a merger was much more the kind that Germany had had with Belgium a few months earlier. As any observer of the situation could judge, it was not going to be an easy arrangement. Sam spent money as through it were produced from a hose-pipe. But so did Zukor, and whenever one of them authorized the payment of a cheque, the other complained he was being ruined.

There was, for instance, the time that Jack Pickford, Mary's little-talented brother, was placed under contract for $500 a week, which to Sam still seemed like a reasonable slice of the national debt, but which to Zukor represented status. The more money he was able to pay, the more was he going to be respected in the industry. Goldfish believed that it meant simply the quicker the route to the bankruptcy court.

Sam cancelled the contract. Zukor ordered it reinstated. They were like two schoolboys poking out their tongues and wiggling their ears.

Both Mary Pickford and Chaplin were making pictures for the outfit—with all the attendant rows that entailed. Mary heard that Chaplin was being paid $670,000 a year. She was getting much less and wanted more.

It was another reason for a row between the two senior partners. Zukor said she was getting enough. Sam said she was 'a big drawing card', which was the term she herself had used. They settled for paying her $10,000 a week—still huge money for the time.

Meanwhile, Sam was doing all he could to let the world know that he was right. He had his own views on entertainment and the people he was hiring as entertainers.

What, for instance, did Mr Goldfish think of stage actors going into the movies? That was the question *The New York Times* asked him.

He said that people who thought that actors prostituted themselves and their talents were King Canutes—which shows that he was already a great believer in hiring people to write his own words as well as those in his scripts.

'Better their chances to stop the rising ocean tide than to retard an industry that is international in scope, that amuses and entertains millions every day, and that is proving to the artist a stable and profitable field.'

He was plainly feathering his own nest with every word he didn't actually say. But there was a lot of truth in those words and the sentiments were plainly his own all the way.

'The photoplay versions of great dramas are shown to millions of persons, whereas the original stage versions are reserved for theatre-goers in a comparatively few cities that can support extravagant theatres. The photoplay also exhibits a cast of the very finest artists, whereas some of the present-day stars of the legitimate theatre are actually limited in their appearances to New York, Chicago and a continental tour once in several years.'

As he went on: 'Ten years ago, the legitimate managers objected to their players entering vaudeville, because they said, it lessened their value. Now the vaudeville managers are joining the same cry against the photoplay.'

The 'photoplay' wasn't the only potential victim. As Sam might have said—and certainly believed—he was being sorely used by his new partner. And he didn't think much of the way his brother-in-law treated him either.

None of that should have come as any surprise. Jesse liked Sam, admired all he had done for the business, but none of that was important when he thought about his own role as brother to Sam's wife Blanche.

No one knew better than Lasky that Sam wasn't spending enough time with Blanche. He had never really considered it much of a love match, but in the early years of the twentieth century, particularly in Jewish circles, it was much more important that a girl should have a sense of security (which the then champion glove salesman had surely been able to offer).

But that wasn't enough any more. Sam hardly ever bothered to spend time with his baby daughter, Ruth, and Blanche suspected there must be another woman on the scene. There was—several of them.

The man who had done so much to invent Hollywood had also now done a great deal towards inventing a Hollywood tradition—the casting couch.

The success of a new actress's future could best be gauged by the amount of time she spent in Sam's office. If he thought a girl had potential, the office door would be locked. The lengthiest and most lucrative contracts went to those who lasted the course longest. Mind you, seduction was harder in those days. Young actresses wore very long dresses over petticoats and laced-up corsets that were themselves endurance tests. If a girl was tempting enough for Sam to survive the test until she got round to stripping completely for him, then, he figured, she had box-office promise, too. So every time he squeezed a girl's breasts, it could be argued he was doing it for the benefit of the business.

It would not have been an argument either Blanche or Jesse—to say nothing of Zukor—would have willingly appreciated.

They had suspected for a long time that when he went on out-of-town trips it wasn't just to sell movies—especially since his secretaries were always new, shapely in the departments Sam considered important, and none of them was renowned for her ability with either a typewritter or a shorthand pad.

It wasn't just 'secretaries' or new actresses for whom Sam had a strictly non-professional interest. When he saw a girl on the screen, he fantasized. When he had her in his office, usually on the pretext of a 'possible' raise or at least a bonus, it was an opportunity to put those fantasies into practice—and the hands that had sold a million gloves into more interesting uses; usually, to begin with, down the bodices of dresses he would swear he paid for. A conversation about an unsuspecting girl's new shoes would usually end up with a demonstration and a Goldfish hand climbing her leg ever higher.

Not even his biggest 'properties' were immune from this kind of activity. When one of these, the beautiful Elissa Landi, refused his advances—so strongly that Sam was totally mystified as to his next move—she told him: 'I'll have you know I was the star in my last picture.' The high-pitched Goldfish voice piped up: 'You stank in your last picture.' Stink or not, he found the perfume she was wafting in his office that day a great deal more intoxicating.

Mabel Normand and Mae Murray, two top stars of their day, had him smitten—emotionally as well as physically. One actress told of defeating his efforts around the spic-and-span, huge Goldfish desk. When Sam admitted defeat, so out of breath about the only thing he could raise was a squeaky cough, he showed the girl the door with the comment that he had never been so insulted in his life. The girl's own emotions, faced with a lecherous movie mogul, were not questioned.

Blanche, however did question them. She questioned the way he tried to keep her out of their Hollywood house, by having all the locks changed. She questioned, above all, the stories that reached her every time she had a coffee morning for her friends or went shopping.

At first, she couldn't believe it. Jewish husbands didn't do that sort of thing, but Hollywood was a new industry. Sam was still in his thirties and believed in doing everything differently—not that chasing other women wasn't of itself a great deal older than even the glove business.

She commissioned a private detective who reported to her virtually every pair of panties removed for her husband's entertainment. Finally, she sued for divorce. It was the most exciting moment the gossipists had had for years—especially when Blanche's lawyers listed Sam's dalliances and he replied by saying Ruth wasn't his own daughter. Even his lawyers went pale at that, a remark that he would regret almost the moment he said it and which cost him a relationship with the girl practically for the rest of his life. Indeed, for twenty years she didn't even know that Sam was her father.

The court was told he was earning $20,000 a week—a kind of figure no one outside of the big industrial houses of America would dare to contemplate. It was fairy-story money and in 1916 Blanche was determined to let that fairy story work for her benefit.

The final decision was straight out of a studio ledger, with figures so large—for 1916—they might have figured in a movie's budget.

Sam lost. As a result, he was ordered to pay his former wife $2,600 a year alimony and another $5,200 year for life, as compensation for all she lost by no longer being his wife, a situation she was glad to be out of. She had had enough and went back to the home of her mother and brother, the one where married life had begun. She felt hurt, humiliated and totally lost.

In September 1916 Sam announced he had had enough too. He was resigning from the Famous Players-Lasky Corporation, although he would retain his seat on the board of directors.

He would, however, no longer be Chairman of the Board or a member of the executive committee. The right words were being said by everyone with the remotest connection with the outfit, but the financial settlement was what counted on both sides of the fence—and it wasn't terribly hard to work out. Sam walked away with more than a million dollars—which was another Hollywood first. (The company itself was capitalized to the extent of $25 million.)

Sam left but took his speech-writer with him. 'I have contemplated retiring from the active management of the Famous Players-Lasky Corporation for some time in order to mature certain personal plans which are of great importance to me, and which I could not mature if I continued as one of the executives of the company.'

The Kid From Warsaw never spoke like that, never knew words like 'mature'—even if they had fitted the sentence better than they had—but, as he added, he had had to wait until the merger of the two companies was complete before finalizing his decision.

'It is, of course a matter of great regret to me that serving the corporations and going on with these plans of which I can say nothing definite at the present time, became inconsistent. From the time of the beginning of the Lasky Company to now, my heart and soul were in the work which I started quietly and unostentatiously about two-and-one-half years ago.'

These were public words. Privately, things were very much more acrimonious. They had, of course, been that way ever since Zukor first entered the scene. Now, though, no one taking Sam's side was having a civil word for anyone else. And above all, that went for Lasky, who was no doubt taking things out on Goldfish on his sister's behalf.

Matters really reached their head when Sam returned to New York after his three months of negotiations with Paramount. He returned to find a letter signed by both Zukor and Lasky saying he had to go—there could not be both Zukor as President and Goldfish as Chairman trying to run the operation.

Lasky presented the letter himself. He walked into Sam's private office and said: 'I have some bad news for you.'

'How will you vote?' Sam asked him.

'For Zukor,' he said, 'It's better that he remain and you go.'

As Sam told a subsequent hearing into allegations of Famous Players-Lasky developing a film-producing monopoly: 'Lasky and I have been partners for some time. We worked hard and got a 50–50 interest. I didn't think it was a very nice thing for him to do.'

As he probably thought, but didn't choose to say, if he had not used his own name at that time, he might just as well reap the benefit of it now.

'I am very proud of what has been accomplished, first by the Lasky company and since by the larger and more important corporation in which it merged with the Famous Players Film Company a few months ago, and proud, too, of such share of its success as my associates have been good enough to credit to my endeavours. My confidence in its future is amply evidenced, I think, by my retention of all my stock interests in it'.

The remaining members of the board issued their own statement. Goldfish's resignation didn't come as a surprise they admitted—far from it—but they received it with great regret. Not only was it received with regret, it was also accepted that way, too, but only because 'the board felt that any request that Mr Goldfish continue longer as an executive of the company would be unfair to him, in view of his statement that his work with the company would interfere with the maturing of his personal plans.'

Such consideration had been known to start wars, but they were trying to be all sweetness and light as they trampled each other underfoot.

Sam's other plans, meanwhile were—shall we say—maturing.

4
Kid Millions

What was Sam going to do now? No one really expected him to leave the industry he had helped to 'mature' along with his own ideas—except that he intended to do it in a much bigger way than he had previously contemplated.

Let Lasky and Zukor—with DeMille hanging on behind—cook up their deals and try to run the movie industry. Sam was staying in Hollywood, enjoying the benefits of his golden handshake and highly delighted to be free of Blanche. He was going to do big things.

And he was still anxious to do them bigger than anyone had before. The man who had, he always believed, created the long feature film (and although D. W. Griffith had had his own four-reeler before *Squaw Man*, it had been the Lasky film that made all the impact, nearly two years before Griffith's *Birth of a Nation*) now wanted to do it better than anyone before him.

The cinema, he was convinced, couldn't move much further ahead. Those long films with their close-up photography didn't flicker nearly as much as they used to do. After all, what more could the cinema offer? Colour? Sound? As Sam might have said, but didn't—that was a dream for pipes.

What Goldfish believed was that the film-going public wanted great stories beautifully written. How their writing could be translated into slides inserted between the action was not a matter that disturbed him. Nevertheless, he believed that people would be impressed with quality. Tell them they were about to see a film that had been a great Broadway success and he was sure they would pay the money he asked for tickets.

He knew, though, that in early 1917 that might be easier said than done. The man who had just discarded three partners reluctantly decided he had to take on others.

He really was not very sure what he was going to do next. It was still a young business and no matter how cock-sure he had seemed of both his talents and his prospects, the inevitable insecurity enveloped him from time to time.

One thing *was* certain: he was going to stay in the film business. But he was not sure enough of himself to go it alone. He needed someone else to share the burden with him. He didn't have Blanche at a time when he told friends he could have done with her. He was even saying that he loved her—a situation that cut no ice with the Lasky family, all of whom were sworn neither to talk to him nor ever to reveal his identity to Ruth (the child's name had now been changed—to Lasky).

He always believed that to succeed he had to go with a proven winner. Which was how he approached George M. Cohan to join him.

Cohan was the biggest success Broadway had ever known at that time. He not only acted in straight plays, he wrote his own musicals. The songs in them were huge hits: *Yankee Doodle Dandy*, *Give My Regards To Broadway*, *Mary's A Grand Old Name*, and *You're A Grand Old Flag* were among his most successful. He had once been asked if he could ever write a song without a flag in it. He replied: 'I can write without anything but a pencil.'

It wasn't his pencil that Sam wanted, or even his patriotism (although that appealed to him mightily; like many an immigrant, America seemed the best place in the world to him and he wanted people to know just how he felt). What he wanted was Cohan's expertise, his know-how and the people who knew him.

In October 1916 he announced that he was going into business with Cohan, with George appearing in screen versions of all his old successes. It didn't happen, but the idea and the prestige it entailed appealed to Goldfish tremendously. What he was hoping for was to find someone who could provide him with the benefits of a talent he could exploit.

It was Sam's conviction that 'stories came first, films second', that got him involved with the Selwyn brothers, Edgar and Arch. They were very young and very ambitious—and also very clever. So clever that they were thinking along the same lines as Mr Goldfish, which most people would agree was a very clever thing to do indeed.

It was that notion of being on the same wavelength—a concept that hadn't, of course, yet been invented—which attracted Sam. They had a growing library of impressive plays under their belt, ready, before long, to produce on Broadway. Sam, of course, had other ideals—such a ready-made collection of literary wealth was made-to-measure for the screen and could serve as a marvellous stock for the new movie company he was about to set up. He *would* set it up, of course, if the Selwyns came in with him (there could be no other way of getting his still finely-gloved hands on those plays).

Goldfish was as impressive to the young Selwyns as he had been to everyone with whom he had ever conducted business, and he did cut a fine figure. He wasn't tall, but in those days he was slim and still had hair, dark hair which he always believed was an asset towards good relations with attractive women.

His voice was sometimes unnervingly high and that accent did make him a target for every budding impersonator in Hollywood and New York. But what came out in those mangled sentences of his did make a great deal of sense. Business sense. The case he presented to the Selwyns seemed practically unanswerable: they had the plays, he had the movie experience and ability and there was no way they could fail.

The brothers came to more or less the same conclusion. Except that they were not clever producers by taking other people's words at face value. They made their own investigations. In the course of these, Edgar Selwyn went to see Adolph Zukor which, had Sam found out about it, would have sent him into apoplexies of anger.

Considering the circumstances, Zukor was extraordinarily generous. 'Do you know any reason why I shouldn't go into business with Sam?' he asked Zukor.

'As far as his honesty and integrity are concerned,' said Zukor, 'there is none.'

That was the end of the generosity—other than the free way in which he offered advice. 'If you do,' he told Selwyn, 'you'll be a most unhappy boy.'

It was not something that could be accepted quite so lightly and simply. Selwyn wanted to know why—he had plainly not heard the stories that Zukor was very willing to tell his stockholders.

Sam at least was determined. As he was to say: 'I was fed up with having to make compromises with people who didn't know as much about the film business as I did. I was determined to do everything myself, without having to consult bankers, boards of directors or anybody else.'

Zukor was an intelligent man with a clever turn of phrase. He used that ability to explain his anti-Goldfish stand. 'Sam is like a Jersey cow that gives the finest milk, but before you can take the bucket away he has kicked it over.'

The metaphor took a little working out. But it became clear to them that Zukor didn't like Goldfish. Was that the reason he was trying to keep the Selwyns away? At first, the brothers needed some convincing. They were rightly suspicious of a man with such an important axe to grind. But then they thought the rival mogul might have a point. Why get involved with a man like Sam? Why did they even want to get into films? That certainly wasn't their business. Was it? So they said No.

Sam protested. They listened. Then they were convinced. They would, after all, go with him. But what to call their joint enterprise? It was Sam who suggested merging syllables of their two names along with their two companies—although Sam's company consisted only of Sam Goldfish and his secretary. Selwyn and Goldfish? Selgold? No. That didn't have the right ring about it. Gold was what they hoped to make, not sell. Goldsel seemed to make the same mistake. Selfish Pictures? That wasn't exactly the image they were after. Goldwyn? They seemed about right. After all, it had an element of class about it, and that would be Sam's aim thereafter.

He had lost his old sense of overt modesty. Now he saw no reason to hide his light behind any other Hollywood bushel. The Selwyns were content enough. They knew they couldn't go into such an arrangement other than as junior partners and therefore it had to be Goldfish's first syllable which would come before theirs.

None of that is to say that Sam was happy with his name. When Shmuel Gelbfisz became Samuel Goldfish, he had no idea of the effect it would have on the company he would keep or just how much of a joke that immigration man was having.

So the change of name was important to him, even without a new company to go with it.

He knew people made fun of the name. As writer Alva Johnston noted in 1937: 'Sam could not have provoked more merriment if he wore a pigtail or a Lord Fauntleroy suit. On being introduced to Goldfish, you had to say something good or forfeit your reputation as a quick thinker.'

There was, for instance, the assortment of stories of Sam Goldfish at public occasions. 'Mr Samuel Goldfish,' announced the flunky at those Hollywood or Manhattan events, and a titter of laughter ran though the room like the sound of coins rattling at the box-office.

He was getting fed up with it. And he was particularly upset when he went to the theatre. 'Mr Goldfish's seats,' announced the usher—and there was enough amusement caused by that statement to keep an audience happy through the dullest plays.

Sam had never been more mortified than when he arrived, not quite punctually, for a performance of the *Midnight Frolics* presented by Florenz Ziegfeld on the roof of his theatre.

Sam was seated behind a glass partition. He protested—and opened a can of worms sufficent to feed much bigger fish.

Gene Buck, the Broadway wit who was assisting Ziegfeld in the Frolics enterprise, couldn't resist the opportunity with which he was now being presented on a plate. 'Behind glass' he said, 'is the right place for a Goldfish.'

Sam was broken up. The whole world—or at least the world in which he lived—was laughing at him. No matter how much success he had had.

His new film company appeared to offer the chance he needed. If Goldwyn was good enough for his business, it was certainly also good enough for him. A judge of the United States Supreme Court agreed.

Sam went to court in an endeavour to get the change of name legalized—he didn't want any further complications; this was a Goldfish he wanted to discard and not to see swimming up before him in the future.

The appropriately-named Judge Learned Hand listened sympathetically. He said he understood perfectly. 'A self-made man, he declared, 'may prefer a self-made name.'

Well, the name wasn't totally self-made. The Selwyns had a little to do with it, but they were happy to stay with their own nomenclature and look to the future with their new operation. (Not that Sam would lose the old name completely. Virtually to his dying day there would be a wag who would attempt to introduce him as 'Mr Goldfish'.)

And they had an impressive partner. He would go to meetings with distributors or executives in an English-made suit, beautifully pressed. His stiff white collar was immaculately curved and fitted so closely that his black knitted tie had to be knotted below it. That was stylish and very modern compared with the wing collars worn by most businessmen of the day.

Sam knew that if the new company was going to succeed it really did have to do things bigger and better than his competitors did them—particularly bigger and better than the way the Famous Players-Lasky outfit did.

He also knew that the one way of being sure of making films more successfully was to employ the right people—not just the writers whom he had already said were so important. He wanted Broadway producers to bring their art and their experience to film-making. And he wanted the finest artists to design sets that would make audiences gasp. It wasn't enough to depend on the beauty of his actresses or the smartness of his male stars to make this work.

He also wanted new ideas. Arthur Hopkins, who went to the Goldwyn studios straight from Broadway, came up with one idea which was right up Goldwyn's home street—a film without sub-titles, no words to interrupt the flow of pictures. It was an idea which Sam thought was so beautiful, it would entice his audiences, and persuade their friends to come too.

Fighting Odds the picture was called and Sam gave it his full blessing. The Goldwyn Picture Corporation was starting work very big indeed. Everyone would have to sit up and listen. The trouble was that Sam himself started listening—and came up with an entirely wrong conclusion.

The idea was discussed with a party of theatre-owners who plainly disagreed with Sam and told him so. The public wouldn't take it—and they weren't going to give them the chance. Goldwyn, with the courage of their convictions, ordered sub-titles to be added.

They were added after the film had been shot and in between scenes never intended to take them. It was all a terrible mess and the box-office take proved it.

People began to wonder about the so-called Goldwyn touch. Had Sam himself lost it? Or did he ever have it? Was he not just a super salesman who had depended a great deal on his 'chutzpah' and on the help of newly involved professionals like Cecil B. DeMille? That was the talk and, as we have seen, talk worried Sam Goldwyn.

All the odds had been against Sam with the *Fighting Odds*—even his choice of leading lady.

Sam's great weakness was an over-respect for Broadway. What attracted audiences to the live stage in New York would, he was sure, bring them into the movie-theatres being built all over the States as 'picture-palaces'. He was wrong.

He paid a fortune to attract Maxine Elliott to the screen. Miss Elliott was renowned as a stage beauty. Everyone knew that. The way her breasts were pushed out in front by contemporary fashion and her hips magnificently curved was supposed to have men salivating at the notion of seeing her. Her face had been regarded as the most magnificent on which a spotlight had ever been focused. Sam knew her reputation and signed Miss Elliott for a vast sum of money to appear in his film.

The truth is she didn't look the way he remembered her. Or at least, she didn't photograph that way. Her hips were wider than reputation had it, her bust . . . well, it wasn't quite as high as people remembered. And that magnificent face . . . could have done with the ministrations of one of the Westmores who a generation later would revolutionize film make-up. It bore the ravages of time and of twenty-four years of facing that spotlight.

Sam was beginning to be convinced that the priority had to be the stories. He brought *Thais*, a play by Anatole France (allegedly because he was convinced it would capture the French market) and, only after the deal was done, thought about a star.

He next approached another Metropolitan Opera star, Mary Garden, who was so-so on camera, but didn't bring in any customers to the picture-palaces. It seems that potential audiences thought he was presenting Mary Gardner—a name that symbolized the days when going to the movies meant visiting a nickelodeon. Nobody knew what Miss Gardner really looked like because of the flickering of the projector, but they remembered.

Things might have been helped if the extraordinarily bosomy Miss Garden had been a good actress. She wasn't. She was an eminent opera star, who, deprived of a voice, had only that bosom—which was in better shape (literally) than Miss Elliot's—to offer cinema patrons. She threw out her notable mammaries with every gesture on screen, but once the novelty had worn off there was little else to offer. The people who paid for tickets weren't in the least interested in her opera pedigree—Sam's impression of the cultural tastes of Mr and Mrs America was as extraordinarily inflated as Miss Garden's bust—and the confusion with the other lady amounted to a big failure.

The audiences wanted nothing of Miss Garden and Sam worried that perhaps they wanted nothing of him either. But it was the star who bore the brunt of the opposition.

One critic wrote: 'She died like an acrobat instead of a saint.'

Another attempt at converting an opera singer into a film star wasn't any easier. Geraldine Farrar had transferred from Lasky to Goldwyn when Sam formed his company. But nothing she could do at the new studio was any good. Finally Sam reluctantly told her they had to go their own ways.

He had been paying her $250,000 a picture—a literally fantastic sum—and she admitted it was asking too much to keep going.

Sam called on her on a Sunday afternoon, tried to be nice and jolly but was totally unable to conceal his anxiety. Geraldine knew what he was trying not to say and made it easy for him.

'If you do what I want, Mr Goldwyn, you will just tear up that contract,' she told him. 'You have been too sweet to me.' To which Sam commented: 'I have never met a finer person.'

And it wasn't that even he believed his other idea for buying important new plays was, as he had been known to put it, a 'cure-all'.

It had been an accepted wisdom that making a film of a play meant no one wanted to see the original stage version. Now the reverse was happening.

When Sam made Margaret Mayo's *Baby Mine* he found that stock companies were putting the play into production—and so getting the benefit of his publicity. At the same time, people buying tickets for the stage play were saying they wouldn't want to see the film. It was beginning to worry Goldwyn and, in truth, all his competitors too.

Things went from bad to worse. Sam was doing most of his filming, not in Hollywood, but in New Jersey—which was not a very clever thing to do in the midst of a world war when electricity was being cut. He thought it would be more economical to film on the East Coast, so close to the business office. Now he was having doubts. His competitors were using the Hollywood sunshine, which didn't cost them a penny.

He said it was all part of the story of the industry.

'How are the pictures doing?' asked *The New York Times* seven months after America joined the war in November 1917.

His answer wasn't very encouraging. 'The motion picture industry is in a dangerous condition,' he told them. 'Disaster is very close indeed. The war has not hit attendances at motion-picture houses as hard as it has at the Broadway theatres, but that is only because the scale of prices is so much lower and the great democratic audiences of the screen are drawn largely from those who are getting more employment and more profitable employment through the war.

'The success and the health of the motion picture is based on the modest price of admission at which good films can be seen. The dangerous, even disastrous, conditions in the industry of which I have spoken are due to the fact that all manner of competitive extravagance is threatening to destroy that one safeguard—and, with it, the industry itself.'

Now that was strange material to read about Mr Goldwyn, the great believer in the efficacy of spending money. Goldwyn talking about extravagance had the smell of sour grapes about it—although he denied any such intent. Sam's was not suffering more than any other studio; in fact, he maintained it was doing better than most. But he was desperate to point out that there was a 'criminal waste of the producer's money, the exhibitor's money and—in the last analysis—the public's money'. Somebody, he declared, should speak out plainly.

Sam was ready to speak as plainly as his ghost-writer knew how.

He was into his stride and enjoying every miserable fact that he felt it his duty to impart. The newly-named Samuel Goldwyn was taking yet another name for himself—Job.

There were those who, conscious that his operation wasn't doing quite as well as he would have liked, wondered about his right to sneer, but Goldwyn was certain he had a responsibility to his competitors as well as to himself and his own stockholders.

'If you ask me what is wrong with this top-heavy industry of ours, I should say—organization. Fundamentally all our producing organizations are wrong. Fundamentally all our distributing organizations are wrong.

It was perhaps easier to put the blame on the distributors, people he wasn't terribly fond of at the best of times. They were the parasites of the industry as far as he could make out, the middlemen whom he needed because they had the theatres sewn up. If he were able to, he would assemble his own work team to do the distributing. It was, after all, 1917 and he was getting the feeling that this modern age needed a modern man.

'There are about twenty-five distributing organizations in America, all of them maintaining some two dozen branch offices throughout the country. Those twenty-five exchanges serving the State of Maine, to take a single flagrant example, have only twenty-eight cities and town—small ones at that—in which to sell films.'

It is a technicality, but it does give a good indication of the way the film industry was operating. He also admitted that the production side of the business needed improving. There was a lack of adequate finance—'the cost of production has gone up at a terrific rate, a rate that the public has no conception of.'

And then came a fascinating illustration. It was now impossible to make a feature picture for less than $150,000.

As he said: 'The big factor in keeping down moving picture prices, I feel, is the producer. He must organize. The great steel industry was in just such a chaotic condition before the coming of the United States Steel Corporation. If the producing factors in moving pictures do not shortly come to their senses, I predict failure—spectacular failure—for a great many of the plungers of filmdom today.'

And yet, for reasons no one could adequately explain, Sam was trying to keep a smile on his face—even in the midst of extreme provocation. He was also extremely athletic, both sexually (with no marital inhibitions to stop him) and physically.

In 1917 Sam broke an ankle while playing handball at the New York Athletic Club, a place at which he liked to be seen—for it demonstrated a degree of acceptance into Manhattan society that was not given to most immigrants.

It was before the days of plaster casts or other devices. For three months he was confined to a hospital bed, his foot, having been physically reset, resting on a slung hammock.

That was just another problem. Edgar Selwyn and his other fellow-directors, former Broadway producers Al Woods, Sam Harris and Arthur Hopkins, came to see him. 'It's bankruptcy, Sam' they said. 'No choice.'

If Goldwyn had had a cigar to smoke—and if the hospital would have allowed it—he would have been twirling it in his fingers and puffing away merrily.

When things seemed to be going wrong, that was when he knew they could only get better.

'Gentlemen,' he said enthusiastically, 'I can see nothing but roses.'

The only roses his partners saw were in the colour of the ink on the balance sheets, but that wasn't going to be allowed to spoil his euphoria. All outstanding payroll debts were paid that week by practically wiping out his own bank account and he borrowed heavily, mainly from the Du Pont organization.

His optimism was to be proved right. What he predicted became a fact of life.

The 1918 armistice brought a new wave of prosperity to an America on the verge of the jazz age. People wanted to forget and there was no better place in which to do it than in a seat at the movies.

For those people hungry for bright entertainment, Sam gave them all the tricks that he knew.

He also enjoyed the torments of the opposition. Lasky and Zukor between them had the bright idea of engaging Enrico Caruso to make a movie for them. It was ten years before the advent of sound pictures and Caruso without his voice was like a performing seal with its flippers tied. He photographed bearing a close resemblance to a very plump Italian peasant who could have done with some acting lessons. Sam chortled while Lasky and Zukor looked for some way of redeeming themselves.

Goldwyn, meanwhile had *Joan of Plattsburg* and Mabel Normand.

Perhaps it would be more significant to say more simply that Sam had Mabel Normand. He was in the midst of a deep, deep love affair with the beautiful star who could twist him round her little finger.

It began with a typical Goldwyn seduction scene, a meeting in his office, the promise of a new contract, great wealth, a kiss, a plunge down the front of her dress. She didn't try to resist him. She knew Goldwyn's strength and his power.

Before long, she was loving him as much as he loved her. They didn't talk of marriage. Sam had had one experience and didn't want to repeat it. But he brought Mabel furs, jewellery, a car, everything she wanted. He wrote her cheques—which she only cashed when she needed something. Money held no value for her, simply because she didn't understand it. She was, however, a natural actress and *Joan of Plattsburg* was an outstanding hit.

He was not beyond 'borrowing' stars from other outfits, including his previous organization. Pauline Frederick was one of these.

His former partners said he was behaving dishonestly and had enticed her away with promises he would not be able to keep.

Sam denied it vociferously. 'I don't believe you, Goldfish,' said Zukor when he confronted his old adversary.

'Are you calling me a liar?' responded Goldwyn.

Eventually, even Mabel Normand got wise to her lover's attitude to his business. She got wind of what Pauline Frederick was earning—twice as much as the $1,000 a week she got—and demanded $5,000. It wasn't that she was now more familiar with the wiles of big business. She simply was playing the jealous woman, who didn't see why another woman should get more money than she did.

When Sam said No, she took off for Europe and told him she wasn't coming back. In the end, Sam offered her $1,500 a week and she returned. That was partly due to a new Mr Fix-It whom Sam brought in to the operation—his old glove-making pal Abe Lehr.

Abe had remained Sam's closest friend and now he proved a stabilizing force in the company, someone on whom he could bounce ideas. Not that he always took advice. He was no more willing now to abandon an idea simply because Lehr had opposed it than he had been when they had squabbled over Sam's gambling. But he did respect him.

He also respected learning—and writing. A big book always impressed him, even if he didn't actually read it. When he first saw a dictionary, the story goes, he commented: 'My, my what a big book. Who wrote it?'

Lehr was caught off guard. 'Webster' he replied.

'Must have taken him a long time', said Sam thoughtfully.

'Yes,' said his trusted associate, 'a century.'

'My,' rejoined Sam, 'fifty years.'

Now, it can't be proved, but it is quite possible Sam was himself enjoying the joke. He knew that people were beginning to laugh at him and the way he treated the English language as though it were some newly washed laundry just about to be wrung out, but he was taking the attitude that it was better to be talked about than be ignored. And you couldn't ignore Sam Goldwyn, even then.

He did, however, want people to know that he had a love of culture and that writers were the most important people in his stable. Cynics could argue with a certain justification that this was because he couldn't get the stars. But no one had any right to doubt that people who wrote books were installed on a fairly high pedestal as far as Goldwyn was concerned. Other moguls sneered at the 'pen-pushers'. Goldwyn respected them in the way painters and musicians are admired by people who cannot use a paintbrush or hold a note. There was a mystique about these people. Have a writer on your side and you were a man who could hold his head to the sky.

In 1919 he consummated that admiration by forming an organization that so astonished his competitors, they seemed to collectively gasp instead of uttering the gaffaws everyone expected. He formed the League of Eminent Authors—including Leroy Scott, Mary Roberts Rinehart, Basil King, Rex Beach and Gertrude Atherton—and announced they were all going to work for Goldwyn Pictures.

He also launched Eminent Authors as a separate film company. 'Good films', said Sam 'should begin with a detailed scenario and not with a budget.'

He even had the idea of plugging the writer's name above the title, with the star's below (and in smaller type). It was not a good move. It suggested that Goldwyn didn't know as much about his public as he always claimed he did. Picture-going audiences weren't interested in writers, certainly didn't know many of their names. Before long it seemed that this was what another generation of Goldwyn film fans might have called King's New Clothes syndrome—an attempt to hide Sam's inadequacies rather than boast his advantages.

But it was enough to cause a few furrowed brows among his competitors. Before long other studios were signing up names like Somerset Maugham, Arnold Bennett and Elinor Glyn to write for them, with about the same kind of results and the same amount of publicity. There is no doubt, however, that Sam benefited from the first jolt of Press attention.

The publicity was immense—and so was the trouble the writers caused him. Few of them had any idea how to write for motion pictures, silent motion pictures. And what they did write came only after a series of rows that were so heated and so loud, Sam seemed to have invented talking pictures before the men from Vitaphone.

But he kept to his original intentions, stubbornly refusing to admit he could ever be wrong on a matter that the Press had confirmed was so right. He was so confident that he *was* correct that he gradually fired all his staff scenarists—including a certain Darryl F. Zanuck, who was promptly taken on by Warner Bros. and before long would run Twentieth Century-Fox.

He made almost the same fuss of his writers as he did of his starlets—the *almost*, of course, says what he did *not* do—cherished and cosseted them. Whatever they wanted, they were able to get: comfortable offices, attractive secretaries using near-silent typewriters (or as nearly silent as was possible in the early 1920s) and the privilege of being photographed with Mr Goldwyn himself. He told them that everything would receive his own personal attention.

What is intriguing is that Sam, still the uneducated product of the Warsaw Jewish quarter and the steerage passage from Liverpool to New York, knew what good writing was—and not simply because of the name on the front page of a script.

Basil King was the first of his writers to disappoint him. He read King's first attempt at a script for a now forgotten movie and was so upset he almost cried. He called King into his office and decided that the best approach was to be kind. There was no need for hysteria, for uncontrolled anger. He had to be polite, even praising.

'Mr. King,' he told him, 'you are undoubtedly the greatest writer in the world.' King glowed. 'But,' Sam added, 'maybe this is not good for the movies.'

All his writers were told they were the greatest writers in the world—and then, practically one by one, were informed that their work stank.

His only success—ignoring, that is, the tremendous triumph to the Goldwyn name which his publicity campaign had brought—was with Rupert Hughes. Hughes produced for him a script called *The Old Nest*. The picture made a million dollars—which was enough to convince Goldwyn he had been right all along. Good writers *were* more important than actors.

It was a sentiment George Bernard Shaw might have been expected to share, and probably did, except that he had no desire to go into the movies or work for Samuel Goldwyn.

Sam sailed for London to try to convince the writer of *Pygmalion*, *Arms and the Man* and *Man and Superman* to join him. Goldwyn was not used to being thwarted—in fact it practically never happened. What ensued was really a Man and Superman encounter of classic dimensions. Sam flattered, and Shaw rejected—but in a way that Goldwyn had to admit destroyed him in just the manner he himself usually demolished antagonists.

'The trouble, Mr Goldwyn,' the Irish-born playwright pointed out, 'is that you are only interested in art and I am only interested in money.'

The epigram danced back and forth across the transatlantic cable link.

Sam had met his match. It wasn't his only one. The Belgian writer Maurice Maeterlinck proved to be a Goldwyn disaster of epic proportions. Sam really should have known better, but for some reason ignored all the signs, which were as obvious as if they had been written in yard-high letters illuminated in neon.

Maeterlinck had an international reputation and that was supposedly well deserved. Sam thought that anyone invited over to the United States for a lecture tour had to be marvellous. The trouble was that Goldwyn appeared to stop reading about him before Maeterlinck began and ended his tour in one night.

He had been booked into the highly prestigious Carnegie Hall—another good sign, Sam believed. He was to give a lecture that he considered so important he wrote down every word first—in French. He then had the French text translated into English, a language he didn't know. But he was a writer and an intelligent man and wasn't going to allow that mere detail to faze him. If he were going to read his lecture in English, he had to be able to know how. He came up with a solution to which perhaps only a later Goldwyn star, Danny Kaye, could have done justice.

Because he didn't know English, he didn't know how English should sound. In that case, he reasoned, he would have those sounds translated into corresponding French sounds. For more than an hour the Maeterlinck phonetics had the Carnegie Hall audience at first shifting uncomfortably in their seats and then doing all they could not to roll in the aisles.

It was total gibberish. Maeterlinck didn't know what he was saying. The English people though he was speaking French, the French that he was giving an exposition of that new international language Esperanto.

The only one who wasn't laughing was Sam Goldwyn. He might have heard that the Belgian gentleman had hit a spot of bother; if so he could no doubt get him cheap. The lecture tour was cancelled, but Maeterlinck was still in America—possibly trying to find a way to pay his fare home.

They had a meeting. Sam flattered again. But this time, it was much harder than with, say, a Bernard Shaw. Sam hadn't bargained with the writer's lack of English and if his words of flattery couldn't be understood, what point was there?

He tried again. He had a list of all his writers brought before him and then asked for their contracts to be submitted for the Belgian's perusal.

'Look,' said Sam, trying very hard and with one of his staff now brought in to act as interpreter. 'Look what I am paying them. You'll be getting as much as any of them.'

The look on the writer's face now approximated that of his own Carnegie Hall audience.

Sam thought the time had come to be specific.

'You know Basil King,' he challenged.

Maeterlinck looked at the mogul again and this time Sam had a smile on his face. He knew he had struck home. He was convinced that this time he had said something to impress. The writer studied Sam and, Goldwyn was now sure, was about to say how moved he was by the comparison. Sam repeated it, now confident of the answer.

'You know, Basil King?' he asked once more.

Maeterlinck looked again and said: 'Non.'

'You know Rupert Hughes?'

'Non,' the Belgian replied.

'Well, how about Rex Beach?'

'Non.'

If audiences were going to be impressed by Sam's list of Eminent Authors, this didn't bode well.

'What's the matter with this guy?' Sam squeaked at length. 'Dumb?'

He wasn't dumb enough to pass up the kind of money Sam still thought it wise to proffer. It amounted to well over $20,000 and that Maeterlinck understood only too well.

Nobody had yet thought of what the Belgian writer was actually going to produce, but for the moment that was a mere detail. It was much more important that people should get to know what an important find this was, what a *prestigious* addition Samuel Goldwyn had to his list of eminent writers.

He put the matter in the hands of his publicist, Howard Dietz, who had just earned himself a place in the history of Hollywood. But more of that shortly.

Dietz took his solution to the Maeterlinck problem to Sam's Fifth Avenue apartment on the corner of 40th Street, which, as he remarked, was appropriate since it faced the lions of New York's Public Library.

The reason those lions were appropriate will also become apparent before long.

Dietz's aim was to convince the public how important Goldwyn's new find was—and, equally, to convince the new find how much he was being valued.

So he dreamed up the idea of a coast-to-coast tour for the Belgian writer, using the same car that Woodrow Wilson had used selling America on the gospel of the League of Nations.

Everywhere he went statements were issued saying how proud he was to be in America and how grateful to Sam Goldwyn for giving him this opportunity. (He still couldn't speak English, but having wrestled with Sam's command of the language, this didn't present any great problem for Dietz. He was a skilled ghost-writer.)

Sometimes, he switched the compliments, too. 'America does not give the motion picture the artistic importance it merits,' he was reported as saying in February 1920—and the idea was that newspaper readers would assume he mean to add, 'until now and with the help of Sam Goldwyn'.

Maeterlinck was best known for his successful play *The Blue Bird*. Now Goldwyn was sure that that hit was all the public would remember and would wait, in grateful anticipation, for what was going to follow.

The trouble was, with the contract and the money it involved safely in his pocket, Maeterlinck was no longer prepared to play Sam's game. He was accompanied on the trip by his lecture manager and *he* didn't like the competition that both the movies and this preamble were presenting.

Despite the Carnegie Hall fiasco, the lecture tour would continue before long. Both manager and client were on a percentage and, instead of thinking it was all good publicity, the manager reasoned that people wouldn't want to both read and listen to the writer. Every public statement Maeterlinck made, he said, represented 100 lost lecture seats. So no more public statements.

The whole journey was a battle between manager and publicist—with Sam pacing the floor of his New York office after every call from Dietz, a man who was not used to being frustrated in this way.

The manager actually arranged to reroute the private carriage of the train taking Maeterlinck to a dinner in Dallas. Sam heard about this and instantly had one of his henchmen meet the train at its next stopping point.

The manager was paged. Sam's man greeted him warmly, shook his hand—and then punched him square on the jaw. The hitherto victorious and unsuspecting manager was laid out flat on the platform.

Things were no better in Hollywood, where Sam had now moved his office once more. Maeterlinck produced a story that not only guaranteed Goldwyn an invitation to a creditors' meeting, but which was also enough to have them all certified insane.

The story was based on his *Life of a Bee*. Sam almost had an instant attack of apoplexy. 'My God,' he said, 'He's written a story where the hero is a bee.'

When the message resounded loud and clear in Maeterlinck's office that a bee wasn't exactly his boss's idea of fun, he tried again.

There was probably not a little bit of sabotage involved. Maeterlinck knew that Goldwyn was tied to him legally and had to cough up the money to which he was committed—while he himself regarded everyone around as a philistine. But he appeared to try. Nothing worked out (he might have been sorry if it had).

He produced a scenario that began with a manhole cover being lifted open from below a Paris street—by a dishevelled woman, wearing a beret with a dagger clenched between her teeth.

Sam didn't like that idea, either, and eventually had the courage to tell the Belgian so. He was so glad to get rid of him that he personally escorted Maeterlinck to the local station. There, he helped him on to his train. As it started to steam out, Goldwyn, still clutching Maeterlinck's hand, purred: 'Don't worry Maurice. You'll make good yet.'

There were speedy efforts by Maeterlinck and his sidekicks to recoup some vestige of pride from the affair. The Belgian knew Sam would do all he could to excoriate him. Maeterlinck let it be known that he and Goldwyn could not get on. 'I cannot write for you or for America,' he let reporters know he had already told Goldwyn. 'For you want love stories and you will not permit adultery' (He didn't add 'in your movies', that would have been a more accurate assessment). 'When writing of one, I write always of the other.'

More than a decade later Sam found himself in the seemingly unfortunate situation of being in Cannes at the same time as the writer. 'Would you like to meet Maeterlinck?' a friend asked him. 'No thank you,' said Goldwyn, 'I had enough of that man years ago.'

There were others. Even so, nothing would convince Sam that the writers were not the real stars of his operation, and that belief was to go a long way towards confirming the Goldwyn reputation of searching for a quality that eluded his competitors. But it was trying for all concerned.

Eventually, Sam admitted that the only two of his 'Eminent Writers' who had made good in Hollywood were Rupert Hughes and Rex Beach, although all of them had made at least $10,000 a year from him irrespective of whether they had anything accepted for the screen. He lost 'heavily', he would say, on two stories by Basil King which were made into films. Mrs Atherton had already given up the ghost of film-writing before Maeterlinck was handed his marching orders. She said it did not suit her style.

Mary Roberts Rinehart decided she could make more money simply by selling the screen rights to her work.

She was the writer to whom Sam offered the prospect of what he believed was total co-operation. Except that what he said was: 'I want to cohabit with you.'

What were needed, Sam said, were 'freshly creative imaginations'. (That, at least, was what *The New York Times*—in an article replete with references to King Richard III and for the offer of his kingdom for a horse—said he was calling for. What he actually told his ghost-writer boggles the imagination.) 'If you have this power, I await you eagerly and, upon finding you, I shall act like a famed gentleman who had a high mountain and all the kingdoms of his world at his command.'

And that was really what Sam believed. His writers were the ones he was sure would bring him not just money, but all the prestige he dreamed of commanding. When, in June 1920, he signed up Booth Tarkington to write for him—he bought the rights to the author held by his cousin Tarkington Baher—he trumpeted the news the way the other studios were to announce over the years the acquisition of a Garbo or a Monroe.

Will Rogers was one of Goldwyn's stars at the time, wearing his cowboy hat and twirling his lasso. He was delighted to be signed to star in *The Legend of Sleepy Hollow*, based on Washington Irving's story. He didn't fancy being asked to take part in anything produced by the League. As he said, 'I'm all off living authors' work. Me for the dead ones!'

They had had correspondence with each other in 1919 when Rogers was due to star in his film *Jubilo*. Sam didn't like the title, which was based on a story by Ben Ames Williams, about a tramp. He decided to change it. Rogers took the view that the title would be changed over his tramp's dead body. 'THOUGHT I WAS SUPPOSED TO BE A COMEDIAN BUT WHEN YOU SUGGEST CHANGING THE TITLE OF *JUBILO* YOU ARE FUNNIER THAN I EVER WAS' Rogers wrote in a telegram. He finished his message; 'WHAT WOULD YOU HAVE CALLED *BIRTH OF A NATION*?'

Sam must have pondered that thought. He kept the title.

As a result of *Jubilo* Rogers was now firmly established as one of Sam's aces. Lon Chaney Senior joined in 1920, another big Goldwyn coup. Things were looking up.

In 1921 he introduced Conrad Veidt to American audiences by bringing over the German film *The Cabinet of Dr Caligari*, which some regard as the first ever avant-garde movie. He didn't understand it. He knew most of his audiences wouldn't understand it. But he also knew that people would say that Sam was doing a great deal for the arts. Prestige was as important to him as cash.

5
Beloved Enemy

He was personally involved in every aspect of his filming now.

That was why he was so keen on publicity. The man who had been so shrinking a violet (which is perhaps not an ideal term to use when thinking about Samuel Goldwyn) that he wanted his brother-in-law's name on their joint company instead of his own, had turned full circle. When people talked about Goldwyn, he believed they wanted to see his films.

Like his writers and his stars, his publicists had to be the best, which is how Howard Dietz came on the scene and how he made his huge contribution to the history of the cinema.

He did it simply by inventing what would today be called a 'logo' for Sam's company—a lion mounted in the midst of a wreath bearing the legend 'Ars Gratia Artis', 'Art for Art's Sake'.

It would later become Sam's greatest contribution to MGM (although that is jumping the story somewhat), but when Dietz came up with the idea he did it for his boss alone, a time before anyone had any idea of a Metro and a Mayer joining forces—supposedly—with a Goldwyn, which is also jumping ahead.

Dietz later said he got the idea of the lion—immediately named Leo—from a college comic called *The Jester*. As he said, a lion was the emblem of Columbia University, New York, and had been pinched by them from King's College, London.

He was already a lion among publicists, probably *the* best in the business. (Eventually he would become even better known as a lyricist; *Dancing In The Dark* was to be probably his best.) Few of his tasks presented any great problems to him—although it was as much due to Dietz's own precision and persistence as to the luck that Sam had in employing him. He almost didn't.

Quite some time after selling him the idea of the lion, Dietz applied for a full-time job with Goldwyn's company. He waited a whole day in Sam's outer office to be seen and was ignored. Finally, in desperation, he got hold of a typewriter and a sheet of Goldwyn notepaper—security plainly wasn't all that sophisticated in those days—and wrote a letter, telling stories about Sam's great successes in business to the editor of the *Evening Mail*. The letter was published; so were three others. Then, Dietz took his courage (which was clearly self evident) into his typing hands and wrote one in Sam's own name to the head of Eastman Kodak company, asking, nay begging, him to produce a non-inflammable film. He then sent it to Sam saying what marvellous publicity it would make.

Goldwyn not only had to agree—he kept it in his pocket for two days, showing it to all whom he met till it virtually got too grubby for use, before posting it. He then appointed Dietz to his job as publicity chief, pushing up the offered salary of $50 a week to $200.

Dietz was to say that Sam was a tough man to work for. A man who frequently lost his temper—especially when he knew he wasn't in the right. A man who despised clock-watchers, and expected his employees to be on call whenever needed.

You couldn't be a clock-watcher if you were a Goldwyn publicist—even if you weren't Howard Dietz.

Who are the thirteen best actors and actresses in Hollywood? That was a notion one publicist named Pete Smith asked Sam to contemplate. He suggested that if Goldwyn listed the thirteen in a press handout he would distribute, it would generate a host of articles in his favour (which goes to show how things have changed in the past three-quarters of a century).

Sam thought about that and had to agree that the idea had some merit—except, he pointed out, it might make the thirteen performers love him, but all the rest would be so insulted they would start saying the most outrageous things. So Sam had a better idea. He told the press agent to list twelve of his favourites—and said the thirteenth name was to stay a secret.

For days, papers were trying to guess who that number thirteen really was.

Not that Sam always had the right ideas. On one occasion he asked for some publicity pictures of himself to be taken. Then he ordered them to be printed extra large so that the papers would have to run them over two columns instead of just one. He couldn't be convinced that the papers would print their pictures as big as they wanted them, irrespective of the size of the original prints.

Other plans had more logic to them.

It was his idea to work harder than ever to sell the product in England. Few of his competitors had grasped the importance of the British market or how easy it really was to tap—there wasn't even the need for new sub-titles; he had been told the English people understood English, too.

Not only did he look for titles that would appeal particularly to British audiences (*The Gay Lord Quex*, which would have to be renamed today, and *Lord and Lady Algy* were two of these) but he went to London to sell them. Only he, he figured quite correctly, could get the message across satisfactorily that what he had to sell was the best that had ever flashed on to a British cinema screen. Sometimes, he wasn't as convinced as he sounded. On one celebrated occasion he cabled back to America: 'I went to see *Lord and Lady Algy* three nights ago and I still am sick.'

Wags suggested that Sam really thought he was being invited to a party given by the nobility, but he was far brighter than that. He also had a number of aristocratic friends who genuinely admired his abilities and his spirit. Newspaper magnate Lord Beaverbrook was a close friend. He and Sam had a mutual respect for each other as superb communicators.

You couldn't catch Sam Goldwyn out. Sam got up early in the morning, went to bed late at night and was still miles ahead of anyone trying to pull anything on him.

There was just one man, or so the rumour had it, who was able to defeat Goldwyn at his own game—a much older, much sicker-looking man called Abraham Finkelstein, whose immigrant background wasn't unlike that of Sam's own.

Finkelstein had been tall once, but now he was badly stooped. For all this apparent frailty he ran all the movie theatres in Minneapolis; small fry to a Goldwyn, but when Sam heard that Finkelstein refused to pay the price he was demanding for film rentals, it was worse than a danger signal. It was a challenge Goldwyn couldn't resist. He went to see the man.

Sam saw the apparently ill and elderly Finkelstein and immediately sized him up. He was easy meat. They spoke and Sam flattered. Then it came to business. Mentally, he gave himself a couple of minutes to do the deal. But those minutes went by and Finkelstein was not bending (except from the shoulders). Sam was demanding that the exhibitor pay his price, but there was no way he would agree to do it.

Finally, Finkelstein decided to end the matter. Sam was talking—persuasively, he thought—and in full flow when the older man pressed a button on his desk. Almost simultaneously the door of his spacious office flew open and two men in white coats entered and led Sam out. They said they were from the local mental hospital.

Finkelstein laughed as Sam was frogmarched to his car, calling the Minneapolis mogul a 'momzer' and every other Yiddish phrase he thought reasonable—adding for good measure that the old man was the one who needed to be locked up.

Now was this a defeat that he was going to admit? Not if he was named Sam Goldwyn, it wasn't. He went back to Finkelstein and said he would drive him out of business. He himself would open his own theatre in Minneapolis and no one would go to see any of Finkelstein's pictures.

That, he figured, would scare the man into acquiescence. It didn't. But it did soften his approach. He invited Sam to come for a ride in his car. 'I'll show you the best sites where you can build your theatre,' he told him.

He did. But Sam didn't build a cinema there or, unlike the other movie moguls, anywhere else for that matter. But he did take a substantial interest in the Capitol Theatre on Broadway, which in 1920 was the largest in the world, with 5,400 seats.

Before long he was controlling it—with Howard Dietz deputed to find ways of bringing people to the theatre. Dietz dreamed up the idea of flashing a magic-lantern slide, proclaiming 'Go To The Capitol' high into the clouds. It didn't work, so Dietz moved it around. The lights flashed blindingly through the windows of *The New York Times* building. The *Times* men only saw the joke when the letters were redirected—at the walls of the rival Paramount Theatre. There, they came out sharp and crisp. The Paramount was furious, but the *Times* wrote a big piece about it.

The old folks at home in Warsaw would have called that chutzpah, too. It was still one of the principal requirements in selling both movies and the places that showed them. Sam sought ways to show that he was spending money—but spending it effectively—and his staff knew it.

Sometimes they exploited that knowledge to their own ends. Like Pete Smith, the publicity man.

He became both the hero and the fall guy for a publicity idea that didn't exactly have the mark of genius about it. He gazed admiringly at a banner hung from the parapets of two Hollywood buildings. It was extolling a new movie produced by a rival studio. Sam liked that. He liked it so much that he said he wanted to do the same thing—only, of course, bigger. To him, the only way such an advertising scheme could work would be to have dozens of banners, stretching across buildings on every corner leading to the theatre when Sam's next film was being premiered.

The publicist had doubts about that. Before banners could be hung up, there had to be agreement from the owners of the buildings he was using. Smith worried about the days, if not weeks, spent in horsetrading or finalizing the sums involved.

But that wasn't a good enough reason to talk Sam out of his idea. There had to be something better to offer him. Then he had his stroke of brilliance.

'Mr Goldwyn,' he said, 'it is just a great idea. The banners won't cost very much. We could put up hundreds of them for only $30,000. Just think how that will impress people.'

Sam didn't want to spend $30,000 and Smith knew he didn't. 'That's a stupid idea,' he told him. And that was that. It seemed he had no financial worries, but he resented, as he saw it, wasting money. That was why, in November 1920, he sought to strike out the $5,200 a year he had been ordered to pay his former wife. Blanche had remarried and there was no reason to keep paying alimony to her, he argued.

The court didn't agree. Blanche's money, said the judge, was not alimony at all, but was in consideration of what she had lost by divorcing him—and her agreement not to make any claims on his property.

But the judge ordered that the additional $2,600 alimony payment should stop. It didn't stop Sam regarding the judge—to say nothing of Blanche—as a sworn enemy.

As far as business was concerned, Sam still thought that the real enemies of the film industry were the actors. For a time it seemed that any union of film moguls would incorporate in its rules one that decreed that no actor should be allowed near a movie studio. He would have loved to have kept his away from his lot at Culver City.

His main war, however, was over what he called the 'star class'. He was content to bring in new faces, but was afraid of the personality cults that stars engendered.

The Goldwyn studios had ceased to be quite the independent fiefdom he had planned. In December 1919 the toll of the war years was being felt and, reluctantly, Sam had to accept that, in addition to the Selwyns, he needed more money brought in by more money people.

He was getting desperately worried—more than he at at any time let on—and was searching for desperate measures. The obvious answer was to go to the banks. But the big corporations were not interested in fly-by-night film producers, whom they regarded with a distaste that seemed to owe more to their WASPish background (and to Sam's Jewish antecedents) than to commercial practice.

Sam eventually found someone who would help: Amadeo Peter Giannini, whose Bank of Italy operated from California (later he would change its name to the more patriotic Bank of America, but his earliest customers were immigrants from Italy). But now, even this, was not enough.

Still, however, there was the lingering belief that plays and stories were the things to bring in the customers. And bringing in the customers was the principal object of the business.

So he co-opted Lee and Jake Shubert to become officers of his board—a seemingly shrewd move because it meant they would make the screen rights of their stage shows available for Goldwyn's use. After Florenz Ziegfeld, they were the best known impressarios on Broadway. They were the ones who had spotted the potential of Al Jolson and made him the star of their Winter Garden Theatre. No one ever accused them of being nice—in fact, they were known to do dreadful things to erring performers; one top star complained of being seen off at Grand Central station by the brothers and then shunted to a siding where he stayed all night locked alone in the private railway coach which he had previously taken as a great compliment. Needless to say, the brothers were highly successful.

When the Shuberts suggested to Sam bringing in a man called Frank Godsol to ease his financial troubles, he jumped at the idea without checking the credentials of the man the theatre said was a financial wizard.

It turned out that Godsol was a con artist of mammoth proportions and had been convicted for fraud in France. He became Vice-President of the Goldwyn operation and singularly failed to bring in a penny extra cash—until he confirmed that he knew the Du Pont family.

The cousins Henry and Eugene Du Pont were cajoled by Godsol to infuse *their* cash into the Goldwyn studio. They did, with help from E. V. R.

Thayer of the Chase National Bank. All three took seats on the board and issued firm declarations.

There had to be a change from the previous and existing policy of everybody being fairly content just so long as the next film could be financed from the profits of the one that had just gone on release.

But Sam was less than happy about what so many new people were going to do to his 'family'. As he said: 'This business is dog eat dog and nobody's gonna eat me.'

He no more thought of himself as a dog than he had ever done. But he was worried about the tactics of the backyard being brought into Hollywood. Goldwyn was, however, enough of a realist to understand that this latest development was nothing less than essential.

It did provide an injection of necessary capital. It did make Goldwyn one of the soundest-based studios in America. But it seemed to end the independence for which Sam craved. He hadn't left Lasky to let yet another crowd of people tell him how to run his studios.

The rows became inevitable and more and more heated. Finally, on September 3 1920, it was announced he was resigning as head of Goldwyn Pictures, giving way to Messmore Kendall. It was all due, he had no hesitation in revealing, to 'a disagreement with the Board of Directors on a matter of general policy'.

What that matter of general policy was was not revealed at the time. Later, it became obvious that the Du Ponts and their friends were very unhappy indeed with the financial outlook of the company. They wanted the studios run smoothly like a bank. And that was not the way Goldwyn wanted it at all. It is safe to say that Sam felt he needed to spend money which would, in turn (or so he believed) bring more money to the studio. Certainly he thought it would bring more quality to the studio and the Goldwyn name.

And there you have the difference between Sam and his fellow-directors. He had much more than a financial interest in the enterprise. They only wanted to see economic prosperity. He needed to feel that his own name was being enhanced by what the studios at Culver City, and expanding all the time, did.

Another member of the Du Pont family, Coleman, who had been brought in by the cousins, became President of the company. He had no more knowledge of the film industry than he had Sam's love for his 'baby'. Not only did the studio not prosper now, it was going deeper into the red. The board had a meeting, asked Sam if he would come back. He said No. They promised full autonomy—which they knew all the time was what he wanted above all else—and he said Yes.

Now, it seemed, he was firmly established in the studios at Culver City, which impressed everyone who went there—including the actors and actresses whom he hoped would not become stars.

He had invented a policy for the benefit of his audiences. 'I felt that the public were getting tired of seeing the same old faces on the screen and being served with the same old cut-and-dried plots refurnished from magazine stories. So, for a (step) toward better things, I used a new broom on the Culver City lot.'

Nothing he did or said had to be too far divorced from its publicity value. He was now using that new broom to try to extricate himself from the mire into which his Eminent Author friends drove him. Now he was going out of his way to use the least eminent authors who had ever picked up a pencil. He sponsored a competition in the Chicago *Daily News* and offered $30,000 in prizes for 'fresh ideas for story plots'.

It showed that Goldwyn—with Dietz's help, no doubt—still had ideas that got people talking about him.

His main fight, he kept saying now, was against those 'cut-and-dried' plots. He wanted more films that did not have happy endings—that was a risky thing to aim for; people, particularly women, wanted to leave theatres thinking that the characters up there on the screen lived happily ever after.

Sam ordered his minions to forget the last-scene embraces that ended in fade-outs. They may be popular, but they were what had been done last year and the year before that and the year before . . . . As he might have said, the business had matured by now.

More and more, too, he was considering himself to be something of a patron saint to his industry, caring about it and telling people how much he cared.

When the film director William Desmond Taylor was murdered, he believed that the whole industry was being attacked and that spelt damage to the profits of Goldwyn Productions as much as to any other outfit.

'The film industry should not be condemned because of one or two unfortunate occurrences,' he said in February 1922, just months after the Fatty Arbuckle scandal.

Nor was it true that film producers were trying to suppress facts about the business and the people in it.

'The industry comprises a population greater than that of almost any city in the world' (it didn't; but that was of no matter), he said. 'No city ever goes through the year without many regrettable happenings. It is as unjust to say that the moving pictures need cleaning up as to speak of cleaning up the United States. The good and helpful things the industry is doing for the betterment of the world are never chronicled on the front page, but let anybody connected with the movies get into trouble and not only he but also the whole industry is in the headlines for many days.'

He was addressing his remarks to his fellow-producers. The situation, Goldwyn said, was a fact of life, encouraged 'by the emphasis you and all your competitors put on publicizing your wares'. It was not something Mr Goldwyn would want to be told himself. There was a great deal of wanting one's sugar cake and eating it at every meal about running a major Hollywood studio.

'When the industry was fortunate enough to secure so great an executive (words he would be eating before very long) as Will H. Hays for co-operation in its problems, the wildest rumours of political plans and fantastic statements that he was to be insured for $2 million were published everywhere,' Sam went on.

The former Postmaster General of the United States had been brought in, in the wake of the Arbuckle Affair, to clean up the industry. As President of the Motion Picture Producers and Distributors Association—to be known as the 'Hays Office'—he introduced the 'production code', which ordered a list of do's and don'ts ranging from the length of a kiss and the amount of cleavage a woman was allowed to show to the demand that a villain would always be seen to meet his just end.

'I cannot ask the newspapers to ignore the occurrences, but I do ask the public . . . to realize that the . . .industry is made up of all sorts of people and that being a moving-picture man is no more indication of character than being a plumber, a steel man, a banker, a merchant or what-not.'

Whatever Sam was he certainly was never a what-not.

He encouraged writers to produce not just an outline or even a script. He wanted the titles, the continuity, the direction—which a skilled director might or might not accept.

None of this really helped, however. Godsol thought he knew where his bread was buttered (and smothered with the finest caviar) and joined forces with the Du Ponts every time the money men got into rows with Sam. And these were more frequent as the months went by.

Everything they said was contrary to what Goldwyn believed was good for *his* studio. Finally, in March 1922, he decided he had really had enough. He announced his resignation. This time he meant what he said. Nothing would convince him to join that crowd of people who would have been happier making a profit operating funeral parlours than savouring the heady delights of running a major Hollywood studio (albeit at a loss). They knew nothing about films and it irked him that they would try to tell him what to do.

At a meeting more stormy than any shipwreck sequence ever filmed at Culver City, he shouted his decision. 'And,' he added for good measure remembering last time, 'don't try coming back to me on bended elbows.'

6
We Live Again

Sam was going to use his own elbows to ease out the competition. Until he thought again about that. No. It wasn't the kind of business he wanted to get into, after all.

He was staying in the business. But in a different way. He'd had enough of partners. He was no longer going to chase the We-can-make-more-pictures-in-a-year-than-you-stakes. Sam Goldwyn was going to become an independent producer. And so an independent producer he became.

But something strange was happening. The old studio was merging with two others and Sam wouldn't have liked being involved in that at all. And that was a circumstance that led to a very interesting situation indeed. Suddenly, Sam's own name was being incorporated into what would become—in the public's eye—perhaps the best known studio of them all. His name would be right at the centre, right above the lion that had been his own emblem. And he would have nothing to do with it at all. Soon, they would buy him out and he wouldn't even have a financial stake, other than the $52,000 a year 'salary' they would pay him as part of the deal.

Metro-Goldwyn-Mayer—or MGM as most people were to know it—would for ever be thought of as Sam's company. But it never was. He had just given it his name—which was something MGM wanted to keep. While doing so, they demanded that he himself give it up. Shmuel Gelbfisz who became Samuel Goldfish who turned into Sam Goldwyn was now being told to call himself something else.

What he called Louis B. Mayer, who was the real studio boss there, is a different matter entirely.

They hated each other. Charles Chaplin had had fist fights with Mayer long before Goldwyn got into scrapes with him, so it was not difficult to hate Louis B. There was constant vituperation between him and Sam—probably due as much as anything to the fact that Mayer would always feel that MGM was helping to publicize Sam's name (Sam felt they were exploiting *him*).

'It didn't stop Sam and Irving Thalberg being very close friends, however,' David Rose, the producer who was to be Sam's business adviser, told me.

Sam and Mayer had been known to spar with each other, verbally, for years. Sam objected to what he considered Mayer's pretensions to grandeur, a snobbery that was totally foreign to his own ambitious search for prestige. Above all, there was a lack of chemistry between them, or what there was usually produced an explosive reaction. Once, in the Hillcrest Country Club locker-room, Sam was so infuriated by what he alleged Mayer had been saying about him that the row developed into something altogether more physical. The short, fat Mayer punched him into a hamper of wet towels—and then walked out before Sam could recover his composition.

Goldwyn subsequently tried to deny any kind of feud, in the course of which denial he revealed feelings that were altogether more real. 'We're like friends,' he insisted—but couldn't get more detailed than merely 'like' friends—'we're like brothers. We love each other. We'd do anything for each other. We'd even cut each other's throats for each other.'

What probably stirred his emotions was one of those paradoxes of show-business life. He didn't want anything to do with the people who were running an operation that bore his name, but still resented, inwardly, that *they* were there. Suddenly, he was the scorned suitor who hated the man who had got the girl he himself now genuinely hated.

Everything about Louis B.Mayer he detested. The way he ran his studio, the way he did business with people outside of MGM, even the kind of hats he wore. When he saw Mayer wearing a straw Panama, he burst into uncontrollable laughter.

From that moment on Louis B.Mayer was known as 'Panama'. He never appeared as anything else in internal studio correspondence.

Mayer gave the impression of being the man who not only ran the newly-formed MGM with the lion that Sam had so proudly boasted symbolized the strength of the Goldwyn studios, but who also owned it, too. That was never true, although the full truth of that situation would take a couple of generations to be felt. He was a minority stockholder and just as much power could be wielded, when he wanted to do so, by Marcus Loew—like Adolph Zukor, a former fur trader. He had turned the movie-theatre industry into his own, from penny arcades all the way to the picture-palaces sprouting up in American cities like giant mushrooms after a storm.

Loew was the first to see the value of combining a studio with a theatre chain; so to go with the theatres there was the Metro Pictures Corporation. When the studio got bigger, it gobbled up the Louis B.Mayer Pictures Corporation.

Now the merger with Goldwyn left Loew the real power of the operation. It may be Mayer who wept oceans of tears when a Joan Crawford failed to show appreciation for all that his millions were doing for her. It was Loew who controlled the purse-strings.

MGM would for ever more show Goldwyn's contribution to the film industry, but he would never have anything to do with what that particular studio put out.

Sam was going to stay independent or he would get out altogether.

The previous firm had become part of what was now called Metro-Goldwyn-Mayer. The previous firm was the Goldwyn Picture Corporation. Now he was calling himself Samuel Goldwyn Productions Inc., a step that was to take a little time to register with his rivals.

On 5 July 1923 Sam gave a dinner at the Ritz Carlton Hotel in New York for twenty-six of the top movie men in America. They included his dubious friends Adolph Zukor—just a month after giving evidence to the inquiry into the huge wedge of the movie market owned by Zukor and his partners—and Marcus Loew.

Sam told them he had done a deal with the First National Corporation to have his films released by them and spoke with a great deal of emotion and gratitude for the promises of co-operation the industry itself was offering one of its own.

Then came a revealing statement which could have been dreamed up by no ghost-writer or press agent. 'I feel', he said referring to his recent departure from Goldwyn Pictures, 'the same sort of victim as Frankenstein'. (That was precisely what he would be if Louis B.Mayer had his way.)

Now he said the film men had agreed to a policy of 'give and take'. What was not certain at that date was who was going to do all the giving and who was taking.

By the autumn of that year it was clear that he was expected to give a great deal and take practically nothing in return—that is, after he had banked his cheque from the new men at MGM.

In early September MGM announced they were suing Sam. Now that was to be anticipated. The new studio clearly didn't like the idea of the name Goldwyn being borne by two completely different and disconnected studios.

The MGM lawyers said that Goldwyn was nothing more than a 'synthetic trade name'. As they tried to point out, the name 'has been given a commercial value by its advertising, a value independent of the individual who assumed it'. They added: 'On the market it is presumably worth more than Goldfish.' It was like the man who designed the STUTZ car, a name made from his initials. When the name was patented at the time of the merger with Selwyn, Sam had, in fact created a trade mark.

Now all of this would have sounded a little crazy to Sam, who had already announced that his first production vehicles would go out under the banner of 'Samuel Goldwyn presents. . . .' The first one, *The Eternal City* was at the moment being advertised as a Goldwyn film. In addition, another movie, *Potash and Perlmutter* had already been made. *Potash and Perlmutter* was an interesting choice. It was an old Broadway success about two Lower East Side Jewish characters, the kind of tale Sam and practically all the Jewish moguls in Hollywood would turn away from. They didn't want Jewish stories about people with Jewish names. It offended their sensibilities (and their claims to be as American as the old families who wouldn't let them into their golf clubs). Nothing was going to get him to change the card at the opening of that or any other movie.

As he might have said—but didn't—his name would smell just as sweet whatever he chose to call himself. He had chosen Goldwyn and was going to keep things that way.

He had had permission from the Supreme Court on 16 December 1918 to change his name, six months after the patent registration.

That did not, of course, mean that people would stop joking about him. On the contrary, they went out of the way to get him to say funny things—or things that everyone but Sam thought funny.

It was about this time that an article in a humorous magazine portrayed a Jewish character who looked as though he had walked straight out of a *Potash and Perlmutter* script. In one memorable phrase the fellow said: 'I'll tell you in two words—"im-possible".' Charlie Chaplin read this, told a friend and said: 'It sounds like Sam Goldwyn'. From the moment on, perhaps the most famous Goldwynism of all was born and attributed to a man who didn't even know about it.

MGM, on the other hand—fighting as the Goldwyn Pictures Corporation to stress their unhappiness at Sam's stubbornness—were having none of it.

In return for a $52,000-a-year salary he had guaranteed never to use or allow to be used his name in connection with any other motion-picture company.

Now this was a freshly dyed red rag to an already very angry bull. He had a name of his own and nobody else was going to tell him he couldn't use it in whatever way he chose. He chose to stay in the film business. He was going to have no more partners—so as far as he was concerned that was going to be the name of his company.

He was ignoring the possibility of taking some neutral name—à la Columbia, Twentieth-Century, Republic, First National and so on—because he chose not to use any other name. That was his choice, nobody else's.

Sam didn't say so at the time, but he was clearly also not ignoring the fact that there was every commercial reason to keep calling himself Goldwyn. If his opponents objected to that, that was their worry not his.

His old friend Judge Learned Hand stepped in at this point and said that Sam would not be allowed to use his own name. Smiles, handshakes all round the courtroom for the MGM team. But then Judge Hand added: 'unless he follows his name with the words, "Not connected with the Goldwyn Pictures Corporation".'

Eventually it was agreed that all his films had to begin with the words 'Samuel Goldwyn Presents . . .' Sam liked that. The name 'Samuel' differentiated between his operation and that of his predecessors.

Since it was the name Samuel Goldwyn that was the money-spinner and since the Goldwyn Pictures Corporation no longer existed other than as a corporate entity, and since everyone who ever thought about it would assume that Sam was the genius behind MGM, it could be assumed he was quite a happy man at that outcome. He was.

Then the matter went to appeal. MGM said Sam had forfeited all rights to his name when he left the old firm. The Appeal Court upheld the earlier ruling. They said that the Federal Court ruling did not deny Sam the right to use his name in exploiting his own films and if this were an error it would not now be corrected. Neither did it rule on whether or not Sam was even entitled to use the name Goldwyn for his own purposes.

Of course, people would go on saying they assumed he had a lot to do with MGM. He parried their remarks by adding something like: 'Yes MGM are great. And you know what? They haven't harmed me a bit.'

If that was so, then it was a case of mutual help. MGM wasn't doing so bad either, operating from his own old base at Culver City.

It hadn't yet taken on its glittery image, the all-white set hadn't been invented and, four years away from Al Jolson's *The Jazz Singer* for rival Warners, of course there could be no musicals in silent pictures.

Sam, having decided that he wouldn't be part of a big studio, had to make up his mind precisely what he did want to be. Making one or two films a year was just part of what he had in mind.

What he really wanted to do was to be an innovator. Being the only independent producer worth the name in the midst of giants was pretty innovative in itself. But it wasn't enough. He wanted to operate his outfit in the sort of way no other studio operated.

For a time that meant working out of New York. Why bother with Hollywood, after all? Sure, it was nice out there. The weather was perfect, the mood relaxed. But Sam didn't terribly want to be relaxed. When he relaxed he was like a hospital patient suffering from an onset of St Vitus's Dance.

And then all his competitors were there. Did he want to spend every day of his life worrying about bumping into Jesse Lasky or Adolph Zukor or, worst of all, The Panama? He didn't. And then these were modern times. By January 1924 prosperity had arrived and with it all those marvellous inventions. Electric lighting had been perfected so well, who needed to bother about the additional sunlight available in California? Not Sam.

He hadn't yet been there for a whole year and, you know what, he told himself, he liked things that way. New York was exciting. It was where everything happened. It was where the best stories were written, and certainly where the best plays—the kind that he could make into the best movies—were performed.

Then he thought about it some more and decided he had to come to a totally different decision. Hollywood was the capital of his end of show business. Being out of the centre of things would be totally destructive to what he had in mind.

'The people in Los Angeles live and think motion pictures.

'They really start work in the studios at 9 o'clock in the morning, to do which some of them have to arise at 7. If you want a thousand people out there, you can depend on getting your thousand and also know that they will report punctually on location.'

That was the reality of motion-picture making. As he told *The New York Times*: 'In New York, the weather is always an uncertainty and often it is necessary to wait until the very morning of the day's work before ordering the crowd to report. If they are instructed to appear the day before, it sometimes happens that the weather changes and the conditions are such that they have to be sent away, the producer paying each individual's expenses and a little money besides.'

And it was better for the actors and the others taking part in a film, too. They had homes in LA. There were some who had made money there from other sources than their studio salary. Ruth Rowland, an actress who only really worked in film serials, had made millions out of real estate ventures.

And he went on, almost apologizing for the decision he had made which would quite certainly deprive the New York area of a number of new jobs:

'A little girl comes out to appear in a picture. She is accompanied by her mother, and later the father and the rest of the family get rid of their homes and go to California. Their relations eventually are attracted by the idea of living in Los Angeles and soon you find that this one girl's career has brought whole families to the West.'

There were ways in which he *was* going to be different, however. The man who lauded the arrival of the former Postmaster General was going to have nothing to do with the Hays Office.

And he hinted as much in 1924. 'If you have drama, you have love, 'he said in another *Times* interview. 'And it is almost that you have a triangle. You can't expect us to knock everything interesting out of a good story because some persons hold up their hands in horror at the mere suggestion of an illegitimate child. Griffith's greatest success was *Way Down East* and in it there was a child born out of wedlock. Pictures have shown a vast improvement in the last two or three years. But if the producers have their hands tied with expurgations of a story they cannot put forth artistic pictures, as the very features that cause the narrative or the drama to be conspicuously different from other efforts are perhaps incidents which censorial bodies have objected to and successfully excluded.'

It was necessary, he said, for the cinema to reflect life. But if it were going to do that, it had to be free of the constrictions of a censor. 'We *must* take life and reflect it.'

Even though Sam's words had just as clearly as ever been polished up by his tame ghost-writer, the sentiments had to be his. He would never have allowed anything with which he didn't agree to go out under his name, even if the god Publicity was the one to whom he performed at least daily worship.

There was the question of *Rain*, a play he had not bought, but which he admired. It wouldn't be welcomed by the film men—was that *why* he hadn't bought it? But, as he pointed out, was there any valid reason why Somerset Maugham's Sadie Thompson story should be allowed on stage and not on screen? It would, he said, 'not have much left of interest in it by the time it had been through the censorial scissors of the different bodies throughout the United States'.

There was, of course, a good reason for him to bring up the whole matter. His latest film was *Cytherea*. 'There is a great moral in this picture,' he pointed out. 'It points out that there is such a thing as retribution for stealing a wife or a husband. It is not a sermon, but a gripping story.'

It is only fair to point out, however, that Sam was saying a great deal about a lot of different things. For instance, he didn't think much of women who 'bobbed' their hair—a view that would provide him with a certain problem before very long.

'It spoils charm,' he declared. 'It robs women of their feminine charms.' Short hair, he said, made girls masculine and 'temporarily unbalanced'.

After having made these important pronouncements, he began to realize the publicity value in speaking out on such matters of moment. If, as he declared, a woman who bobbed her hair was imperilling her femininity, then this had to be a matter that concerned the religious authorities. And if it did, why not bring them into it? And since Sam always, but always, believed in going to the top, where better than the Vatican? He dispatched an emissary to ask the Pope to back his view. Alas for Sam, the Pope was not terribly concerned with bobbed hair. Or if he were, he was spectacularly well advised not to involve himself in a controversy that would benefit no one except Mr Samuel Goldwyn (who wasn't even a Catholic).

There were those, of course, who when faced with some of Sam's more excitable moments of conversation, could have come to a similar conclusion. But then, as he told one writer: 'When I want your opinion, I'll give it to you.'

David Rose, who was also Douglas Fairbanks's business partner and became a vice-president of United Artists and general manager of Goldwyn's studios, told me:

'He knew what he wanted and got it—a terrific guy, the greatest film exploiter in the business. When he had something he thought was good, he made the most of it.'

Even as early as this his instinct for stories was what carried him through.

Statements like giving people their own opinions made some of the other, intentionally more serious, things he said all the more fascinating.

His son Sam Junior was to tell me for a magazine interview that Goldwyn's trouble was that his brain thought faster than his tongue. People would go on manufacturing 'Goldwynisms' on Sam's behalf until—and after—he died. The junior Goldwyn said that he knew of twenty-eight of them which were genuine.

But it was a keen brain, let no one doubt. Any man who could become champion glove salesman of the United States had to have something. His ideas on film producing, despite all his subsequent problems, were incredibly far-sighted.

That was clear from the way he tried to extricate himself from some of his problems.

The most serious of these was that, having been eased out of three companies he had founded, he was once again in the business of having to go out looking for new talent. But he had a good eye—usually for a pretty girl—and that served him well.

This was the time when Hollywood was trumpeting—as only it possibly could trumpet in those days—the arrival on the scene of the most beautiful woman in the world, the apparently unsophisticated Swedish actress Greta Garbo.

Naturally, Sam would have liked to have had Garbo under contract himself, but those unpleasant people at MGM had beaten him to it.

Sam's answer to that little local difficulty was to go out and search for his own Garbo; one who would be bigger than Garbo.

Goldwyn really believed he had found her in Budapest during the summer of 1924. He was on holiday in the Hungarian capital—although any holiday for Samuel Goldwyn was a mixture of business and pleasure.

He was always on the look out for beautiful girls, for instance, although whether that was inevitably with business in mind is not a matter that has been proved beyond question.

It was when he was standing outside a shop window that those two needs—commercial and physical—appeared to merge and be answered.

There, in an exquisite frame, was the portrait of seemingly the most beautiful girl he had ever seen. The features were perfect, the complexion, as he could judge, even from the portrait, was the kind that sent most men into agonies of love and desire. He was among them.

For minutes on end he stood looking at the picture. He walked away and then went back. He looked once more before reluctantly accepting he had to move on for a lunch appointment at his hotel.

He thought about the picture a great deal, but no more than other people might think of a work of art. It was of a beautiful girl, but he saw no great point in even asking the price of the picture. He wouldn't find a great deal of satisfaction in just having it hanging in his Hollywood office.

Sam did, however, think of going into the shop to ask the identity of the model, but other things took over and he chose not to pursue it any further.

The time eventually came when he had to leave Budapest for home. He was finding great difficulty in getting on to a train. It was not that the train wasn't there or that he didn't have a ticket. More, the ticket inspector wouldn't allow him on to that train. They said his passport wasn't in order—a fact for which it has been suggested any Jew travelling in Hungary at that time ought to have been prepared.

But while waiting and arguing—and his arguing with an immigration official must have been at least as equally amusing as seeing him in combat with a Hollywood writer or PR man—his mind was distracted by a vision on the platform. It was the girl in the portrait. No question about that, except that this time there was a whole woman there—with curves as ravishing as the face. She was also very, very real.

Sam stopped arguing, accepted he would have to catch another train, have some additional documents appended to his passport . . . yes, yes, anything at all . . . and impatiently made his way to the girl.

He doffed his Homburg hat, made a little bow and introduced himself. 'My name is Sam Goldwyn,' he told her. 'Mine,' she replied, 'is Countess Vilma Banky.'

The 'countess' part was enough to frighten off many a man whose intentions were less than honorable. But Sam was determined to set the record straight. He gave her a card. He offered her money to come to Hollywood.

It was the money and the sort of figures spoken about—$250 a week to start with, rising to thousands once a screen test had been passed—which convinced her that the real Sam Goldwyn he was. It was a name she had heard, for she really did have ambitions of one day appearing in the movies and she did dearly want to go to Hollywood. Most of these negotiations had to be done in mime, with a constant flow of scribbled figures on a piece of scrap paper Sam had handy. The lady didn't speak more than a smattering of English. But what on earth did that matter? He was going to make her a motion-picture star, not an actress on Broadway.

It was the idea of her being a countess that counted quite as much as her figure and her facial beauty. He had her in mind for a certain kind of film. As he had told executives before his departure: 'We want a lady. Someone who's couth.'

When he offered her $1,000 on account there and then—a sight that could easily have been misinterpreted as he withdrew the dollar bills from his wallet—she was certain. If he wasn't Samuel Goldwyn the movie producer, he was surely very rich. And if Sam's accent didn't make Americans think he was American, Vilma didn't take him for anything else.

So she went and Sam introduced her to all his cronies, to his publicity people, to the newspapers. The fact that his new star was a Hungarian countess was not lost on the people Sam wanted to impress most.

He was going to star her in his forthcoming production *The Dark Angel*—not an inappropriate title, since it could be suggested that all the countess needed was a pair of wings and an angel she would be.

She was also going to be a silent angel. Sam hadn't reckoned with the problems of making a girl who hardly spoke a word of English into a star. Stars had to talk to newspaper people. How would she manage? He eventually decided it didn't matter very much. When the writers saw that face, gazed at those curves, they would be so capitivated they would write whatever the Goldwyn publicity man told them to write.

Sam himself thought more about that face, those curves . . . which were perhaps becoming a little too curvy. Her hips were just an inch or so wider than they had been when he met her on the station platform. And those breasts were . . . or was it imagination?

Goldwyn asked her to cut down on some of the eating he had seen her do in public. He tried to get over the message as easily as he could, and that wasn't easy with a girl who may have understood more than she pretended to.

'Say "lamb-chops and pineapple",' he told her. It is fascinating to contemplate the elocution lesson and its effect. Samuel Goldwyn was giving lessons in spoken English. Or was he? He really did want Vilma to go on a diet restricted to lamb-chops and pineapple.

That, he had been advised, would dissipate the fat. Miss Banky (calling her 'countess' was no longer important) said 'lamb-chops and pineapple' to herself and lost the required amount of weight.

The information was casually released to the Press—with the added news that she was about to star in *The Dark Angel*, a picture for Samuel Goldwyn—and suddenly there was a tremendous rush on both lamb-chops and pineapples. It became known as the Vilma Banky diet.

But even more important to Sam was the effect of the film in which Miss Banky was teamed with a tall, exceedingly good-looking Englishman named Ronald Colman. Sam thought that he, too, would be a star. Just how big a one he couldn't possibly have guessed.

For the moment the Press were enthusing on the British influence, although in those silent days when one could only guess the nationality of the stars, it wasn't Colman they were talking about.

The New York Times, for instance, opined that Vilma Banky 'the Hungarian actress who was engaged by Samuel Goldwyn, is a young person of rare beauty who might be American or English, with soft fair hair, a slightly *retroussé* nose and lovely blue eyes which have the suggestion of a slant. Her acting is sincere and earnest and her tears seem very real. She is so exquisite that one is not in the least surprised that she is never forgotten by Hilary Trent (Ronald Colman) when as a blinded war hero he settles down to dictating boys' stories.'

Well, now Sam was ready to start dictating all the Vilma Banky stories he could get his publicity department to dream up on his behalf. But there were other interests and other problems to solve.

The worst of these, as he saw it, was to find the right stories. (He really never changed in this solid belief that if he had a decent story written by a more than decent author his problems would be over.) It now seems strange that writing for silent films which, on the surface of things, seems to have so few opportunities for good authors, was considered by Sam to be so vital.

He was now saying that he thought plots were 'too syrupy'. Speaking as the first producer to recognize the value of the writers whom he imported into the studio, Sam said: 'Nobody can deny that the novelists of today are careless in plot development, treatment and characterization. Their trend of technique is to attack to a fixed formula, so factory methods dominate to the exclusion of artistic endeavour. Even many so-called successful writers, as far as financial returns are concerned, turn out stereotyped efforts, giving the story a new locale, new costumes, but the same old lifeless situations.'

Did Samuel Goldwyn in 1924 know the word 'stereotyped'? It seems doubtful. But he did know what he was saying. He did read books—not all the volumes that flooded into his office from authors who claimed they were able to write the way he wanted them to, but an occasional novel that took his fancy. The plots of other books he had summarized for his attention—and he knew instinctively whether filming them would be good for his burgeoning studio.

Sam also saw things from that financial point of view. He knew that authors ought to look further ahead than the tops of their pens or of their slow, ungainly manual typewriters.

'The average author of today writes only for the novel form. He ought to have in mind the serialization in newspapers and magazines to increase the number of his readers. He should consider the screen as the greatest agency for shattering provincial barriers.'

He thought Elinor Glyn was one of the few 'great authors' who took the cinema seriously. That one should have been spotted by the publicity man. Calling Elinor Glyn a great author was not calculated to win the literary approval of newspapers like *The New York Times*, although they made surprisingly little of it.

Sam knew the sort of people he was after, however. Early in 1925 he thought it would cause a veritable sensation if he brought Sigmund Freud to Hollywood. He was right, it would—had Freud only agreed to come.

Sam took off for Vienna in a blaze of self-inspired publicity. Freud was every intellectual's favourite talking-point, although the rumour was that he himself was in financial difficulties. If this were true, Goldwyn would be killing a fair number of birds with one stone. He would offer to help the father of psychoanalysis out of his money problems, he would have the fair chance of a good film plot (deriving from some of Freud's theories and fantasies) and at the same time reap a publicity harvest that would last seemingly for ever.

He would also promise not to let him have the benefit of his frequently expressed theory—that anyone who went to a psychiatrist ought to have his head examined.

In his mind's eye he saw himself photographed with the great Freud as they entered the train at Vienna station, as they boarded the ship, as they docked in New York, as they drove into the section of First National studios which Sam was using for his own films.

When he arrived at the Austrian capital Goldwyn sent the doctor a telegram, asking for an appointment. Instead, Freud dictated a reply: 'I do not intend to see Mr Goldwyn.' Not 'I do not want to see him', 'I do not intend to see Mr Goldwyn'.

That was one of the hazards of doing things Sam's way. Leaving in the midst of a publicity storm, he sometimes ended up soaking wet in public.

So he denied he had had any thumbs-down from Freud. 'He was ill,' Sam explained. And then, he added, he still wanted to bring him to Hollywood as a 'scenario writer'.

But, all in all, he had been very impressed by what he had seen in Europe—and not just by Vilma Banky and others like her.

Europe was a good market for American films and the Europeans knew why. American dressmakers, he maintained, set the fashions for all the world's women—and only through the movies; that was not a theory with which it would have been sensible to take issue.

He saw that Germany was the real treasure-house for the future. In those last nine years before Hitler there seemed every reason to believe this was so. The Weimar Republic was already in trouble, but nobody thought it would crumble and, indeed, its theatres and cabarets looked healthier than ever before. So why not the cinema? Sam predicted that, before long, Germany would be as good a market for Hollywood's products as England was already. In return, 80 per cent of America's imported films would come from Germany.

Goldwyn might not have been able to forecast the rise of Hitler, but he should have been able to assess the rumblings coming from Warner Bros., that little studio on Sunset Boulevard, which before long would decide that films should talk.

He did assess them—and came to the conclusion that talking pictures were a fairground fad which would never get into the cinemas. If he thought otherwise, he might have concluded that the foreign film and the foreign film market would soon be stone dead.

People, meanwhile, were wondering how long Samuel Goldwyn could keep going. He was doing very, very well—surprisingly well. The 'experts' who had concluded that he couldn't possibly continue in the face of the massive competition offered by the big studios were being forced to eat their words. But for how long? *Could* an independent outfit like his really succeed?

Sam was saying that he could and, indeed, there seemed good reason to believe him—particularly when offers came for mergers that would only be levelled at a really successful rival operation.

Even MGM made an approach for him to consider coming back to Culver City. Sam liked that, as he was entitled to like and appreciate the irony of the offer. 'I'll come', he jested, 'if they change the name to Metro-Goldwyn-Mayer-Goldwyn.' That would have been gilding the lily the way he wanted it done. But he and 'the Panama' could never have worked together and Sam knew it. Mayer probably knew it, too, but with his son-in-law Irving Thalberg in charge of production (the aphorism 'The Son-in-Law Also Rises' was coined with Mayer and Thalberg in mind, to say nothing of Mayer and Selznick and the Warner Bros. and their various sons-in-law in the business), that he wouldn't have been on offer for very long.

Sam was still determined to have no partners—in his own operation. That did not, however, stop him joining the board of directors of United Artists, which now consisted of Rudolph Valentino, Norma Talmadge and William S.Hart as well as the founders, Charlie Chaplin and Douglas Fairbanks and Mary Pickford.

It signalled a change from First National as the distributors of his films and promised first-rate studio facilities for his operations.

It seemed to change Sam for a time. He liked the rarified atmosphere of a 'WASP' operation like UA—although there were stories of Chaplin being Jewish, he was for ever denying them—and was excited by being in the Fairbanks set in particular.

When Chaplin grew a moustache, Sam followed suit. It seemed to help put him on an equal footing with his partners. It didn't work. Fairbanks was superbly handsome and his own moustache only enhanced his good looks. Most people imagined that Chaplin had one anyway—even if of a different shape from the one on screen—but a moustacheod Sam looked pretty ridiculous. That was, though, of no significance.

Even if his upper lip wasn't, Sam's other plans were blossoming magnificently.

He was making another *Potash and Perlmutter* movie, to be called *Partners Again*, and had signed up Henry King, one of the brightest young directors in the film capital, to make *Stella Dallas* for him. At least three other pictures were on the cards. Five important new films needing new facilities and a new distribution agreement if Goldwyn decided he had had enough of First National. He decided just that.

He also decided he had to make other changes. In the spring of 1925 he was getting married again.

7
I Want You

It was no secret in Hollywood or anywhere else where people talked movies that Sam Goldwyn had an eye for a pretty actress. The Vilma Banky success proved that in abundance. Other men eyed beautiful women either from afar or close at hand and came to their own conclusions—they would get to know them, make love to them, perhaps marry them. Others would simply admire and not even let that admiration show.

Sam had the gift of seeing a woman in three dimensions, with the full colour of her own personality glowing and radiating, and could imagine her being projected, flat, on to a black and white screen. If she passed that mental test, she was set for a glorious career.

On the other hand, there were those girls introduced to Sam's casting couch who were never promised a bigger role in life and who never really expected one either. He would make love to them once—perhaps twice—and that was considered that.

When he met Frances Howard at a party it cannot now be said with any certainty into which slot he placed her. He had seen her in a recent film called *The Swan*, playing the part of a princess, and she had been opposite the important star Richard Dix in his movie *Too Many Kisses*.

Sam had also seen her play a flapper in a stage play called *The Best People*. She plainly was not to be considered seriously for the casting couch—although she was pretty and shapely enough to catch his eye from a professional as well as a personal point of view.

For a moment, he had forgotten they had already met. When they did, it was a business occasion, and Sam had so many business occasions and interviewed so many young actresses that one frequently blurred into the other.

This first meeting followed the time he saw her on stage in a play called *Intimate Strangers*. He ordered a talent scout to call her for a meeting at the new Goldwyn Manhattan offices. He asked her for a photograph and fixed up the interview with his boss.

They were introduced. He took one look at her, muttered something like, 'I don't like bobbed hair,' and turned away. Exit one disappointed and offended young actress.

From that moment on she had only one word to describe the film mogul, 'appalling'.

Now she and the 'appalling' Mr Goldwyn were together in the same room at the same party, given at the Manhattan apartment of publisher Condé Nast. She knew she looked good that night in a white crèpe dress that cost $310—a veritable fortune, but the kind of investment that was as important to a budding actress as having a set of decent photographs taken.

And *he*, too, was behaving differently, more relaxed, more romantic. Even so, he wasn't totally endowed with good manners on this occasion either.

She told him she had signed a five-year contract with a studio—Famous Players-Lasky of all outfits, so there wouldn't have been much he could do about inveigling her into his own movies.

That being so, what would Frances Howard see in Sam Goldwyn?

He insisted he didn't remember meeting her before. But again he said how much he disliked the way she bobbed her hair.

Add to this the fact that she was slim, tall, well spoken, from a 'good' family and intensely Catholic and you have some idea of the problems likely to be in store.

Then there was Sam's growing stomach, his balding head, and the high voice with an accent you could cut with one of the knives being used to slice the beef at the party they were attending.

But Sam was no more a man to be thwarted in matters of the heart than he was in subjects concerning the script conference or the bank balance.

He had another meeting in view just as soon as it could be logistically arranged—everything had to be fitted into the Goldwyn logistic calendar. (He would tell people: 'I have a rule for you . . . always know what your plans are.' Sam had 'rules' for everyone working for him, even though they were sometimes rules he would break himself. He didn't ask people to do what he did, simply what he told them to do.)

Sam wasn't a man who liked yes-men. It was said that he liked no-men even less, but that was a Goldwyn attitude of mind he wanted to get around; it conveyed strength. He also conveyed that attitude in himself.

Somehow, he believed that he had to talk to a pretty girl the way he addressed a directors' meeting, straight-forward, attacking from the offensive. 'I think you're an awful actress,' he told her.

In cool print that looks a pretty dreadful thing to say. Sam thought Frances would find it intriguing and would quiver the way a Goldwyn starlet might shake when the boss spoke.

The pretty young Miss Howard was equally shocked when he told her so to her face. The extraordinary cheek of it, she must have reasoned. The uncouth, uneducated so and so . . . . She tried to think of something biting to say in return.

All she could manage was 'I'm sorry you think so', turn her pretty back and walk away. That wasn't what Sam thought she would do. He expected her to merely quiver and try to find some way of begging him to forgive her—that was what his own actresses usually did.

So he pursued her. He happened to mention he was going to another party after the Nast affair. He had been invited to one at Gloria Swanson's place—to celebrate her recent marriage to the Marquis de la Falaise.

Everything told her to say No.

Sam Goldwyn was not the sort of man she wanted to be seen with. After all, he did have that reputation . . . and he couldn't get her a place in pictures, because she had that already with Mr Zukor and Mr Lasky. All this rushed through her mind at the speed of frames of film being threaded through a projector. Her answer *was* No—except she didn't have time to say so. Mr Nast said that he, too, was going to Gloria Swanson's party and, if she would do him the honour, he would be pleased to escort her.

Goldwyn knew that Nast was doing him a favour and didn't quibble with the apparent pre-empting of his own invitation. She went to the party and Sam found himself next to her.

The story is that Sam was so smitten with the young girl—she was just twenty-one at the time—that she knew he wanted to take her out before he even asked her. She couldn't forget what he had said about her hair and her acting and she certainly did not consider him physically attractive. She said No, and then went on to report to the writer Anita Loos—who was soon to be best known for her *Gentlemen Prefer Blondes*—'Guess who wants to take me out? That awful Sam Goldwyn.'

That awful Sam Goldwyn was turned down. But he had been turned down before and always came back, pressing his claim again and again. Only Sigmund Freud had been known recently to get away with refusing a Goldwyn entreaty and this one was different.

They may have been of different backgrounds and had about twenty years difference in their ages, but Sam was fascinated by Frances Howard and wanted her to know how he felt.

He phoned her in the week and this time she said Yes.

They fixed a time and he said he would take her out to dinner. How would she fancy the Colony Restaurant? Frances may have been invited to the best parties, but she came from a fairly impecunious background and she wasn't used to going into expensive restaurants.

Sam asked where she lived. She told him between Eighty-First Street and West End Avenue. That was not good news to the man who liked to think he bought the finest stars and writers in the world.

Frances might just as easily have told him she was sharing a tenement on the Lower East Side with three other families and a tailor's sweat-shop. Eighty-First Street and West End Avenue was not the sort of address he wanted to be seen in. It wouldn't look good. People would say that Samuel Goldwyn was either slumming or being forced to look for a woman who was beneath his self-established station in life.

He had to think of an alternative to actually going to 425 West End Avenue, where Frances lived with her mother Mrs Helen McLaughlin.

He thought for a long moment and then suggested that she meet him at his hotel, the Ambassador on Park Avenue. He wasn't suggesting anything immoral, he stressed. He didn't want her to go to his room or anything like that. She should just take a taxi to the hotel and he would be waiting outside.

If Frances hadn't seemed a yes-woman until that moment—and she certainly hadn't—this was now a testing time. Much to her own surprise, to say nothing of his or of anyone else who was to hear this story subsequently, Frances agreed. She would meet him at the Ambassador.

They met, he gave her a polite kiss on the cheek and the taxi took them to the Colony Restaurant.

It was at the restaurant that Sam realized finally that she was different from those other girls he had dated or eyed—even those whom he thought he could turn into stars.

He told her that she should forget about being a movie star. That wasn't the role he had in mind for her—did he know more about her potential as an actress than she thought she knew herself? Probably. No, he said, he wanted to take her to Hollywood, but as his wife. As for that contract she had with Lasky . . . it wasn't going to be worth the paper it was printed on—which sounded a lot better but a lot less funny than the statement that was later to be attributed to him.

She accepted. Within a month, *The New York Times* announced: 'Samuel Goldwyn To Take Film Bride.' Even Sam had to be satisfied with that—and no doubt to feel grateful that the appeal court had allowed him to keep his name. 'Samuel Goldfish To Take Film Bride' wouldn't have looked nearly as good. And would Frances Howard have agreed to become Frances Goldfish? One can now only speculate.

For the moment, none of that was important. They were seen together at the finest restaurants. Night after night specially reserved 'house' seats at the most popular theatres on Broadway were unexpectedly occupied by Mr Goldwyn and his new fiancée.

Sam even agreed to take Frances to the opera—which this man, who might have been thought to have pretensions to the fine arts, usually admitted was not his favourite bag. On this occasion he said he thought an evening at the opera was just about the best way he knew of having a good time.

As Frances later told him: 'Like a fool I believed you.'

The invitation to *Tannhäuser* came from Sam's friends Dr and Mrs Giannini. Dr Giannini still owned the Bank of America and Sam was conceivably his best customer, paying a great deal of interest on the money he was allowing him to borrow.

Before Goldwyn had a chance to say anything, Frances said, 'I'd love to,' and Sam had to reply, 'Yes, I'd love to, too.'

He didn't love to at all, and that became evident from the moment the curtain went up.

She spent the rest of the evening watching her fiancé yawn, squirm and shift uncomfortably in his seat.

The nice thing to do after an evening as someone else's guest was to invite one's host and hostess out for supper. Instead, Sam thanked them and pushed Frances into a taxi.

'How'd you enjoy it?' he asked her.

'Fine,' she said. He squirmed again.

In fact, he was mentally weighing up in his mind whether or not he could really take as a wife one who liked going to grand opera. Being a man who believed it wise to say exactly what he felt when he felt it, he turned to his fiancée and said they both needed some serious thinking. *He* did. In fact, he said: 'I've been thinking this whole marriage project may be a mistake.'

And he went on to compound what Frances may have thought was an unpardonable indiscretion: 'Here you are, just getting a good start in your career; and here I am . . . I've had a pretty good time so far in my life and—well, what do you say we call this whole thing off?' As he said, he had been single for a long time and it might be difficult to adjust.

Many a blossoming romance has skidded to an unalterable halt because of pride. But would a young girl who had already agreed to meet a man on their first day, taking her own taxi, allow pride to break up an engagement?

'Call it off?' she rounded. 'Not by a long shot! You asked me to marry you and you're going to. So just make up your mind to that.'

And she added: 'Sam, you can't get out of this.' But when it seemed that that was precisely what he wanted to do, she grew red in the face and refused to look at him.

When the taxi drew up outside Frances's door, she pushed open the door and ran inside, a handkerchief to her nose.

It was only a matter of minutes before the telephone in her apartment—one of the old sit-up-and-beg type phones, with the earpiece on a separate latch from the main stalk—rang. Sam was on the other end, apologizing for upsetting her. Frances sniffed and was about to accept that apology when Sam added that he was a little shocked to discover she had such a strong temper.

At that, she slammed down the phone again—and then left if off the hook, so that he wouldn't be able to get through once more.

But she didn't do it very satisfactorily. In the early hours of the following morning she was awakened by a nudge from her mother—who didn't approve of the relationship at all.

'That Mr Goldwyn's on the phone again,' she said. 'Who does he think he is?'

She got to the phone. She said no, she wouldn't meet him again—ever. No, she couldn't see him that day, she was having some publicity photographs taken. No, she couldn't take a taxi to the photographer and go via the Ambassador Hotel. No . . . . But of course she did.

It was a windy day. When the taxi arrived at the hotel Sam was waiting outside the Ambassador, his coat flying gallantly in the wind like a flag on a ship.

He was struggling to keep the 'flag' from turning into a parachute and carting him away.

To try to keep the coat and himself together, he was pressing his hand close to his chest. In his hand there was a bunch of gardenias.

'They're a bit brown round the edges,' he told her apologetically. 'I'm afraid all the decent florists are shut.'

It was enough. Once more she said she would marry Sam. But what about his notion that they ought to call if off? That no longer applied—just providing he didn't have to spend too many nights at the opera, which might have suited the Marx Brothers but was distinctly not Sam's idea of fun. Besides, how could you transfer a grand opera to a silent movie? Others *had* tried. Sam wouldn't even think about it.

That was the funny side of things. But there were many more serious matters. For one thing, there was that matter of different backgrounds. Frances was young and Catholic—which meant that she went to Mass on Sundays; in those days, all Catholics always did. Sam was already middle-aged, still spoke with his Polish-Yiddish accent and although he hadn't been religious since he ran away from both home and his father's volumes of Talmud, he wasn't going to deny his roots.

It may have seemed uncomfortable at times, and he tried to insist that he was an American first and foremost, but he wasn't going to say, no he wasn't Jewish. After all, he was still keeping his sister Nettie in Warsaw and all sorts of other family members who frequently wrote to their rich relative in America telling him how hard things were (he replied brusquely, but always enclosed a valuable cheque). Those links with his past were hard to break, even if he really wanted to do so.

So what about any children they might have? Frances insisted they be raised as Catholics. He agreed.

Mrs McLaughlin was less easily pleased. She behaved precisely the way Sam's own mother would have done had she been alive and discovered her son was about to marry outside the faith. He understood that, but it didn't make for good relations between them—and he was almost the same age as his future mother-in-law.

There was, as Frances later reported, an 'explosion'. There were tears, shouts, incredulity. Frances was marrying not just a man of a different religion, but of a different class.

To her credit, Sam's millions—or, more accurately, the Bank of America's millions—didn't seem to matter very much to the older woman.

Sam himself tried to soothe things, told Mrs McLaughlin he loved her daughter, would give her a good home and, yes, promised that any children they had would be brought up as good Catholics.

She was still opposed to any marriage and said as much. They weren't going to get married. And then she softened: 'Even if you do,' she said, 'it won't last.'

'It will,' Frances insisted.

'No, it won't,' retorted her mother.

'I hope it will,' said Sam, which didn't satisfy Frances very much at all.

Neither of them was saying very much publicly about their romance. Only one or two very close friends had been in on the news. The plan was that Sam would go off to Los Angeles in a matter of days, that Frances would follow him and their marriage would take place in California soon after her arrival.

But, as in all the best love stories, the expected did not happen like that. The wedding took place a week after the *Times* announcement and in Jersey City, New Jersey, with the ceremony conducted by Judge Leo Sullivan at his office.

Edgar Selwyn, who was no longer his business partner but remained his closest friend, was best man and Frances's sister Constance was maid of honour.

Sam had said from the time he informed Selwyn of his plans that he was telling no one about the marriage and that he wanted it kept secret. So how did it get into *The New York Times* that morning? Sam said he couldn't think . . .'Can I control the Press?' he asked insouciantly.

The question was rhetorical, since there was practically no occasion when he didn't positively jump at a chance to get his name in the papers. Once the wedding was publicized in this way, there was no hope of keeping the crowds away.

He and Selwyn arrived at the judge's offices to see that the way was being cleared for them by mounted police. They even called up police reserves to disperse the crowd which had gathered in the streets surrounding the building. They thronged the corridors leading to the judge's office.

If anyone had doubted the drawing power of a mere producer, this was the answer. The papers had said that Frances Howard—or Frances Howard McLaughlin as the marriage documents would declare—was a pretty girl, but those thousands wouldn't have turned up just to see another pretty girl. It was the distinctly unpretty 43-year-old Goldwyn they wanted to view.

Of course, when Frances did arrive in her green silk dress with its matching felt hat, they felt they had been justly served.

Sam gave her a diamond-and-sapphire brooch as a present and there was a small reception to follow at the Ritz-Carlton Hotel. Among the guests, appropriately enough, was Condé Nast. The only one who didn't have a constant smile on her face was the mother of the bride.

All the way to the ceremony Mrs McLaughlin had kept nudging her daughter and insisting: 'It won't last.'

Frances was determined not to allow any of this to spoil her big day—even if it wasn't a big white affair in the Catholic church (her mother had doubtless dreamed of a society wedding at St Patrick's Cathedral on Fifth Avenue) it was still the most important day in her life.

Every time her mother said, 'It won't last'—and she kept saying it—Frances replied: 'Wait and see.' If only to spite her mother she determined there and then that last the marriage indeed would.

e words 'Samuel Goldwyn Presents . . .' usually meant quality. There were doubts about this. But the message effective

Sam and Frances arriving at Southampton on the *Queen Mary* in 1938

Reunion for the veterans of the Famous Players Company. Seen here are *(l to r):* Cecil B. DeMille, Winifred Kingston, Raymond Hatton, Julia Faye, Jesse L. Lasky, Jane Darwell and Sam

ry Cooper and Teresa Wright — *The Pride of the Yankees*

agy Carmichael only had a small part, as Butch the bartender, in *The Best Years of Our Lives.* But it was ssibly the best part of *his* life. Here he plays for Harold Russell and Fredric March

Ronald Colman — the perfect *Raffles*

Running a film studio was all about talent. A fair sprinkling of it was seen in Sam's answer to Florenz Ziegfeld — *The Goldwyn Follies*

ɪrence Olivier and Merle Oberon in probably the best remembered scene from *Wuthering Heights.* Sam called it *'hering* Heights

ı believed his stars had to be fostered. That went for business associates too. Here he welcomes Flo gfeld, his daughter Patricia and wife Billie Burke to 'erly Hills in 1929

Jesse L. Lasky — the brother-in-law and business partner. It wouldn't be long before Sam decided he didn't want either

(opposite) Publicity — food and drink, some thought, to Sam — was never hotter than in *Ball of Fire,* with Gary Cooper and Barbara Stanwyck

(above) Jean Simmons and Marlon Brando. Unconventional casting for *Guys and Dolls*

(left) The Goldwyn happy family — Sam jun., Frances and Sam in 1949

Goldwyn's finest hour — receiving the Oscar for *The Best Years of Our Lives,* judged the best film of the year. Other Oscars went to the handless Harold Russell for best supporting actor and to William Wyler for best directo

Danny Kaye — one of Sam's greatest film discoveries — here in *Hans Christian Andersen*

8
The Wedding Night

Frances Goldwyn took to Hollywood like a fluffy duckling to a smooth millpond.

As the wife of a big film boss—and Sam was still that, even though he was 'just' that independent producer—there were a great many people ready to do her honour. When she arrived at the Los Angeles station there were bands and flowers all the way.

At Sam's Hollywood home—which she didn't like one bit—the servants were lined up to welcome her and promise to do her bidding.

Suddenly she was queen consort of a realm she didn't know. The customs of her new 'nation' were as strange as the geography. But almost from day one she let everyone know that she was in command.

Before she herself could recognize that fact, however, she had to be introduced. Or perhaps rather she had to be Introduced. The capital letter indicates the significance of the occasion, which was very much part of the Hollywood scene.

On her very first evening in California the Goldwyns were invited to dinner. It wasn't going to be easy.

As she told readers of the *Woman's Home Companion* twenty-five years later, 'my mind separated into two parts: curious delighted anticipation and serious consideration of what I'd wear.'

That was the sort of problem any woman in a new home could face. In Hollywood and as the wife of Sam Goldwyn it was much, much more problematical. She was on show and she knew it all too well.

She chose a dress of pink chiffon. Embroidered shells covered the whole ensemble—which caused the gossips to gossip and the papers to report the arrival of a young lady who was likely to be something of a fashion leader.

She recalled that her toes and fingers had turned to ice. Her throat was dry and she worried about meeting the stars, assembled for her benefit—like both Norma and Constance Talmadge (wearing 'carelessly expensive orchids').

There was the silent star John Gilbert and the eminent German director Ernst Lubitsch. And then there was the man who was her childhood idol Earle Williams. His isn't even a name to most people today, which says quite a lot about the personality of a man who had good looks . . . and very little else.

Frances discovered that on this first night in Hollywood when he was placed next to her at the dinner party. For most of the evening he sat stolidly looking ahead and munching the celery. Then Frances casually happened to mention that she had a photograph of him and he had always been the one she loved to see on screen. Suddenly Williams was a changed man. He talked incessantly and about one subject—himself. That was indeed a lesson on Hollywood.

Pola Negri was there, too, ravishing in a silver lamé turban and looking the way only a film star of the 1920s could look.

Frances was made to feel comfortable. But she didn't yet feel part of what was loosely called the scene.

As she said, she heard a voice inside her which kept on saying: 'You're not Frances Howard, who was going to be a great actress on the stage—the real stage, where you have to be a good actress to be a quarter as famous as those people here. You suddenly up and got married. You chucked what you'd been working for like a beaver ever since you were fifteen . . . and you can't pretend you didn't agree to stop being an actress to become a—just a wife, any more than you can pretend you didn't help Sam along proposing to you.'

Everybody wanted to know as much about Frances as about her husband. Not everyone was always as kind about Sam as Frances liked to be. Neither of them, for instance, liked very much a profile on Goldwyn that appeared in the new magazine *The New Yorker*.

The anonymous writer commented:

> To be under his command even temporarily is a living hell, but to meet him as an equal is refreshing after the surfeit of over-educated, clever young men with nothing to say who seem to fill the world at present.
>
> It is almost painful to see him groping, struggling, bludgeoning his way to clarity, agonizing over ideas he feels but cannot express, a man struggling with his own greatness, a man whose night school education is inferior to his destiny. There are so many stupid people in the movies who cannot see beyond their noses, narrow-minded and timid little men, that Mr Goldwyn stands out from among them, a dramatic figure—an inspired buccaneer.

Sam was reportedly more upset by that *New Yorker* piece than about anything ever written about him before or since. He liked to be thought of as both a dramatic figure and that 'inspired buccaneer' but to be thought of as bludgeoning his way to anywhere, struggling to do anything, was against everything he stood for.

He never did anything, he would like people to believe—although there were those who didn't believe it—without calculating and thinking it over carefully in advance.

'What,' he supposedly said, 'do you want me to put my head in a moose?'

For a time that article in what he knew to be the highly sophisticated *New Yorker* magazine made him worry about his image very considerably. No Goldwynisms—they weren't yet called that but Hollywood people in the know would have recognized them—were to be reported. Frances probably had something to do with that; she didn't relish the idea of people thinking she was married to an uncultured man.

What she liked about him were those things that the Californian gossips chose to ignore—his fastidiousness, his sensitivity, his eye for detail.

Sam knew when a thing wasn't right in a film—if a set didn't ring true, if a woman's hat was on wrong, if a leading man's hair-style didn't go with what the story and its period were trying to convey.

His executives might have a similar view but be unable to put their fingers on the precise problem. Sam would say 'the hat' and everyone would realize that that hat did make all the difference. If the difference were considerable, he had no compunction about ordering the scene to be reshot—and unlike the bigger corporations, even in 1925, it was his own money he was spending, not that of any invisible stockholders.

What, on the other hand, Sam might *not* have been able to notice was precisely what was wrong with the hat. It didn't take many months before Frances was realizing—and Sam along with her—that here she had an important part to play.

She watched the rushes when he saw them, read the scripts when he was handed a bunch of them. If the hat or the hair was wrong, she would point out the precise details. Sam Goldwyn who had fought against partners in his operation now had one at his side a great deal of the time—in the shape of Frances. By all accounts he liked it that way.

In years to come their son Sam Junior was to say that Frances made all the final decisions. Certainly, she gave a lot of advice which was to prove useful to her husband, guiding him, sometimes persuading him, sometimes offering a restraining hand.

There were those who detected Frances's influence in the way Sam dressed. She doubtless approved of the care he took in his appearance, but he had dressed that way long before she came on the scene. A man who sold gloves had to look as though he wore nothing but the best of them himself. And gloves were just the finishing touch, after all. His suits had to be made to measure either in New York or in London. They had to be pressed perfectly, with nothing in his pockets to affect the straight line he sought—like royalty, he never carried money for that reason, a fact that would bring him a few problems over the years. His shoes were hand-made in London from lasts shaped from his own feet.

He was equally set on punctuality. Nobody ever came late to a Sam Goldwyn meeting and lived to talk about it—professionally, that is. If you were late for a business meeting without good cause, he just didn't want to do business with you. If you arrived late for a dinner party at his home, it is quite likely he would tell his butler to inform you that the affair was over. (Only Frances's sense of tact prevented many a serious break in friendship over this.)

You might say, however, that this was part of the search for perfection which separated Sam Goldwyn from the other men in Hollywood.

It was also one of the reasons why what Sam said was taken so seriously, not just by the other men in the film industry but also by the Press.

This was one of those periodic occasions when the film men worried about their future. In 1925 it was radio that they saw as a distinct threat to the way they earned their money. It wasn't necessary to be concerned, Sam reassured them. It was no more an encroachment on their world than the aeroplane was likely to affect the automobile industry. They were wise words—and an exact comparison.

But, wait, it wasn't radio as such that Sam was talking about, the kind of radio that was already being swallowed up by hundreds of thousands of Americans who would make their evening's fun sitting around a crystal set, with earphones sprouting from their heads. Sam was predicting television—in 1925.

Al Jolson had just experimented with this possible new entertainment medium, two years before he made the first talkie. A flickering green image of the 'Mammy' singer had been transmitted from the Hotel Astor in New York to a nearby building. It *was* just an experiment and nobody had appeared to take very much notice, but what rumours there had been spread with the speed of instant anxiety.

Goldwyn took it as his duty to put a fatherly hand on their collective shoulders and tell his colleagues to calm down.

As he said, 'If the transmission of motion pictures by radio is perfected, feature pictures will be necessary as now, in order to make them more than a passing fad.' That was in itself a remarkably prescient thought. He was forecasting the TV and video age more than a quarter of a century before anyone else saw it as a possibility, let alone a serious threat.

But that was far away and he wanted people to know it.

He went on: 'Now it is readily apparent that if no radio were so highly developed that one could see productions in his home by simply turning the dials, there would be no incentive for us to expend the great amount necessary for production.' Did anyone see Sam or his competitors for that matter cutting their budgets?

He was, however, wrong on one count. He said that radio hadn't yet hurt the theatre. It had. Both radio and his own business, motion pictures, had already by then handed out a death sentence to vaudeville, at least. The circuits still operating these theatres all over America were recording weekly tumbling attendance figures.

Sam didn't see it that way. He was optimistic, buoyant—no doubt due in part to being with Frances. The theatre had the edge on listening to—or possibly one day watching—entertainment at home. As he said: 'There is a certain psychology about the showhouse, a love of the lights, the carefree camaraderie of the audience and the appeal to the optic sense aside from the actual sight of the screen drama, which will never be supplanted by any domestic makeshifts.'

He was, however, giving notice that if these 'domestic makeshifts' did become realities, he was going to take full advantage of them.

And neither was he any easier to please. He was spending upwards of $900,000 a picture, and in return he demanded perfection.

Before *King Harlequin* could go into production he and Henry King, the director, worked on four drafts of a script in a suite at the Los Angeles Ambassador Hotel. 'The interest is not sustained,' he kept saying before script number four was finally approved.

It wasn't sustained any better in a film called *Woman Chases Man*. Sam first offered the job of writing the picture to a highly successful playwright named Eddie Chodorov. Sam had bought the rights to a stage play and asked Chodorov to turn it into a movie.

He read the play—and hated it. The mistake he made was to tell Sam he hated it. In fact, he didn't just hate it. He detested it. He didn't think it had any merit at all and said so.

Sam flew into one of his not infrequent rages and ordered the writer out, all the time muttering something about the man having no idea what a good film was.

The film was written by someone else, went before the cameras, was released—and bombed like a First World War air corps plane hovering over the German lines.

Years later—so long afterwards that both men had lost a great deal of hair by then and what they had had changed to silvery grey—Chodorov's name was mentioned in another connection to Sam.

Again Goldwyn flew into a rage. 'Don't talk to me about Chodorov,' he said. 'Chodorov? That man was associated with one of my biggest flops.'

There were other things that were going a lot better for him, however.

For one, his own domestic arrangements were subject to a certain change. In 1926, almost exactly a year after his marriage, Frances was no longer able to spend quite so much time in helping Sam in the business. She gave birth to their son, whom they called Sammy, or Sam Junior—a name which showed just how far Goldwyn had departed from his Jewish origins. It has always been a cherished Jewish tradition that a son is never named after a living father. But still, this was Hollywood, America, and the twenties were roaring.

Ronald Colman was by now Sam's number-one star, a man who had to be cosseted, who was only to be allowed to appear in movies that Goldwyn himself judged to be right.

That applied, too, if and when he lent him out to other studios—for the sort of money which Sam thought suitable, and Sam's idea of suitable was, of course, huge.

It happened when Warner Bros. decided they needed Colman to take over from Clive Brook in Ernst Lubitsch's version of Oscar Wilde's *Lady Windermere's Fan*.

There were problems. Sam insisted on Colman getting top billing, which was difficult because the female star Irene Rich had a contract with Warners which specified that *she* always had to be the top star. The matter was only sorted out when Miss Rich said she wouldn't insist.

Sam, however, of course insisted on seeing the script. When he did, he rang the director, angry as only a mogul with problems could be angry.

'Why didn't you tell me it was a villain you wanted him to play?' he demanded of Lubitsch.

Lubitsch answered that he was a lover, and added for good measure: 'He loses the girl!'

Sam was convinced. No man who gave up the woman he loved could possibly be a heel. The loan out was agreed.

Sam insisted, however, on one more detail: He had to have a credit that said: 'Ronald Colman appears through the courtesy of Samuel Goldwyn.'

It riled Lubitsch, who believed that no one appeared in his movies by courtesy of anyone but himself. But Warners said agree and agree he had to. However, every time he directed Colman, Lubitsch let him know how upset he was.

'Remember,' he would instruct, 'Mr Colman, you walk across the room, you stop by the table, you pick up the book, then you look into the eyes of Miss McAvoy through the courtesy of Samuel Goldwyn.'

Sam was, as usual, full of new ideas, always able to spot a talent no one else seemed to know was there.

In 1926 the Goldwyn studios were planning a Western in which Colman, perhaps improbably, would star opposite Vilma Banky. It was to be called *The Winning of Barbara Worth*. As usual, Central Casting (an organization Sam would soon leave; he didn't think they were the best route to get crowd actors and preferred to use his own 'stable') were put on to the job of providing the extras.

Among those whom they sent him was a young man fresh out of Helena, Montana, who had tried his luck at being a newspaper cartoonist. He wasn't, however, that lucky and decided to search for something else—which was how he got to Hollywood and became an extra on *Barbara Worth*.

Sam, as usual, went on to the set and surveyed the scene in front of him just as the director was lining up the action about to be shot. He spotted the new extra and had a word with him, watched the way he stood and how he spoke—although he didn't say much. In any event he made him second lead in the film. That was how Gary Cooper got his start.

It would be years before Cooper worked for him again, but the story made just the sort of publicity Sam craved. And he sold the film with all the enthusiasm he could muster—which was always enough to make every other studio boss feel inadequate.

He arranged for the Governors of all Western States to see the movie at a summit meeting he himself called in Hollywood—ostensibly to discuss water conservation. The problems of getting water were front page news in the papers and so was *The Winning of Barbara Worth*.

Not a few people now believed that the clever thing to do was to find a way of Winning Samuel Goldwyn.

9
The Masquerader

Sam had set himself up as everybody's film guru. What Goldwyn said seemed to go. When Charlie Chaplin was sued for divorce by his first wife, Mildred Harris, Sam was served with a 'John Doe' warrant compelling him to give evidence for her. She wanted him to tell the court what he knew about Chaplin's assets and business dealings, since he was a close friend of the man who had just made *The Gold Rush*. Hollywood was looking more incestuous by the day. Sam said he knew nothing.

Chaplin was grateful—and Chaplin's gratitude was not to be scorned. He admired Goldwyn, and there weren't many people whom he did admire.

(Charlie also, incidentally, did the best imitation of Sam's voice anyone knew—and *everybody* who knew Sam tried to impersonate him.)

Sam's opinions, however, were not always the right ones. Occasionally even his own business and publicity ideas were as nought.

For instance, he was delighted to lend Vilma Banky to a rival studio so that she could play opposite Rudolph Valentino in *Son of the Sheikh*.

Banky was his prize 'possession'—the terminology is apt; once under contract to a studio or producer like Goldwyn stars were virtually owned by their employers.

In a previous film it was Sam who ordered her hair to be changed—and rearranged it himself. As Frances later said he got 'a few hairpins sticking out in the wrong places' but the style he himself designed was the one for which she would later be famous.

Now he was banking on Banky, as it were. The 'marriage' of his female sex siren and of Valentino, the man who had millions of women quivering at the mere sight of his profile would be great for publicity—especially if there would be a real marriage.

He worked out in his mind that the two would hit it off instantly, she the beautiful Slav, he the romantic Latin. Just think of the explosive publicity drive that would result! Unfortunately, the attempt at forced love was no more successful than putting two strange pandas together in a cage in the zoo. They seemed to like each other, but no more.

The world's greatest lover, it seems, had another love.

Valentino had met Pola Negri and they were more and more involved every day. Any reluctance he might show towards Vilma Banky was not evident from a theatre seat, however. Her bosom heaved and she breathed heavily every time he approached.

But his reluctance to become seriously involved with Miss Banky presented tremendous problems to Goldwyn. Having his star rejected by Valentino meant very bad publicity indeed. So some extra effort was needed lest the public discover that she had been spurned and, even worse for Sam, that what Goldwyn said didn't always go.

For a time he tried to get Ronald Colman interested in marrying the beautiful countess, but while Colman was as enticed by Miss Banky's face and those magnificent curves as any warm-blooded man, he wasn't prepared to marry her for the sake of Sam Goldwyn and his business.

Sam asked a visiting French newspaperman if he could help. Henri Letellier was no more willing to admit defeat on a matter of professional expertise than was Goldwyn. Sam asked him if he knew someone who could whisk Banky off to Paris.

Letellier suggested a Baron Valdemar, who might be willing to play this particular ball. He was.

M. le Baron sent Banky a cable. He said he had fallen madly in love with her and wanted to tell her so to her face. The phony romance was front-page news on two continents.

When it seemed that the story was cooling down somewhat, the Baron—acting on the advice of Mr Goldwyn—challenged Rudolph Valentino to a duel for Vilma Banky's honour.

The Baron tried to come to America. But for some reason—it is not beyond the bounds of possibility that Sam had something to do with it—he was not allowed into the United States. He kicked his Gallic heels on Ellis Island while Sam lapped up every minute of his discomfort and Miss Banky continued to be mystified. (After all, she hadn't been consulted.) The Baron then went to Mexico.

At least, that is what the public heard.

He was allowed to disappear at about the time Vilma fell in love for real—with the actor Rod La Rocque. The name was as phony as Vilma's relationship with the Baron, but he was a star and when Sam heard they were going to get married, he organized the wedding.

He picked the church, the minister, the guests and, of course, made sure that the Press were in on it. In on it? There was never a better time for getting stars on to the front pages of the country's newspapers and Goldwyn knew that white veils and the throwing of rice was the best way possible to do so.

The fact that the lace cap of her veil was the exact one she had worn in *The Dark Angel* was not lost on either Sam's publicity department or the newsmen—and particularly the newswomen.

Louella Parsons was matron of honour—could anyone think of a better way of getting exposure in her column?

Cecil B DeMille was best man—which might have been complicated since La Rocque was trying to break a contract with DeMille and being friendly enough to appear at the wedding could have compromised their relationship. Sam worried about that and found a legal loophoole—the Banky-La Rocque wedding was on a Sunday and nothing that happened on Sundays was legally binding (although strangely this did not apply to the wedding itself).

Ronald Colman was one of the ushers.

The bridesmaids were straight out of a movieland fan album: Dolores Del Rio, Marion Davies, Norma and Constance Talmadge, and both Frances and Mrs Harold Lloyd.

Immediately after the ceremony the bride was asked what name she had in mind for her first child. She smiled sweetly at the reporter and then with a serious look on her face answered: 'I think you ought to ask Mr Goldwyn.'

The general impression seemed to be that if Sam Goldwyn thought it a legitimate way of promoting his stars, then it must all be Okay. The world was a lot more innocent in those days, but there was never to be a better time to publicize movies, those mythical shadows no one was ever expected to think actually mirrored reality.

The crowds assembled for that wedding in Hollywood treated it the way they would a premiere at Grauman's Chinese Theatre—which is precisely what they were expected to do.

They stood at the edge of a red carpet, roped off by the police, and 'oo-ed' and 'ah-hed' as each celebrity entered. They fainted on cue. They screamed. All that was missing were the searchlights—a wedding had to be in the daytime—and the microphone at the entrance to the theatre at which a famous columnist interviewed the people coming in.

That was how Sam Goldwyn wanted it to be. No one imagined he took it seriously, but the general public—those who were expected to spend 10 cents or so for a theatre seat—didn't know and took in every unreal, glamorous second of it all.

As far as the Press and the industry was concerned, that meant Sam had to be taken seriously—as seriously as he took the whole Banky publicity stunt, which he had dreamed up himself. Whatever he said was deemed to be Important.

(For once, the publicity paid off in every regard. The marriage was one of Hollywood's happiest and lasted until La Rocque's death in 1969.)

His views on television had put a lot of people at ease. That, though, wasn't always what he tried to achieve. More frequently he was issuing dire warnings. What he wasn't always able to achieve was consistency.

The Motion Picture Producers and Distributors Association were in the process of drawing up that 'production code'. He hadn't liked it when he heard of it. Now he was doing one of his celebrated U-turns. (He had been known to do them in the course of a single sentence—to begin by saying he wanted to do something and then end by giving every reason for thinking the opposite.) The man who had come out so vociferously against censorship was now welcoming it warmly when it came to one of the main planks of the Hays office's platform for cleaning up Hollywood—nudity.

Sam's old partner Cecil B. DeMille had not been averse to showing a breast or two in his movies, and other directors had done the same. Few had gone as far as displaying as much as an inkling of pubic hair, certainly to nothing like the extent prevelant in films today, but a little nudity spiced enough movies to make them attractive sales propositions. Sam decreed he would have nothing to do with such things.

'Stars can no longer substitute legs for brains,' he declared.

'Photographs of the nude or semi-nude female's form divine are *passé*', his statement read—again it is debatable whether or not he would have used the term '*passé*'. But he was just warming to a subject which he knew would get him almost as much exposure as one of those naked breasts. 'They are not only a possible deterrent to public morals but also a mighty poor type of exploitation.'

Since Sam was now spending $900,000 a film, it could be taken as read that he wouldn't embark on anything involving exploitation without weighing up the costs extremely carefully.

Having said that, and everyone having believed him, he was due for another U-turn. Remember there was no threat to the film industry or theatre by radio or any other medium?

A year or so later he was saying precisely the opposite, although he wasn't blaming radio. This time he said that the film industry was heading for disaster and ruin because vaudeville theatres were mixing films and stage shows together.

That was bad for business and meant that the public wasn't getting either good vaudeville or good films.

'Furthermore,' said Sam, 'the motion-picture fans will resent this poor quality as they have already resented being exhausted by an hour of cheap vaudeville before the picture starts. There is room for vaudeville separately and for pictures separately but the two do not belong together.'

If this *was* a change-about, there was an excuse for it. *The Jazz Singer* had been premiered in October 1927, two months before Sam made his statement and he was frightened that the silent movie, at least, would be sent back to the fairground where it had all begun.

As Sam said: 'If the combination continues, the film industry will be forced to make poorer pictures because of the heavy vaudeville cost burdens borne by the theatre-owners.' What Sam hadn't yet seen was that the new talking pictures had spelt the end of America's foreign language market. Sam was worrying about losing that, but not simply because of pictures that were going to be recorded in English. He thought the quality of films made for vaudeville would affect that market more.

'Good pictures', he said, 'have given us a splendid foreign market. But we will lose our supremacy if we are forced into cutting quality.'

If only that was all that people talked about in connection with Goldwyn. Even those who respected him—and most in the industry did—loved retelling those stories. When he took Frances on a cruise to Europe and a coterie of Goldwyn executives went to the dock to see them off, it was Sam from his position on deck who shouted 'bon voyage'.

Later, on that same trip Sam needed to talk urgently to Marcus Loew's son Arthur in New York. It was the middle of the night on the Eastern seaboard, but that didn't seem to register with Goldwyn.

When Sam got through—via three or four different operators, for this was years before direct dialling—Loew shouted angrily down the mouthpiece: 'For God's sake, Sam! Do you know what time it is?'

'Frances,' Goldwyn said to his wife, 'Arthur wants to know what time it is.'

Now it is possible Sam knew he was being funny and enjoyed the joke a lot more than Arthur Loew did. When he smiled Sam's face was already beginning to resemble the squashed lemon used on soft-drink advertisements. It is also possible he was quite naïve about the whole matter. Which was something he was never likely to be when it came to making films.

The trip to Europe on the *Berengaria* was not entirely a holiday. He was there to 'study film conditions', he made clear.

Britain came very firmly into his sphere of attack. Arriving in what had been his most important overseas market, Sam said he had a lot of sympathy for 'their efforts to legislate health and vigour into their infant film industry'. Since the British film industry offered no competition whatsoever for what Goldwyn had been turning out, he had every right to be sympathetic. However, it was the way they sold his own pictures that worried him.

He tried to say that wasn't his worry. What bothered him was the kind of pictures they made. The only solution for Britain's problem was by producing good movies.

As he said: 'Americans would rather see a good English picture than a bad American one. English people would rather see a good American one than change or alter that.'

What Sam really was hitting at was Britain's quota system—which insisted that a certain percentage of movies shown in British cinemas had to be home produced. This gave a green light to some really dreadful pictures being made—the words 'English picture' were themselves as perjorative in England as in the United States.

Some American studios got round the quota system by making movies in

Britain themselves. That was not a bag Sam could either afford or want to get into.

Quotas, he stated, were a 'weak way of doing things. It is quite obvious that the real method for England to adopt would be to produce good pictures. You can't stop a good play or a good picture. The exhibitors over here (the interview was for American consumption and what he was saying was absolutely untrue) don't care where a film comes from so long as it will draw the people. Nobody worried whether *Passion* was German or not. It was highly praised and the consequence was that Ernst Lubitsch, the director and Pola Negri, one of the principals, were brought to Hollywood . . . All the laws in the world will not improve a product.'

Mind you, one of the problems, as he saw it, was the way the industry was run in those days. 'Before Wall Street came into the picture business it had been developed here by men who started at the bottom, men who have proved that they not only realized the possibilities of pictorial stories but who worked to improve their product.'

There was a different problem in France. The Government there ordered that for every four American films shown in their country, Hollywood had to buy one French movie for showing in America.

Sam didn't like that idea one bit. As he said. 'It is ridiculous for us to take films that the American public will not see . . . and when the French or any other people produce films that Americans will see, the pictures will sell themselves.'

The British and French film industries may have worried Sam enough to cry crocodile tears. However, Germany gave him much more concern—not for political reasons, not because he was insulted, but with Frances on hand he couldn't enjoy all the facilities offered him.

He was swamped in Berlin by young girls displaying tempting favours that he couldn't possibly accept with his wife around him.

Of course, they all wanted jobs in the movies and, like girls yearning for Hollywood through the generations, they found ingenious ways of secreting themselves in a producer's bedroom.

As he described it the girls were accompanied by a 'small mountain' of pictures and applications.

But he did say he was on the look out for new talent, the kind he could use in Goldwyn films. He came back to America on the *Mauretania* saying he had found two of them.

One was a beautiful young French girl called Lili Damita, who had been working in Germany. He thought she was just beautiful, even more enchanting than he had found Vilma Banky. (Errol Flynn was to agree. Damita gave him the kind of welcome to America Flynn wanted. They had a highly publicized affair which later became an even more publicized marriage. The number of plates they threw at each other kept local china stores in business for years.) She was never to be a great star, but she did look good on the screen and benefited from the Hollywood treatment.

The second Goldwyn import was rather less of a hit. Walter Butler, he said, was going to be Ronald Colman's successor. That was wishful thinking—or was it? Colman was going so strong, the very idea of a successor seemed ridiculous. Butler never made it—at least as Walter Butler. By the time he appeared in his first Goldwyn film, *The Awakening*, he had changed his name—or perhaps Goldwyn and his publicity department had changed the name—to Walter Byron. He appeared in several films, and *The New York Times* welcomed him as a major new discovery, but he never became a huge star.

Sam was, however, on stronger ground looking for an English actor than searching for a continental. He hadn't yet realized that was precisely what he would not be able to do in the future. Something had happened to the movie industry which practically in one fell swoop was killing the notion of pictures starring actors and actresses who couldn't speak English.

Sam could rightly say that he usually saw the way things were going and made sure he was ahead. But even he made mistakes, particularly when it came to going 'talkie' after the huge success of *The Jazz Singer*. Sam was caught metaphorically with his pants down just as much as any of his competitors were. None of them had taken sound films seriously and when Warners had what they themselves called their 'supreme triumph', all the moguls were wringing their hands not knowing what they should do next.

Almost a year after its premiere, in a *New York Times* interview in August 1927, Sam was saying how upset he was.

He dismissed the fuss over *The Jazz Singer* as 'hysteria' and because he *was* Sam Goldwyn no one suggested this was just sour grapes. He genuinely believed that Warner's new idea—which wasn't a new idea at all; even Edison had been putting forward notions for sound movies since the turn of the century—was just a bright flash in a pretty shoddy pan.

'It's a pity', he said, 'that so many picture-makers are just sheep'. Everyone wanted to get on a profitable bandwagon. When he made *Stella Dallas*, every other studio tried to copy the idea and bring out 'mother' pictures.

'The present state of excitement over the sound picture is virually due to the financial success of *The Jazz Singer*, which it should be remembered featured that inimitable artist Al Jolson. What would this picture have been without Mr Jolson? Certainly, it might have made money but it would never have been the outstanding hit it was all over the country without that stellar performer.'

But he told the *Times*; 'I am by no means opposed to the sound film, but I do think that the hysteria that reigns here at present may mean that so many inadequate talking subjects will be issued that people will eventually long for the peace and quiet to which they have been accustomed with the silent features. They can make all the sound films they want, but I wonder how many pictures will be made with the new medium that will be as beautiful as Chaplin's *Gold Rush*.'

Despite his comments about 'hysteria', it has to be accepted that many of the moguls felt the same way. They were just a little too unsure of themselves to put their money where their hearts were.

Sam called for more time in bringing out talking pictures. 'A great deal of experimenting is needed. For improvements will be made from week to week. A talking picture that is considered good may be virtually behind the times soon after its release and, when its makers are still working along the same lines, another producer may have found a way to picture a sound subject that puts the other man's films in the background.'

Alas, Goldwyn's thoughts were based more on hope than reality. He was asking his fellow producers to follow him down the road, but the others were walking in a different direction. Before long, he realized he had to run to catch up.

But for a time Sam continued to make silent films—right in fact until Jolson's *The Singing Fool* and its *Sonny Boy* theme song in 1929 finally convinced the other producers to convert to sound.

None of them thanked the Warners for what they had done—but Sam was not alone in wishing he had thought of it before they did. To many it seemed that, instead of being a huge forward leap, bringing sound to the screen was a big step backwards.

Just as Sam had predicted, the cinema had 'matured'. Directors had introduced new lighting effects, new camera angles and wonderful scenic effects with movies shot on location in the wide outdoors. There were Cecil B. DeMille's Biblical epics and Griffith's Westerns, to say nothing of Goldwyn's own productions.

Sound couldn't cope with these. Microphones were attached to wires and wires had to be connected to booths and the booths to the mains plugs. You couldn't do that in the open air. And then there was the question of where you were going to put those microphones.

The OK-for-sound episode in *Singin' In the Rain* was perhaps only a little exaggerated. Nobody had yet invented the overhead boom and microphones really did have to be hidden in the strangest places—which was why so many scenes featured actors and actresses huddled over telephones. Mikes were secreted in actress's corsages or inside their bras—which may have made for fun for the sound operators but provided all sorts of other headaches, and not just for the actresses. Yes, heart-beats were picked up by the mikes; yes, when a girl played with her pearl necklace it did sound like the collapse of a skyscraper.

None of this really explained Goldwyn's reluctance to make what were now being called 'talkies' (as distinct from mere 'movies').

He was always a man of fixed ideas—didn't he say, 'I never put on a pair of shoes until I've worn them for five years'? But now he couldn't be sure what his ideas should be.

He was much more afraid of the costs involved in wiring theatres for sound, which might be—he even hoped would be—a temporary phenomenon. What was more, if he were going to make a sound film he wanted it to be handled by a man who knew more about recording sound than anyone else. He engaged Gordon Sawyer, who achieved what Goldwyn was heard to say were 'genius results'.

What Sawyer could not do to that new-fad thing called a sound-track was really not worth doing. Except in one particular instance—he couldn't do anything about Vilma Banky.

Miss Banky was still Sam's biggest star and his biggest drawing attraction. She wasn't exactly in the full bloom of youth any more and perhaps she hadn't restricted herself sufficiently to those lamb-chops and pineapple pieces, but every time she appeared on screen that bosom heaved and the men in the audience fell to pieces.

Unfortunately, when they saw her in *This Is Heaven*, they—and their delighted wives and girl-friends—fell to pieces for an altogether different reason: her accent. For reasons that have never been sufficiently explained—perhaps because of the way he knew that he himself spoke—Sam never gave Banky's voice a second thought.

He knew she had a Hungarian accent, but what did that matter? It mattered a great deal. In those early talkie days, people went to movies as much as anything to discover just how their favourite stars did talk. Until then, most people had no idea she was Hungarian. They probably assumed she was American—all God's children had to be American, didn't they? That was the Hollywood ethic, after all. Those who didn't think she was from their side of the Atlantic doubtless took *The New York Times* critic at his word and decided she was English. But Hungarian? Sam was distraught, more so than at any time since his advances on Banky's part were turned down by Valentino. Then he could cope. Now, he wasn't so sure. He called Vilma into his office, plied her with compliments, told her how ravishing she looked, asked about her husband, wanted to know if the bouquet he had just sent had arrived. (He had personally chosen the blooms; the very best orchids and fresh flowers which his personal florist could provide.) He gave her champagne and still more compliments. Then he suggested that perhaps the time had come to part. Vilma knew what was coming and was prepared. Her temper was kept intact, unruffled, inside that statuesque bosom which had represented so big a Goldwyn investment.

No, she said, she did not agree. She was happy working for Sam—and, besides, she had two years of her contract, worth $250,000, to go. If Goldwyn chose not to use her for those two years, it was . . . well, unfortunate for him.

The lawyers were called in and agreed, it was unfortunate for him. It would, however, have been even more unfortunate to risk using her in any other films. She sat out those two years and enjoyed Sam's money and was barely heard of in films again.

There obviously had to be a total rethink about all the people on the Goldwyn books. Just about the only one to come out with a clean bill of health was Ronald Colman—so clean in fact Sam suddenly realized that only now would he be able to use the English actor's finest asset—his voice.

He was a handsome man, but the voice was even more enticing to women than his face and Sam was out to exploit it as much as possible. He put him in the first of a series of *Bulldog Drummond* movies, which made more money for Sam than he really deserved. It wasn't much of a movie at all, but hearing Colman talk was enough.

The voice did, however, give Goldwyn a problem—and if Sam thought he had a problem, he was convinced everyone else who saw the movie would have one, too.

For the first time, he had passed a script, allowed it to go into production and then discovered (seemingly too late) something wrong.

He was watching the rushes, listening to the tinny dialogue coming from the speakers in the projection-room and trying to decide whether he liked talking pictures or not. Then, it struck him. He heard one of the characters complain about 'the infernal din.'

A quick check was made with the script. Yes, Sidney Howard had written that word.

'What does "din" mean?' Sam asked on aide.

There was a quick discussion. 'Din' is not an American word. It's very English and although this was a picture about Englishmen, Goldwyn's principal aim was to sell it in America.

'It means "noise",' the aide came back. 'Well,' said Sam, 'make him say "noise" in that case.'

Making him say 'noise' was reputed to have cost anything betwen $15,000 and $25,000. The set had already been struck and therefore had to be rebuilt. Many of the actors, who had been working on a day-to-day free-lance basis, had already been sent home and therefore had to be bought in all over again. But Sam Goldwyn didn't want his audiences, hearing a Sam Goldwyn film talk for the first time, to leave the theatre muttering that they didn't understand his dialogue.

At the premiere—at which Sam insisted Colman escort Frances—the actor was mobbed.

The New York Times described it as 'the happiest and most enjoyable entertainment of its kind that has so far reached the screen'.

He then put his British star into *Raffles*, which was to become another classic film subject, remade a dozen times in one guise or another.

Sam was never totally satisfied with this movie—and once again his first doubts were sparked watching the rushes. (Rushes and pictures about

Englishmen didn't seem to work for Sam.) Next to him was the director, Harry D'Arrast.

Sam was constantly picking on details which he said he didn't like. D'Arrast was distinctly upset. 'You and I don't speak the same language, Mr Goldwyn,' he said.

It was enough. Sam retorted: 'I'm sorry Mr D'Arrast, but it's my money that's buying the language.'

The director was fired on the spot and replaced by George Fitzmaurice, with whom he had a happier relationship.

Colman's association with Sam was always, however, stormy. When he had problems that needed sorting out he used mediators. The director, Arthur Hornblow, was frequently brought in to fulfil this role. Sometimes it was enough. Occasionally it was not.

On one occasion the studio rocked to the sound of a minor earthquake—but one so close that it was very noisy indeed. 'Don't worry,' said Colman to a young girl shaking with fright, 'it's only Sam Goldwyn seeing some more rushes.'

Now, though, there were other things to look for. Sam wanted a bigger business base and by cementing his relationship with United Artists he had it. By becoming part of a United Artists—but only to the extent of having a financial interest and using the company to distribute his movies; Samuel Goldwyn Productions were his alone—Colman and his other actors and actresses joined John Barrymore, Dolores Del Rio and the Talmadge sisters whose work went out under the UA imprint.

It was to prove a stormy time for Sam—and lead to five years of bickering with his partners, all of whom were supposed to produce films, too. Before more than a couple of those years had elapsed it seemed obvious to Sam that he was doing most of the work and they were reaping all his benefits.

They were distributing his films and he was using their studios on North Formosa Avenue—for which Sam was paying a handsome rent. He was turning out perhaps three or four pictures a year, whereas, between them, they hadn't made more than five in as many years.

But at the beginning he seemed content enough.

He was making talking films and pretending that he had never opposed them. He was making them only in English despite the worry about losing continental markets. As always, he had an answer to the people who couldn't understand how he could so readily take back what he had preached before as virtually holy gospel. But there he was saying it: 'I believe in the future of talking films.'

And he was saying it only six months after condemning the 'hysteria'.

'The day of the director is over,' he declared. 'That of the author and the playwright (has) arrived.' So he was trying to recoup some of his lost prestige by repeating what he had been known to say occasionally before.

To prove how much he believed in that philosophy, he had just given a great new deal to the English playwright Sidney Howard.

Not only had he guaranteed Howard a lot of money; he had also promised not to alter a single word of his dialogue. Now that was an important step, but seen in the context of the times, an understandable one. The playwright didn't now just have to suggest pantomine and contemplate sub-title cards.

Now, he was being asked to write a play, a screen play, literally—and few people knew better than a playwright how to do that. Or at least that was what Goldwyn believed.

Language was everything. As Sam said: 'I shall make talking films in English exclusively and distribute these products abroad, because I feel that there is a definite demand in foreign countries for films with English dialogue. I believe that, through the help of audible pictures, English will become the universal language.' It might even become Goldwyn's language, some voices were heard to suggest.

It made sense, because an independent producer, even a millionaire one like Sam Goldwyn, couldn't afford to do otherwise. Paramount, as the Zukor-Lasky operation was now known, and the other studios were making French and German versions of pictures they had already shot in English in an attempt to retain the overseas market, but Sam saw before his competitors that this was an uphill climb. They may use the same sets and the same crowd scenes, but changing directors and stars for the same stories was a thankless task.

One thing which was never allowed to seem a thankless task was working for Sam and even just listening to him.

One of the reasons Sam was so successful was because he had an innate faith in his own importance. Where he went he assumed he was being treated as a monarch on a state visit.

Immediately after booking into the Hotel Blackstone in Chicago he picked up the phone in his suite and commanded the switchboard operator: 'Get my office.' Now, the poor girl didn't know who he was, let alone the number of his office. When he told her his name she still didn't know his office number. She asked him for it. He didn't know. Like carrying money in his pocket, knowing telephone numbers—even the one at home—was not for him.

Once in conversation with Harpo Marx and a mutual friend, the man asked for his phone number. 'What's my number, Harpo?' he asked. Marx told him. Later, going home in Harpo's car, he asked again: 'What's my number?' Again, Harpo—the silent one of the Marx Brothers—told him. 'Write it down for me,' he said.

One thing he was not going to forget was the change in the film industry.

Now having accepted talkies, Sam was going to sell them the way he had sold his gloves. He knew that Ronald Colman was his strongest asset and he was telling everyone that listening to the Englishman's voice was the experience of a lifetime.

So when his sound films were released, nothing was left to chance. Sam even thought of the English audience—and arranged a transatlantic radio interview with a writer from the London *Daily Mail*, to coincide with the opening of *Bulldog Drummond* there.

At the premiere itself Sam and Frances were seen to embrace their star, in the company of fellow-English actor Clive Brook and two—wait for it—real English bulldogs.

The only thing that worried Sam was that Colman and the other actors who really did have commercial voices would be wanting more money. If he couldn't get out of it, he wanted the details finalized in water-tight contracts. His lawyers knew he had to get everything down on paper—for, as he told them at this time, 'a verbal contract isn't worth the paper it's written on'.

When a British company offered him $25 million to make films in England he had to admit that the suggestion was tempting to anyone who ever had to look for his own finance. But, for the moment, he was staying in Hollywood. One view he hadn't changed was that it was necessary to be at the centre of things.

Yet he went to England to prove that *Bulldog Drummond* was as good as he said it was. He said so with all the enthusiasm of another kind of bulldog-owner about to exhibit at Crufts.

Arnold Bennett, Noel Coward and Hugh Walpole were among those who were given personal shows of this magnificent new artistic product. Bennett told him that talking pictures were very much better than and a lot different from anything he had ever imagined. Of course they are, said Sam. I always knew they would be; the trouble was nobody was listening . . . .

10
The Goldwyn Follies

If he hadn't recognized it before, Sam Goldwyn now knew that things were going to change, and he was using all the expertise at his command to help them along.

He wasn't going to sacrifice the one plus factor he always felt he had at his command—quality. His demands were going to be as stringent as ever. If half a film had to be reshot to make sure that that quality was visible, he would still do it. But now there had to be new thoughts.

Sound meant more music, and surprisingly the musical hadn't taken off the way people assumed it would. The Jolson pictures should have given the green light to more and more spectacular musicals to follow, but on the whole it didn't happen—as much as anything else because it was still difficult to guarantee that sufficient microphone hiding-places could be found to take in all the big spectacular numbers. No one had yet contemplated dubbing the music afterwards and the mike boom was still on the way.

MGM were, however, already leading the pack in this regard. *Broadway Melody* with its single line of high-kicking chorus girls fronting a top-hat-and-tails Charles King singing the title song was really the first musical spectacular. But even before it was premiered in New York in 1929, Sam knew that he could do better.

Sam announced that he and Florenz Ziegfeld were joining forces. The man who had engraved over his lintel the legend 'Through these doors walked the most beautiful girls in the world' was plainly someone to respect.

Ziegfeld personified the great showman. His *Follies* were the great spectaculars of the first decades of the century, because when a girl on stage stepped out of a picture frame the frame was carved by craftsmen out of the finest wood, and his girls wore hand-stitched pure silk gowns—and underwear—because he believed it was important they felt as good as they looked.

That was the kind of man with whom Sam Goldwyn wanted to ally himself—the quality man. They were going to make big beautiful musicals with big beautiful girls—Ziegfeld's girls all had to be at least six feet tall—and, what is more, the films were going to be shot in colour. The idea made the mouths of both men water.

Just as important, Ziegfeld had been a great discoverer of talent. Eddie Cantor, Ed Wynn, Sophie Tucker, Fanny Brice had all been Ziegfeld stars. So had Will Rogers, who had already found his way into the Goldwyn stable.

It would never happen. Ziegfeld's only film association—apart from being played twice on screen by William Powell and then by Walter Pidgeon and a string of lesser actors in virtually every turn-of-the-century musical of the forties—was when he produced *Glorifying the American Girl* for Paramount.

That had been his slogan on Broadway. Now, hard up as he always was, he was going to Hollywood to glorify the American picture, and Sam wanted him to do it for him.

They talked of his forgoing his usual Palm Beach winter holiday and going to the Pacific coast instead; of this being the first Broadway-Hollywood link up of the talking picture era; of an improvement in standards previously undreamed of.

They were going to be partners in a Ziegfeld-Goldwyn Corporation. Sam wasn't saying that he was putting his entire operation into Flo Ziegfeld's hands, but the impression was there, especially when Goldwyn said that he and the man the show biz world knew as Ziggy were going to be 50–50 partners.

Did Sam really want another partner? Those who knew him should have known that was hardly a starter, but Sam seemed to be sold on the notion.

He said he had got the idea seeing Ziegfeld's show *Whoopee*, starring Eddie Cantor.

Goldwyn did make *Whoopee* into a movie and did star Eddie Cantor in it but Ziegfeld's 'partnership' was limited to selling screen rights and allowing his star to sign a contract with Sam.

He was, however, paid by Goldwyn to be a co-producer into which role he thought he fitted as well as he did in his Broadway office. Sam wasn't so sure. He suspected that Ziegfeld wanted to be a producer.

While Ziegfeld was working in Long Island, Sam was busy selecting the chorus for his film. Ziggy didn't like that. *He* was the one who knew how to select girls. He had made a profession out of it. Yes, said Goldwyn, but I know more about films—and which girls look good on the screen. And to prove it he chose the most beautiful girls he had ever seen—including one called Paulette Goddard.

Ziegfeld wasn't impressed. The filming should be done on Long Island, so that he could supervise things the way he did on Broadway. Besides, there were all those girls he had used on stage dressed as Red Indians. Sam couldn't possibly match those.

'Sure I can, Ziggy,' he told him by long-distance telephone. 'I can get Indians—all I want. All I've got to do is ring up the reservoir.'

Finally, Ziegfeld journeyed to Hollywood—and brought his own chorus with him. They were the girls he wanted for a Ziegfeld film. Girls with legs carved by a sculptor. Girls with gently curving hips, girls with the narrowest of waists, girls with the biggest but shapliest breasts ever photographed.

The Ziegfeld party arrived—at Flo's own expense—at the Goldwyn studio ready to see the walls tumble around him like Joshua at Jericho—except that Sam was determined that this would be a battle he would not lose.

He put his own girls on display next to Ziegfeld's and a team of so-called independent experts were brought in to judge who were the prettiest. They all agreed that Sam's were—Ziegfeld had to concede that was so and even took some of them back with him for his next stage *Follies*.

Meanwhile, Sam had established a new trademark for his musical films. He called his chorus the Goldwyn Girls.

Sam wanted to control the Goldwyn Girls the way Ziegfeld had run his. He didn't ask for hand-stitched silk underwear, but he did demand a veto on the costumes they wore.

A fashion show was organized for him. Sam sat behind his big desk as a procession of lovely girls came before him, twisting, twirling, moving rhythmically. In the end, the costume designer asked him what he thought of the show.

'The show was great,' said Sam. 'The costumes stank. Start again.'

The costumes were changed. He was like that with writers too. On one celebrated occasion he asked a writer to alter a script. He wasn't impressed. 'All you did,' said Goldwyn, 'was change the words'.

There were other equally significant developments as a result of making *Whoopee*. Sam employed an old Broadway hand, a very old Broadway hand named Thornton Freeland, to direct, and in charge of the choreography he put a young dance director who convinced him he could do big things with motion pictures. His name was Busby Berkeley. Berkeley had been in charge of the dancers of the stage show. Goldwyn, who was—like all his competitors—fishing around for people who could help him in this totally new medium of sound pictures, thought it made sense, and it was a lot easier to take someone who had already worked on the show. How Berkeley would change things given a camera lens to play with, Sam could hardly even suspect.

It could, of course, be put down to luck, to one of those chances which just as easily could not have come off, but bringing in Berkeley was an inspiration. For the Goldwyn Girls he already had a few bright ideas which had not been tried out before, like photographing them in geometric shapes from above.

The result made Berkeley the most talked-of dance director in the business. Eddie Cantor suddenly became an international star and *Whoopee* didn't do so badly for Sam Goldwyn either.

It wouldn't take very long before the picture looked very primitive and dated, but it already showed the kind of promise Sam liked to have made for him. He thought it added a touch of prestige to his name, and that was the sort of touch he liked.

Now, he was announcing he was planning to introduce a 'kind of Pulitzer prize' for films. Somehow or other he didn't think the Academy Award's little statuette was important enough. He was proved wrong before he could bring his idea to fruition—otherwise we might have had Sammies competing with Oscars.

With that idea out of the way Sam was trying again to inveigle more prestigious names into his studio. He attempted once more to persuade George Bernard Shaw to come to Hollywood. But when they eventually met at Shaw's home at Ayot St Lawrence in Hertfordshire, the great Irish playwright wasn't interested. A real writer, he said, wouldn't waste his time on pictures.

It wasn't like that any more, said Sam. Pictures now talked. That won't last, said Shaw. You haven't seen the best of them, insisted Sam, who promptly suggested a list of possible movies that the great man might be interested in seeing. He never did find out if his idea was taken up.

Goldwyn wanted the best in every field in which he believed there was a movie connection. In January 1931 he announced a contract with Mme Coco Chanel to go to Hollywood to advise on film fashions.

She would not only work for Goldwyn films but help provide the best of clothes for United Artists in general. As Sam said, 'She will reorganize the dressmaking department of United Artists Studios and endeavour to anticipate fashions by six months to solve the eternal problem of keeping gowns up to date.' That was indeed a problem. By the time films came out, an entirely new 'line' had been established by the Paris fashion houses and the clothes worn by the actresses on screen suddenly looked appallingly dated. This way, Sam had a sneaking hope that Chanel would let him have some inside information. Of course she didn't, and of course the arrangement wouldn't last. But it was yet another very good story.

Sam was meanwhile buying up properties like a real estate magnate—or at least like a real estate magnate might have behaved before Wall Street went crash in October 1929. Sam lost some money but he was not one of the real victims of the big slump which followed.

He bought the 1929 Pulitzer winner *Street Scene*, which King Vidor was to direct, with Sylvia Sidney starring, and he took over New York's Gaiety Theatre to show his latest Ronald Colman film *The Devil to Pay*—all positive signs that as the 1930s were born, Sam Goldwyn was doing very well indeed.

Actually, it wasn't at all difficult to do well in the movie business during the Great Depression, because films were the Great Diversion. They were also the great levellers at a time when rich and poor suddenly all became poor. Families scraping for a crust somehow or other were able to rustle up the cost of a movie-theatre ticket. At the same time, men too ashamed to let their families know they were unemployed would leave in the mornings and spend most of the day in the warmth of a cinema. It was an escape from reality in more ways than one, and while this situation existed, the film industry had to find ways of catering for it.

Every new idea was trumpeted from on high as though it were announcing the Second Coming—and to Sam that was precisely what was happening. If every film he made was to him some kind of mystic event, the one that followed it was going to be a circumstance of amazing significance. In this, it was one way in which Sam was scoring over his contemporaries. Since they were each producing twenty times as many pictures as he was, everything Goldwyn came up with was regarded as an event. And since the newspapers were happy to co-operate with him—much more than they did with those assembly-belt studios—it was Sam's name that the public got to know. By now, he was the most famous producer in the United States.

In May 1931 Sam was proud to reveal he had just done a deal with Sinclair Lewis to film his *Arrowsmith*. The movie, about an altruistic doctor, was directed by John Ford—Goldwyn saw the worth of the hard-drinking, hard-talking Irishman who was to become best known for his John Wayne Westerns, and was not to be disappointed. Sidney Howard wrote the screen-play imaginatively and Ronald Colman starred—having the women of two continents alternatively weeping and sighing in the aisles.

Ford was to tell Colman's daughter Juliet Benita Colman, for her book *Ronald Colman: A Very Private Person*: 'When you work with Sam, there are always problems if you allow them to worry you. He would come on to the set after I had started work, and I would sit down and order tea or something. He'd say, "Why aren't you shooting?" And I'd say, "Well, if I came into your office while you were working and watched you work, you'd be very much annoyed. This is my office and I am working here and I am not going to be rude and work while you, the president of a company are here, sir. Very bad manners!" He couldn't understand that, so we'd wait until he'd left, then we would resume shooting.'

Before that film could be made Sam was delighting in having Gloria Swanson star in *Tonight or Never*.

Meanwhile, the boss of United Artists, Joseph Schenck, said he wanted Sam to become his head of production. That idea was not to Goldwyn's liking. He hadn't come that far to be someone else's partner, let alone employee. On the other hand he was delighted to benefit from what United Artists put out and to have his films distributed by the organization.

Now he was planning to feature Al Jolson in *Sons o' Guns*, based on the Broadway show of the same name. It looked like a concrete way of cashing in, finally, on what he had missed in 1927. He admired Jolson, knew what he could do and also suspected that the great star was on the slide—and he might therefore get him a bit cheaper than he had previously been. That was not to be. What he did get, however, was Jolson's principal rival, Eddie Cantor, in another movie, *The Kid from Spain*.

It was all looking so good—if only the critics weren't trying to make things difficult for the Hollywood men. 'The time', he declared in December 1931, 'has come to rise in vehement defence of the industry against carping, ridicule and nagging.' (The ghost-writers had been busy again, but that didn't matter.)

But then, like most of the film bosses, Sam had a slight dose of paranoia. When he wasn't falling in love with a new writer or player who was going to change everything for his organization, he was fighting him with the gusto of a newly appointed general on the way to war. Now he was saying that the English star wasn't quite the perfect gentleman his image suggested. In fact, said unnamed quarters in the Goldwyn studios, Colman was known to like the product of the grape and grain a little too much. Colman was furious—so angry, he grew red in the face just like the drunk Goldwyn was alleging him to be. He sued for libel.

These statements, charged the star, were 'reflecting on his character and ability' and portrayed him as 'drunk and dissipated'.

Colman's lawyers, for their part, said that Goldwyn's organization was trying to get the actor to 'perform acts which he said he was not obligated to perform'. In the parlance of half a century or later that sounds a lot more damaging than it actually was. Colman was principally against the publicity stunts that the studio wanted him to engage in.

And it added up. When Colman didn't co-operate Sam decided to go into a different game entirely, although based on the previous one. If the actor wasn't going to do publicity the studio's way, the studio would release statements in his name which they thought would have him begging them for a more considerate approach. Sam's publicists quoted the star saying things he had never said—which wasn't unusual; this time, though, they were even more damaging than the original allegations.

The statements the company issued allegedly on Colman's behalf were grotesque. They suggested that Mr Colman took to drink as his way of 'getting into' a part. One of them actually stated: 'He feels that he looks better for pictures when moderately dissipated than when completely fit.'

Colman said he neither felt that nor said it and demanded an immediate retraction. The retraction was refused and the actor sued for $2 million. Of course, it turned out to be no more than a small tempest in one of the commissary's china cups, but it worried Sam for a time and thrilled the newspaper readers of America no end.

There were those in Hollywood for whom resorting to the law courts was as much a studio sport as tennis or the casting couch. Sam, on the whole, didn't take that route.

He once boasted to a lawyer that he never sued anybody. Then he casually added: 'Three or four maybe. Right now I'm being sued by Paramount for five million dollars.' 'And', he said, warming to his theme greatly, 'its going to be the biggest law suit ever.'

Sam always took the view that it was necessary to keep employees on their toes and not appear too nice. 'I have a rule for you,' he told an executive, 'a happy studio makes bad pictures.'

That did not mean he bore grudges. There was a certain Goldwyn staffer who was summoned to the home of the master and given a telling off that made the recent thunderstorm sound like a cool breeze rustling leaves on an autumn day.

He went on, he ranted, he raved. His excitement grew with the passing of each second on his watch. The man quaked. Sam was in full flow when Sam Junior, Sammy, walked in to say goodnight to his father.

Sam smiled, patted the child on the back, his voice regained its usual timbre—which was high in a different way. He kissed the little boy. Then he looked towards the still shaking 'guest'. 'And', said Sam, 'kiss Uncle . . . goodnight.'

'Uncle' smiled as Sam smiled, sat back in his chair and relaxed. Then Goldwyn returned to the subject in hand. The man jumped out of the chair as though he had just sat on a fire-cracker.

Other times were more fun—although not necessarily for Sam.

On one occasion Frances gave him a surprise party. He arrived home to hear her say she had something she wanted him to see. If he'd just sit in the living-room and wait, she'd show him. And to make things a little more exciting, she blindfolded him as she led him into the luxurious room. He couldn't see a lounge that had been filled with guests who had been instructed, under pain of excommunication from the Goldwyn set, to keep totally still and quiet.

Sam wasn't very comfortable that evening. He had stomach problems. He was standing by his chair, walking round it—unaware that there was a crowd just inches away—breaking wind incessantly, like volleys from a cannon. For a minute, the 'firing' ceased. That was when Frances returned, tore off his blindfold and shouted: 'Surprise! Surprise!

Charlie Chaplin, who was one of the guests, dined out on that story practically until he died.

Goldwyn didn't very often give the impression of being happy himself—in the studio. One day, he walked around the Goldwyn lot, stopping everybody he came across. Naturally, these people—some top executives, some mere underlings—were alternately delighted, then extremely apprehensive about being accosted by the great man. It was not an event that happened very often. Most of them didn't think that Sam knew they existed. Being approached by the boss was instant recognition.

It was a bright sunny day, as it invariably was in Southern California, but for each of them he had the same question: 'Do you think it's raining today?'

Was the boss out of his mind? Was he trying to catch them with the latest 'in' joke they hadn't heard? They had to answer No. One man even went as far as to say: 'Of course not. There isn't a cloud in the sky.'

'I don't mean here,' Goldwyn replied. 'I mean in New York. Our picture opens in New York tonight.'

If it didn't work in New York he would have to go back to his drawing-board and think again about some of the people on his books.

There would have to be a look at some of the figures paid to studio people, writers and players alike. All of them were well paid and, as he also said, 'Talent which does not draw at the box-office is over-paid at any price.' He thought the other studios were putting out too many movies—no company ought to make more than twenty pictures a year, he said.

It was a theme to which he was constantly returning. Except that when he said it again just over a year later in 1933, he said that there should be only fifty films made each year—by the whole of Hollywood.

So many people were drawing money from Hollywood, he maintained, that he 'couldn't see the trees for the woods'.

It was a difficult time for the world. The Jewish world, to which he and all the other big Hollywood figures now tried to feel themselves outsiders, was in anguish over the happenings in Germany.

Adolf Hitler had come to power and almost immediately instituted a boycott of Jewish businesses and of Jews in high places. It would get much, much worse, but to most people outside Germany it seemed horrific enough.

The Hollywood bosses had to decide whether to ignore it from the comfort of their new existences or to suddenly reveal some sort of relationship with their collective pasts. (They weren't given much choice. All their films were now banned in Nazi Germany.)

Sam was one of the first to act. He turned down totally a suggestion that he should reciprocate and ban German directors or actors from his lots. It was an idea which had been seriously put to him. No, said Sam intelligently enough. 'Any country which penalized talent would eventually (have) to pay a great penalty itself.'

But, he said, he was going to start a movement which would invite to Hollywood all those 'who because of their Jewish heritage are being deprived of a livelihood and an outlet for their talent'.

It was a brave move, for not everyone was agreeing with him.

'We not only invite them here,' he went on, 'we need them. Despite the great strides motion pictures have made here I still believe we are undermanned.'

It was another one of those contradictory statements, but even if he had said only a week earlier that he had too many people earning big salaries, the sentiment now was appreciated.

He was about to eat his words on that other subject on which he showed all the consistency of a moving see-saw—censorship. In October 1933 Sam and Joseph M. Schenck, president of both United Artists and the Twentieth Century company, announced they were leaving the Motion Picture

Producers and Distributors of America—otherwise known as the Hays Office.

It wasn't just the Office's censorship code that worried the two moguls. They were equally disturbed by the alleged dominance of New York distributors.

A week earlier they withdrew support from the motion-picture code set up by the National Recovery Agency—President Franklin D. Roosevelt's famous NRA established as part of his New Deal to get America working again after the Depression.

The Agency had recommended maximum salaries being instituted for top actors and executives. Sam, who had been saying much the same thing for years, did another U-turn. 'I'd rather pay an artist $250,000 if he earned it than $2,000 to one who hadn't.' Then he added in a statement that would for ever after be used in evidence against him: 'You can't make a crime out of earning capacity.'

In this regard he was being heavily backed by the very people with whom he usually came into conflict, the Screen Actors Guild, the Screen Writers Guild and hundreds of extras who were in work. The out-of-work writers and actors were all for the NRA.

An emergency meeting of the Office was called to which Sam and Schenck were invited. Harry M. Warner made an impassioned plea for the Hays Office to be given a chance and asked for the two production heads to think again.

Sam decided he had thought and left the meeting with words that have now gone into every book of quotations worth buying: 'Gentlemen,' he said, 'include me out.'

11
The Devil To Pay

It wasn't the only dispute that Sam had with a Warner brother.

A short while afterwards he and the Warners had a meeting at which agreement between Jack and Harry Warner was as rare as between their company and any other picture operation.

Jack Warner Junior was present on one occasion when his father, 'Colonel' Jack Warner (Senior), and his uncle Harry were in dispute with Sam. 'I can no longer remember what it was about,' he told me.

'But I've never forgotten the meeting I went to with my father and uncle and Sam Goldwyn, Louis Mayer and all the others. They were in the midst of a big argument. They made a proposal,' Warner recalled, although the proposal itself is now lost in antiquity.

Goldwyn looked at them and then marched towards the door. 'I won't make an agreement with the Warner Brothers,' he told them. 'Making an agreement with the Warner Brothers is like pissing into the wind.'

'At which point', Warner said, 'the room shook. We were having an earthquake. And I remember thinking, Sam's words were heard up above. There was so much pissing into the wind that it caused an earthquake.'

For all that, there was a sense of respect between the Warners and Goldwyn that didn't exist with other studio heads.

'The brothers Warner had a great deal of respect for him. He wasn't in the same league as Louis Mayer, for instance, or Harry Cohn, for whom they had contempt. They agreed with him on a lot of things. There was a shortage of raw product, stories and stars and they were competing. But Goldwyn was blessed with one thing—it was his money that ran the company and he could make the decisions. The brothers often said that they wished they were like him, with no responsibility to stockholders, for instance. He could pick and choose. Secretly, my father and uncles wished they could be Sam Goldwyn, for all his atrocious accent and mangling of the English language.'

And also for his sense of style. 'He wouldn't be seen dead in some of the sports jackets my father used to wear.'

Neither did they stay away from each others' parties. These were occasions that always produced stories—and even if they *were* friends, they didn't hesitate to tell them against each other afterwards. Like the time Greta Garbo was invited to a Goldwyn party.

Naturally enough, the mogul was sizing her up all the time. He didn't think she had star quality, he decided after that night. That was partly because he couldn't take his eyes off her feet, which he decided were too big. But there was something else, too: he found her in the kitchen talking to Sam's maid—and that was distinctly *infra dig* as far as he was concerned.

Warner must have enjoyed that when he heard about it—and also about the event at his own home when one of the most celebrated of all Goldwynisms was uttered for the first time.

It is not only celebrated, but much discussed and variously attributed. As with most of them, it is sometimes accepted as apocryphal. But Mrs Jean Negulesco, wife of one of Warners' top directors—he had already established himself but was to go on to make a varied selection of movies from *Johnny Belinda* to *How to Marry a Millionaire*—swore to me that she was at the centre of the incident.

It happened on the evening Jack Warner was holding a house-warming party at his magnificent new house on Angelo Drive in Beverly Hills.

Sam was admiring the garden with Mrs Negulesco. In the centre of the lawn was a sundial. Sam was fascinated by it.

'What's that?' he asked her.

'Oh, it's a sundial,' she answered.

'A what?'

'A sundial,' she said. 'You see, every day the sun casts a shadow from the piece of metal at the top. Since the shadow changes all through the day, you can tell what time it is.'

'My!' said Sam, 'what will they think of next.'

'Oh yes, it happened,' Mrs Negulesco told me almost half a century later. 'It happened. It was my conversation with him.'

Jack Warner himself would frequently go to Sam's house with producer Charles K. Feldman to play gin rummy.

'Sam was a terribly heavy gambler,' his producer friend David Rose told me. 'He lost fortunes—at poker, gin rummy; mostly gin rummy. He played for ten dollars a point. At one time he lost a million dollars in a few days. He was in New York one weekend and lost $330,000 to a fellow to whom he couldn't hold a candle to when it came to gambling, Matty Fox, later to be a TV magnate.

'He would play for anything, get mad, double up the stakes.'

It would be like that all of his life. Years later, when Frances went to London to try to wrest Deborah Kerr from Gabriel Pascal—she lost to MGM—Sam lost half-a-million dollars playing cards in the three or four days she was away.

He once lost $10,000 playing with Alexander Korda. In his charming book *Charmed Lives* Michael Korda recalls Sam giving his uncle a cheque and adding in writing: 'Signed with blood.' It was written in red ink. The following night the situation was reversed and Korda wrote: 'Dear Sam, this cheque is signed in my blood, too.' Since Korda was now *Sir* Alexander, a knight of King George VI's realm, he wrote his note in blue ink.

The writing of cheques—in blue or red ink—were frequent occurrences at the Goldwyn home. And from the earliest days of their friendship, Jack Warner was one of his most regular fellow-players to receive and write them. His son-in-law, Bill Orr, recalled those occasions for me:

> Sam used to play while other people in the house were watching movies. His card-room was just off his screening-room. So Sam would sit with his back to the screen, but have his opponents facing it—so that they would be distracted.
>
> Jack used to tell of another occasion when they were playing for high stakes and Charlie Feldman was in for a big score. Sam, who didn't smoke, lit up a cigarette. He put his match down on the score-card which then burnt up. 'Oh', he said, 'I'm so sorry. . . .' Sam didn't smoke, but it got rid of that score.
>
> All those men were competitive with one another, wanting to do better than the other guy. But Jack had no quarrel with Sam.

David Rose remembered when he and his wife returned to their house at Palm Springs from a trip to Mexico.

> Sam was waiting for me. He had been at the racquet club but he now wanted to play cards with me.
>
> It was about nine o'clock and I was tired, but I agreed to play until twelve. I got lucky as hell. Everything I did was right. Twelve o'clock came and my wife was waiting. She wanted us to stop.
>
> Sam wasn't keen. He suggested that Rose just wanted to pack up because he was on a winning streak. So the producer took the score-card, tore it up and threw the shreds into the fire.
>
> At dawn, the phone rang, I was asleep. My wife Betty answered. It was Sam and he was crying—he used to cry a lot. He said, 'Tell David to come along. I'll fix breakfast for him.'
>
> I didn't know he could cook. It was lovely. Well, we went out for a walk. We both used to like walking.
>
> Sam said he wanted to apologize. He said he had behaved very badly last night.
>
> Rose told him not to worry and to forget it. But Goldwyn persisted. 'How much do you think I lost last night?' he asked.
>
> Rose replied 'Sam, what the hell . . . forget about it. Maybe $300.'
>
> They left each other. By the time Rose was back at his office there was a cheque waiting for him—from Goldwyn for $300.

People respected him for that. But they laughed at him, too.

At this time a virtual industry was being created in making up the Goldwynisms—like his not being worried about criticism because 'It rolls off me like a duck's back'. Or even 'Never let that bastard into my room again—unless I need him'. If Goldwyn did not say it, it was precisely the way he would have acted. And very sincerely at that.

Making fun of Sam Goldwyn was a defence mechanism for people who had to recognize his tremendous abilities, not least of all his fine tuning when it came to choosing material that was not only commercial but tasteful. It never ceased to amaze so-called film artists how a man so unschooled, so unaquainted with the language he used, could have such a sense of what was right. It was a judgement much admired by his rivals.

But as Jack Warner told me: 'I can't stress enough that Goldwyn was even then in a different business from the rest of them. He was like Tiffany's compared with Macy's basement. He could pick and choose and did. And he wasn't answerable to anyone but Sam Goldwyn and his wife. Without her, I don't think you'd ever have heard of him.'

Frances helped him at home and at work. Before long she had an office alongside Sam's at the studio on the United Artists lot and she would sift out a pile of scripts or script ideas before Sam himself had a look at them. She would come to the office after Sam—long enough after to make his lunch, which she brought in in a picnic basket.

If he did things on her advice, they were things that upheld his belief in quality. Once having got the finest sound engineer in the business working for him, he built the finest stages. He was the first to dub music on to the sound-track after a scene had been shot and have his singers and dancers mime to a pre-recorded track. By then, too, the boom mike had been invented—no more microphones hidden in girls corsages picking up heartbeats. The only heart that could be heard beating was Sam's—while he tried to decide whether a shot was going to be good enough.

Or if he were going to go against his principles and engage in yet another law suit. In January 1934 two of America's top show-writers, George S. Kaufman and Robert E. Sherwood, sued Goldwyn for money they claim was owed to them for work they did on *Roman Scandals*.

Sam said they only offered a treatment, and a rough draft at that. The writers said they did more, and demanded $25,000 they claimed Goldwyn promised them.

The two were given credit for an 'original story' in the opening moments of the film, but adaptation, music and lyrics were attributed to other people.

Sam tried to settle out of court—where eventually it was all sorted out—but not for anything like the figure being demanded. The writers' lawyer meanwhile, said that when the profits for the picture were known, he would demand even more cash. That, however, was just one of the perils of making Hollywood movies.

After all this time Sam was admitting he was having enough of writers. They were hacks who wrote pot-boilers, he said, sitting in his suite in New York's Waldorf Astoria Hotel.

Were they not inspirational figures? 'Perspirational,' he replied.

'Hollywood is merely a stop-over place for writers.'

That being so, he didn't believe any of them deserved salaries. They should depend on profits. If their work was good, they'd make a lot of money. If it was bad, they'd lose out.

As he also said, the trouble with these people was that they were 'always biting the hand that laid the golden egg'.

He was being helped, however, by loyal friends. Abe Lehr, the son of the man for whom he worked all those years before in Gloversville, had come to Hollywood and was now Sam's principal assistant and, next to Frances, his number one sounding-board and confidant. He might not any longer have to prevent Sam losing his shirt in a card game, but he could help him take the more sensible road in other, more significant gambles.

He also learned more than a little of the Goldwyn mystique. Even Sam's syntax appeared to rub off on him, the way the kid from their gloves used to do.

Sam asked his opinion of a new film starring Eddie Cantor which was going to be called *Yes, Yes*. Lehr liked the script, but not the title. 'Why not?' Sam asked. 'Too negative,' Lehr replied.

To which Goldwyn was generous enough to comment: 'And they say I say funny things.' The title was, however, changed.

There was always trouble with Cantor films. Sam didn't like the way his movie *Palmy Days* was shaping up. A. Edward Sutherland directed it, but Goldwyn didn't like it and asked his friend Mervyn LeRoy—'Moiphy', as he called him—to do 'a couple of days work' on it. The couple of days turned into three weeks.

'Moiphy' did his best, but Sam wanted more girls in the picture, especially when Cantor did his solos. Cantor protested. He worked alone on stage and that was how it had to be on screen, too.

Goldwyn had to accept that—except that he told LeRoy to 'have a few girls whiz by' when the star performed. LeRoy decided not to do anything about it and nothing more was said.

It seemed that everyone should behave and run their businesses like Sam Goldwyn. The difference was that everyone didn't have what was now being called the Goldwyn Touch.

12
Enchantment

What anybody wanting to be a Goldwyn had to do before anything else was, literally, find a Frances.

She may have come from a totally different background from his, she may have seemed, with her bobbed hair and short skirts, to have headstrong ideas—like going against her mother and agreeing to marry Sam in the first place. But she was within a very short time his inspiration and recognized as such by the rest of the Hollywood community.

She was the wholesale peacemaker on the Goldwyn lot. If Sam was in a shouting mood, she was there to calm him down. If she thought he was being unfair to an employee, she would mediate without appearing to interfere.

She went along with his follies and foibles. At one dinner party Sam discovered that tinned peaches were being served for dessert. A new cook had been taken on and he was furious. Frances called to see the cook. 'The peaches,' she said, 'are not Mr Goldwyn's brand.' Sam's dinner was put on to a happier level because she had been seen to take action and the cook saved face.

Frances would always say that it wasn't difficult making Sam happy. 'Sam really is a devoted husband,' she said years later. 'He is the homiest pigeon sort of man you ever knew.'

Saying that was clever—as Sam appreciated. 'Not all women are as smart as my wife,' he said once. 'But I believe if more men would consult their wives on their problems and make them feel important, there would be fewer divorces.'

There is no doubt he loved Frances, admired her acumen and her beauty. Everything about her seemed nothing less than perfect to Sam. Someone remarked about her hands. 'Yes,' he replied. 'Frances has the most beautiful hands in the world—and some day I'm going to make a bust of them.'

To many of his competitors Sam had already made a bust of the film industry. Given half the chance, as Jack Warner has said, they would have loved to have made movies his way, but like soap manufacturers contemplating giving up advertising, none of them was prepared to be the first to take the plunge.

Sam occasionally did things the other men did—just because he didn't want to appear to be either unsociable or risk losing their esteem. It was a familiar phenomenon to people who studied the way of life of successful men.

That was why Sam played golf. Harpo Marx was one of his regular partners at the Hillcrest Country Club.

One day Sam went on to the green with a bag full of sparkling new putters, hauled all the way by his caddy. He attempted a shot at the hole and failed miserably. In a fit of pique he threw his putter to the ground. Harpo picked it up, did a marvellous shot and reached the hole in one stroke.

Sam was fascinated. It must, he decided, have something to do with the club. He asked Harpo if he could use it next. The shot went home. He was very impressed. 'Say Harpo,' said Sam, 'that's a marvellous putter. Would you sell it to me?'

Harpo shook hands and calmly sold Sam his own golf club. Goldwyn never realized what he had done. He didn't like golf, which was why he took up croquet—a vicious sport the way he played it, not at all the vicar's tea-party occasion legend suggests.

He once rang one of his executives. He knew the man was good at croquet and asked to give him a game. The man was flattered but pointed out he had a film to work on. Sam was impressed. He told the young chap that he thought he had his priorities right.

But he re-thought the matter, changed his schedule and rang Sam to say he could play. Goldwyn was exultant. The game began and his companion began to win—convincingly. Sam was furious. After a few minutes, he said: 'Stop! What are you doing here playing croquet? A man like you should be working!'

It was a message he determined to pass on to his son, Sam Junior, whom he educated at the Black-Foxe Military Academy. A chauffer took him to and from school each day. That wasn't because either Sam or Frances wanted to pamper the boy. It was the age of the kidnapper, in the wake of the Lindbergh affair, and no rich family was taking the risk of letting their children out unchaperoned.

It was a decision Frances and Sam took in unison. Most of their decisions were.

Together, they went to the big film premieres. They travelled in processions of yellow Rolls-Royces, the women in white ermine. The trouble was that Frances was inclined to be shoved around by the crowds when she and Sam got out of their Rolls. The crowds hadn't a clue who she was and were impatiently awaiting the stars.

She could cope with it. She smiled and forged ahead over the red carpet. The trouble came when she sat between two actresses, one of them the public wanted to see, the other whom they regarded with indifference. As she said, the neglected girl's false smile would spoil an evening for anyone. But that was just part of being in the business.

It was a totally different world from the one that would follow twenty years later. For the moment, the big studios held sway and independent producers were a rare breed of which the only recognized member was Samuel Goldwyn.

And recognized was the operative word. Unlike all his fellow-Hollywood bosses, everyone seemed to know the name Goldwyn. When in 1935 he announed his intention to produce a film revue to be called *The Goldwyn Follies* hardly a single hair was turned. If anyone—thanks as much as anything to the inspiration of having the Goldwyn Girls—doubted that Sam was the true successor to Florenz Ziegfield, this step would disabuse them of the fact.

It would take three years before the *Follies* happened, but it was worth talking about.

So was the idea of television. Once more, he turned his attention to it. 'I don't think it will work,' he said ultimately. He was thinking in terms of its becoming a big entertainment phenomenon. 'But if it does, we'll buy it.'

Sam didn't like talking about his failures. And when he had them, he tried to pretend they never happened—even though he spent more money trying to recoup his losses than anyone who had ever produced a movie before.

And he worried about them to the practical exclusion of almost everything else. He would lie awake at night, disturbed at the problems of the day. On one occasion he rang an assistant in the middle of the night. 'She has to die,' he said. 'The woman has to die in the end.'

The man hadn't a clue what he was talking about. To Sam that was the supreme insult. His officials were supposed to read his mind as avidly and as easily as they read his inter-office memos. Since he was now talking about the conclusion of a film they were making, there was every reason to be able to do so.

In the 1930s he was once again trying to prove that the real success of his operation would come from making films of the great classics which he now enjoyed reading. His favourite author, he declared, was Emil Zola—which was a tribute to the man who had defended Dreyfus as much as a paean to his literary worth.

He also saw the commercial value of a movie of *Nana*, which he was convinced was the most explosive story of a courtesan ever put on paper. For the role, he looked for a new actress—and found her in the Ukraine. Her name was Anna Sten.

She was a typical Slavic beauty whose only fault Sam could find was her extremely flat chest. But he was so disturbed by this that he personally ordered the costume department to furnish her with a pair of artificial breasts which could be secreted in her brassière. 'But,' he demanded, 'they shouldn't show.' That in itself was a tough order because Goldwyn, particularly now that he was released from the constrictions of the Hays office, liked a degree of cleavage to be in evidence.

In *Nana* that cleavage was vital, so the costume department had their time and talents cut out. However, since the rest of her was as shapely as Zola had imagined, this didn't present so great a problem. Making the film, however, did.

Even if Sam had left the Hays organization, he still had to bow to most of their requirements—unless he wanted to be banned in every State of the Union. That meant an extremely Bowdlerized version. Then there was Miss Sten herself. She hardly spoke English—there was a lesson there which Sam should have learned back in 1927 but still hadn't.

For a year she was under the guidance of English-language coaches—none of whom could come up with any real answer to the problem. There was another difficulty: Anna's husband, Mr Eugene Frenke, a German doctor who was the Svengali to her Trilby. The trouble was that although she couldn't work without her husband around, she didn't do very much apart from look beautiful when he was there either.

Sam got so fed up with his interference that he had the doctor sent off on location—flattered by his appointment as assistant director on another Goldwyn film.

Nothing would go right. One day, in the midst of production, Anna fell asleep on the bed Nana was supposed to use for business purposes. So sound asleep that she didn't notice an electrician fall from the flies above the set. He lay at the foot of her bed, while she slept unconcerned—until, that is, the studio doctor arrived. He didn't see the electrician and assumed the patient was Miss Sten. Without any unnecessary questions, he ripped open the bodice of the still sleeping actress and infused his stethoscope between an artificial breast and a real nipple.

Anna jumped up and down screaming rape.

Sam was feeling much the same way about his film at this stage.

Quite 50 per cent of the movie was shot when he decided to see a rough cut of what had been produced. He was not happy. He fired the director, George Fitzmaurice, and brought in Hollywood's only woman director, Dorothy Arzner, whom he thought had only one feminine characterstic, her name. He hated her, but quite liked what she produced. Every foot of Fitzmaurice's film was destroyed at a cost of nearly half-a-million dollars.

The film was finally completed. Even so, it was a total disaster. But Sam wasn't giving up yet. He needed a new vehicle for Miss Sten, he now decided. And a new director.

In some ways he was still the guy who had helped make *The Squaw Man*. He didn't really understand or at least appreciate the role of the director now any more than he had all those years before.

There was the time one director called at Sam's request at the Goldwyn office, which with its grand piano and family photographs gave a disarming impression of elegance and serenity.

The man had barely had a chance to sit down when Sam barked. 'I won't pay you a cent more,' he said, banging his fist on his shiny walnut desk.

'What?' the man asked.

'I said I won't pay you a cent more.'

'But you don't pay me anything,' he replied.

'I don't mean that,' Sam responded. 'I mean I know what you've been getting and I won't pay you a cent more.'

It was interesting news, but how did it come about? They had no plans to work with each other—as far as he knew. Only then did Goldwyn reveal he wanted the man to make a film.

Other meetings with top directors were somewhat less intimidating.

Rouben Mamoulian was a man he accepted as important. The Armenian-born director was fresh from filming *Queen Christina* with Garbo and John Gilbert. His job was to direct a filmed version of Tolstoy's *Resurrection*, to be called now *We Live Again*. Fredric March would co-star with—Anna Sten.

Mamoulian upset the cast, but Sam was intrigued and delighted by the way he worked. The director had begun in the live theatre and saw no reason why, just because this kind of play was being performed before a camera, he should be less circumspect in demanding full rehearsals.

Such behaviour had already upset Garbo. But just as he insisted that Garbo should rehearse, so he demanded that Sten and March should, too. Goldwyn liked that. It gave him a sense of confidence, a feeling that he was getting his money's-worth.

Mamoulian worked, he told me, as the 'general in the Army', with all the authority that implied. But he recognized that the films on which he worked had to make money. 'If they don't make money, you don't do anything. The important thing is to make money from something that is fine and with quality.'

Later, he declared that he only made films that he himeslf wanted to make—which considering the films he did direct said a very great deal for his own taste.

It wasn't the first meeting between director and producer. He and Goldwyn had known each other socially.

Mamoulian remembered for me:

> One day, he called me up and said he had a film he would like me to do. It was *We Live Again*, which was Tolstoy's *Resurrection*.
>
> I had never worked for Goldwyn before and I didn't want to do so then. I was very tired after having finished *Queen Christina* and I needed a rest.
>
> There were a number of directors those days who had very independent lives from the moguls, who were able to do things their own way. I liked to think I was one of those.

Finally, he said Sam wouldn't like working with him. He would impose conditions that would make it impossible. He would insist that the script should be rewritten.

> I said that I must have a rest for at least a month. So I told him, 'Forget it'.

But after what Sam had gone through with *Nana*, this was as nothing.

The conditions were met 'and throughout the time we were making the film, he was wonderful. There was no interference whatsoever.'

Whether Sam's reaction to the music recorded for the movie could be regarded as interference is a different matter entirely. As always, he sat in on the rushes of the film. None of these impressed him more than the one of the Russian Orthodox Church scene. He was so excited by this he fairly jumped out of his seat. What he liked most about it was the sound. His high-pitched 'bravo' all but echoed through the projection-room. 'Marvellous,' he was heard to exclaim.

Everybody was delighted by his reaction; particularly the projectionist—who had accidentally run the sound-track through the machine backwards. No one dared tell Sam. Mamoulian enjoyed the joke with the others.

When the picture was completed Goldwyn gave a big party in the director's honour. 'He was so glowing in the praise he made of me at that time, his cup was really overflowing. In the end, I had to grab his sleeve and say, "Sam, that's enough. Thank you very much. Wonderful." '

It looked like the start of a beautiful professional friendship. But they didn't work together for another twenty-three years with slightly different results. For the moment, though, *We Live Again* was a happy enough memory. He even produced a modicum of satisfactory work from Anna Sten. Her beauty covered many of her imperfections.

The story was the old one of a Russian prince who falls in love with a servant girl.

Sam was still convinced that Miss Sten was going to be the new Garbo—studios were always looking for a 'new' someone or other. But he knew enough about psychology to realize that all the emphasis of the Goldwyn machine put on her could upset his male lead.

He set about trying to appease his star by telling him: 'Freddie, you have the best role in the picture.' When he saw Miss Sten look up at this, he added hastily, 'And Anna, you have the best role in the picture, too.'

Frank Nugent seemed to think so, too. His *New York Times* review was effusive:

> With the blessings of Mr Goldwyn ringing in her ears, the enchanted and golden-haired Miss Sten triumphs handsomely in the latest screen edition of *Resurrection*. . . . Miss Sten, of course, is not simply a young

> woman of extraordinary charm and unusual talent, but an experienced actress with a distinguished background in the Russian and German cinema and the Soviet State Theatre.

That in itself was unusual—a Hollywood producer bringing over a Russian actress. Even more unusual, one who enjoyed describing herself as 'Soviet'. She was Soviet about everything except her salary, her rights and the kind of clothes and dressing-room she was given.

Sam tried to keep the momentum of that kind of publicity going and ordered his exploitation men accordingly. One of them came up with this gem of understatement: 'The directing skill of Mamoulian, the radiance of Anna Sten and the genius of Goldwyn have united to make the world's greatest entertainment.'

Sam was ecstatic. 'That's the kind of ad I like,' he said. 'Facts. No exaggeration.'

The film excited critics more than audiences and was a financial flop. So was Anna's next role in *The Wedding Night* in which she played the daughter of a Polish farmer in love with a Connecticut author, played by Gary Cooper.

It was around Cooper that another classic Goldwyn story has revolved. The 'yup' and 'nope' actor who had been educated in England at Dunstable Grammar School was now under contract at Paramount. That was difficult for Sam but not a total disaster. All he had to do, he reasoned, was ring up Adolph Zukor.

'Zukor' he screeched in his less than charming voice, 'you and I have a big problem.'

'What problem?' Zukor wanted to know, afraid that another Wall Street Crash was about to descend on Hollywood.

'You've got Gary Cooper,' Goldwyn replied soothingly. 'And I want him.' (Over the years since then the story has been told again and again. One version has Sam ringing Louis B. Mayer and saying it about Clark Gable. The Cooper story seems the most likely.)

He finally arranged for Cooper to be released to his care with Zukor making the profit on the fee Sam paid over and above his Paramount contract figure.

At about this time he also got a nice young English actor whom he thought looked pleasant and sounded well-bred. His name was David Niven.

Niven was to claim that he got into the Goldwyn operation by being with the right people and making sure he was invited to one of the tennis parties given by Frances at her home.

He also said he got himself into Darryl Zanuck's polo team by (uninvited) joining the Fox executive and Sam on the slab at a Turkish bath.

Since the Englishman had got himself so much into the society of Hollywood, the studios thought it worth the publicity to give him the occasional small parts. Irving Thalberg hired him as a mutineer in his *Mutiny on the Bounty*. When Sam read about this in the papers he offered Niven a contract himself.

Sam paid him $100 a week, for which he expected a fair return in fees, lending him to one or other of the big studios.

As Sheridan Morley points out in his Niven biography *The Other Side of the Moon*, Sam wasn't hiring another Ronald Colman. Niven might make an actor. Goldwyn didn't think he was going to be a star.

In fact he didn't use him until he was ready to make a movie called *Splendor*. This starred Joel McCrea, whom Sam had hired at the same time.

Niven would always blame Goldwyn for not furthering his career as diligently as he might.

But finding work for the young Englishman was not Sam's immediate problem. He was much more concerned with getting *Wedding Night* under way—and while work on the film was progressing, Goldwyn wasn't sure that the whole thing was worth the effort. He said he couldn't hear Cooper for mumbles and couldn't understand Miss Sten for accent—or for the deep sighs that appeared to go with the heaving of that reinforced bosom.

He called a meeting with his director, King Vidor, and his various aides and gave them detailed instructions of what he needed. 'And I tell you,' he pronounced, 'if this isn't the greatest love scene ever put on film, the whole Goddamned picture will go right up out of the sewer.'

What really appeared to be locked in the sewer was the career of Miss Sten.

The film was a flop and most people blamed it on her, the laughing stock of the town.

Sam himself was still making his earnest declarations. Not everyone was always sure it was wise. One writer said at this time:

> It is Mr Goldwyn's particular virtue, however, that among the major film producers he stands almost alone in his willingness to charge gallantly into print with vigorous and forthright assaults upon the industry's more obvious weaknesses.

Sam was saying that writers earning up to $5,000 a week were 'literary racketeers' who didn't deserve a tenth of that figure. They were ignorant and insincere.

Many a writer was to say that about Mr Samuel Goldwyn. Allen Churchill, at the time a top magazine editor, was asked by Sam to become his New York story editor. The idea was tempting. He knew Sam's reputation for quality. It offered a new dimension to his own career. And, not least, he thought the money would be good.

Sam invited him up to his Waldorf Astoria suite to discuss the project. 'Would you mind', Goldwyn said at one point, 'if I send down for a drink?'

'No,' said Churchill—who then had the doubtful joy of sitting in his chair while Sam sipped a Martini. He wasn't asked if he would like one. That was when he decided not to take the job. He never saw Goldwyn again. To be fair, that indicates more Sam's view of writers at that particular moment than either his generosity or his good manners.

Writers came in for the butt of Sam's views on contracts—never a sacred document as far as he was concerned, verbal or otherwise. After he hired Adela Rogers St John to work for him, he found he could dispense with her services and get Sidney Howard instead.

'No you can't,' said the writer. 'I have a contract'.

'You couldn't afford to complain,' answered Sam. 'You wouldn't like people to know that Sam Goldwyn fired you, would you?' he asked, convinced the upper hand—as usual—was his.

'I couldn't afford people to think that Sam Goldwyn *didn't* fire me,' she answered—and kept her job.

What he said to Ben Hecht and Charles MacArthur is a matter for intense speculation. But they and Goldwyn weren't always the best of friends, to say the least.

His row with Hecht was the more serious one—and, as usual, was mainly over money. Sam issued an edict banning Hecht from the lot.

The writer's revenge was to say precisely about the moguls—not mentioning Sam by name—what Goldwyn had said about the writers. He, too, used the phrase racketeers.

Finally, Sam, observing his religious belief that certain people were not allowed across his threshold until he needed them, decided that he did want Hecht and his partner to work on a picture.

The men held out—until they were able to get a clause inserted in their contract saying that their boss was not allowed to speak to them.

It seemed all right to Goldwyn. He had no desire to speak to these two 'momzers' any way. But, of course, he did have to. He searched for days for ways of pocketing both his pride and the legal niceties of their contract. Finally, he called MacArthur. 'My err-err wife err-err would like to know how to contact your err-err wife. . . .'

MacArthur laughed, gave him Helen Hayes's phone number and their fight was part of Hollywood history. But for ever afterwards Sam called them both his 'racketeers'.

Sam actually liked both men, but the meal he made out of his words on their account deserves to be included in the Guinness Book of Record Menus. The episode earned him the reputation of Sam—the -sign-'em-at-any-price—Goldwyn.

It appeared that Sam was making Hecht the highest paid writer in Hollywood in order for him to be one of his boys. He paid him $260,000.

Sam had a lot of work for him. But he would be allowed to work on his Broadway plays, too.

On one occasion Sam called Hecht out of a dinner-party. He knocked on the front door and was shown in. He didn't know the host of the evening at all. But he still wanted to talk to Hecht, who was dragged somewhat unwillingly from the conviviality of the dinner-table.

He had a script under his arm. 'I'd like you to help me,' he said. 'There are big problems with this and only you can help me.' He repeated that plaintive phrase again and again.

After an hour Hecht said there was nothing he could do. There was just nothing worth saving. 'Thank you so much Ben', Sam responded, 'for helping me.'

They played cards together. Once Charles MacArthur actually had the temerity to accuse Sam of cheating—a not unusual occurrence. 'What's that between us?' Sam asked. Harpo Marx suggested that Goldwyn was the only man who could throw a seven with one dice.

Still Sam liked gambling indoors. He didn't trust horse-racing. He once excused a loss on the track by saying that he had the winner—'till the caddy fell off'.

It was just Sam's way and, if you worked with Sam, the way you did things *had* to be his way, in or out of the studios. If he said someone was a racketeer, you had to believe it.

There were, of course, others who were saying words to that effect about Sam himself—like the writers Mort Eisman and Louis Shayan who complained about the film *Roman Scandals* in which Eddie Cantor was knocked unconscious in an American town called Rome and imagined himself back in the city of ancient history. The writers charged that the film was 'deliberate piracy and an infringement', which was not something that came as much of a surprise to anyone who knew anything about Hollywood. Such things were happening all the time.

Sam may well have described as 'piracy' the way people played cards with him. He played bridge, not because he was very good at it or because he enjoyed it. Much more, because it was the sort of thing expected of a man in his station.

He didn't win very often and a Goldwyn defeated at the bridge table was a sight to behold—if you *could* bear to behold it.

There was a celebrated dust-up on each such occasion with his partner, the beautiful actress Constance Bennett.

Suddenly, there was the sound of an earthquake errupting in the midst of the normally sedate Goldwyn card-room. Constance Bennett was shaking as though that quake had settled on her right foot—which it almost had. Sam was shouting—and shouting so loudly that one could think that his ancestry and that of his parents had been put into question.

When the dust had settled, Miss Bennett asked him what the fuss was about. 'You overbid your hand,' he said.

He didn't have anything to offer himself. 'How did I know?' she asked incredulously. 'Didn't you hear me keeping still?' Sam rejoined, now reason itself.

In July 1935 another kind of 'piracy' was being alleged about Sam's business activities. He bought out the half interest in United Artists' properties previously owned by Joseph Schenck and Darryl F.Zanuck. That made him sole owner of United Artists' stages, props and wardrobes. But Mary Pickford and Douglas Fairbanks Senior retained the title to the land on which the studio stood. That didn't commend Goldwyn to his former partners at all. (In fact, for a long time it seemed that Sam's only friend in the industry was Irving Thalberg, which is strange considering his relationship with the Hollywood boy wonder's father-in-law Louis B.Mayer.)

Meanwhile, there were other properties Sam had in mind. He bought a piece of land on a choice site in Beverly Hills and excitedly came home to Frances with the news. It was going to be perfect for a long white house, the kind he had always wanted. He knews Frances would love it just as much.

She was as excited about the idea as he was. They got into their car and drove in the direction of the Beverly Hills Hotel. An hour later, they were still driving round and round—and gave up. Sam couldn't remember where the place was.

Fortunately for him, Frances was not the type to take such matters as they stood. She studied the maps, pondered the area in which he said the site was located and eventually found it—on what was to become Laurel Lane.

From that moment on it was her baby. Sam, in fact, didn't visit Laurel Lane until there was a house actually built, painted and furnished there.

When that day finally came Frances knew precisely how the former director of *Nana* had felt. If her husband could totally destroy $411,000-worth of movie what would he do to a mere house?

He walked, he looked, he studied, he beamed. She had passed the test. Not seeing the house in the 'rushes' had obviously been a very good ideas—and he kissed his 'director' to prove it.

The only thing he complained about—and Frances was to confess that it 'riled' her—was there was no soap in the dish in his private bathroom. The rest of the house was perfect.

Frances furnished it expensively, but simply. There was none of the gaudiness associated with *nouveau riche* Hollywood. Everything blended beautifully, the furniture with the carpets and drapes. The pictures by Picasso and other masters reflected Frances's tastes in that she knew what to buy, but Sam appreciated them as much as she did.

He claimed to like the simple life. In those early years in the house in the midst of summer he would even sleep out of doors because he liked to enjoy the magnificent grounds to the full. He had a sunken tennis-court, a swimming-pool, all the other requirements of Beverly Hills good living.

But that didn't stop him demanding nothing more than a glass of hot milk when he awoke at seven o'clock. He ate in moderation and watched his diet—with the exception of a daily ice cream soda which was his principal weakness. (He liked the drink so much that on more than one occasion he took a party to a soda fountain to celebrate a film's premiere.)

None of this should give the impression that the usually conceived definitions of society living escaped him.

The Goldwyn house was the scene of some of the finest dinner-parties ever given in the film capital. State governors, generals, members of President Roosevelt's Cabinet and a gross of stars, to say nothing of writers, directors and producers, were guests there, all welcomed with impeccable charm by Frances and her husband—providing they didn't come late. After dinner, there was always the latest Goldwyn film—and sometimes one from the opposition—with which to entertain his guests, seated on the most comfortable motion-picture theatre seats in the world—in Sam's superbly furnished living-room.

That doyenne of film 'ladies' Irene Dunne told me: 'An invitation to the Goldwyn home was like dining at Buckingham Palace. Frances Goldwyn in particular was charming, the service was impeccable. There were always the most interesting people there.'

Sometimes, the really most interesting people were the unexpected ones. Like the man who arrived on the gleaming doorstep one day, so beautifully, smartly dressed that Sam's English butler immediately assumed him to be a senior executive at United Artists.

Frances came into the living-room to welcome the guest. It seemed the right thing to do, after all, it was not just polite, it was politic. She would, probably, have to spend time talking to the man at the studio.

Then he decided to disillusion her no longer—even when she told him that her husband was still in bed upstairs. No, he said. He wasn't from United Artists at all, but from Paramount. And there was a little matter of $5 million to settle. That was the amount which Adolph Zukor was suing Sam for—because he took away Gary Cooper.

Sam's problem had indeed become Zukor's too—only Zukor was insisting Goldwyn paid for it.

Zukor charged him with 'a breach of morals and ethics'—which didn't suprise anyone. It was almost surprising he didn't include the word 'momzer' in the final legal document.

Cooper's lawyers merely said that that sort of behaviour on Zukor's part was one of the reasons Gary had decided to leave Paramount in the first place.

There was also an element of sentiment there—because Sam had taken Cooper out of the crowd and made him second lead in *The Winning of Barbara Worth*.

Zukor charged that Cooper had been a mere inexperienced actor when he was taken on by Paramount and the company had spent a great deal of money making him a top star.

Before long, as always happened in these cases, the matter was sorted out and Goldwyn and Zukor just went on hating each other for no apparent additional reason.

For a time it seemed that that would also be the relationship between Goldwyn and Eddie Cantor, who the mogul had decided was getting a bit too big for his *Kid Boots*—which just happened to be the title of his first (silent) film.

Ziegfeld could have told him of the demands Cantor made for what he regarded as his super-star status. Now he was being equally difficult to Goldwyn, demanding not just more money but the fripperies of that status. He refused for one thing to use Al Jolson's old dressing-room. Jolson's career appeared to be over and he didn't want this failure to rub off on him. (He didn't know that Jolson would before long have the most spectacular come-back in show-biz history.)

Matters came to a head when he pleaded with Sam to buy *Three Men On A Horse*, a gangster story about a nervous kid from Brooklyn who had an uncanny way of choosing winners. Ultimately, the story was bought by Warner Bros. Eddie pleaded with Sam to release him so that he could make it at the Warners' Burbank studios. Sam still said No—but plied him with alternative stories, all of which the star rejected.

Cantor himself now said that he was going to court. There had been too long a period between films, which cost him money—the cash he could have earned on other ventures had he only been free to take them. Such were the hazards of running a motion-picture company.

At one stage Cantor walked out of the Goldwyn lot—where he kept an office of his own—and said he was 'through'.

Rather than go to law, Goldwyn released him from the contract—it wasn't a bad move on his part after all, as Cantor's star was waning almost as badly as Jolson's, although he was earning about $250,000—in salary and profits—on each film.

There was, however, a cash settlement—with Cantor paying Goldwyn for the release, based on the time and effort Sam had expended in looking for alternative projects.

It wasn't the only connection with Cantor that resulted in legal action of one kind or another. That same year James J.Donnelly claimed $102,000 which he said was owing to him for his song *When My Ship Comes In*, which was used in the Cantor film *Kid Millions*.

There were rows, too, over the employment of the writer William Anthony McGuire, who had worked on the Fred and Adele Astaire Broadway shows and for Ziegfeld. Sam and another producer were in competition for his services.

It was suggested that the battle go to arbitration. Sam agreed. 'I'm a fair man,' he said 'I'll submit anything to arbitration. But remember, whatever happens, McGuire goes to work for me.'

Sam, meanwhile, was still throwing a few pies in the sky—which considering he practically believed he owned the sky over his studios was perhaps not so surprising.

When he embarked on yet another world tour in March 1935, he said he was goint to recruit the most beautiful girl he found in each of the countries he was visiting—including the Soviet Union—and give her a Hollywood contract. Now Sam knew how foolhardy that was, what punishing experiences he had had in the early talkie years bringing back girls whose voice-boxes didn't match their bosoms, but still he wasn't going to be put off.

In the end, all with which he returned—apart, that is, from Frances and Sam Junior—was a case of acute intestinal toxaemia. He was taken to Doctors Hospital, New York, the smartest medical institution in the city.

His recovery might have been quicker had he not chosen to play Sam Goldwyn too early on.

Surgery was necessary, but a week after his operation he was feeling fine. So well, that the doctors allowed Irving Berlin and broadcasting executive Bill Paley to come and visit him. They stayed, they talked—and they laughed. So much that Sam's stitches burst. Frances was summoned to the hospital—and told that her husband had only a couple of hours to live.

It wasn't the only problem she faced. On the one hand, her husband appeared to be dying. On the other, it seemed as though his business was at precisely the same critical state, hovering between this world and the next.

She was not the only one of Sam's confidants in the white walled corridors of what could have been a set in any one of a dozen Goldwyn films. Waiting for her when she emerged, ashen, from the doctor's office was James A. Mulvey, whose official position was President of Samuel Goldwyn Productions Inc.

He had a worried look on his face, not entirely caused by the grave condition of his friend.

The matter worrying Mulvey was *Dead End*, which may have sounded prophetic, but which was, at that moment, the title of the latest project on the Goldwyn agenda. Sam had already paid $25,000 as a down payment for the rights to this story, but $140,000 was still outstanding and, unless it was paid immediately, the company would not only lose the original sum but would forfeit its rights to the story, too.

Why bother her—and now?

His answer said a great deal for Frances's role in the business. He had difficulty in stammering out the details, but eventually he made it: 'If Mr Goldwyn doesn't . . . well . . . it's up to you, Frances.'

Frances agreed. It *was* up to her. She said, she told *Woman's Home Companion*, 'Pay the money, Mulvey. Sam's going to get well. He's going to make that picture. And it'll be good. I've got that faith in God and Sam Goldwyn.' Sam got well.

They were saying a lot of that sort of thing in 1937, Sam's silver jubilee as a producer. Not everyone, though, was totally uncritical.

'I for one will be damned if I feel patriotic about Sam Goldwyn's silver jubilee,' declared Edmund Wilson. 'It is plain that today's producers, including the great Goldwyn and the late Irving Thalberg, are the same megalomaniac cloak-and-suit dealers their predecessors were. . . .'

A cloak-and-suit dealer might not have been able to make *Dead End*, although Sam didn't make it his number-one priority.

Coming back to Beverly Hills he took it upon himself to exercise more. He would do more walking. If he had the time he now walked home from the studios on North Formosa Avenue, but that was quite a distance away. So he compromised. He allowed his chauffeur to drive him to within what he considered a reasonable walking distance and to then drive the rest of the way without him.

He liked the feel of the pavements beneath his feet—it was before Hollywood people seemed to be born without any feet at all and with a silverplated steering-wheel clenched in their baby fists—and to have a gentle breeze blowing under the brim of his grey Homburg was his idea of a movie boss's paradise.

He liked to take at least an hour off each day for those walks. But the exercise was not popular with the secretaries and executives who were sometimes invited to come along with him. They had to run to keep up with their master.

He could hum to himself as he reflected on the goodness of the world around him. One evening, he did more than that. He marvelled at the abundance of goodness available to him and his fellow-men in the foodshops of Hollywood and Beverly Hills. With his car purring its way towards the blue horizon, he stopped at a vegetable pushcart and took himself an apple. It tasted as good as the shiny red skin promised it would be.

'That'll be five cents,' said the owner.

Five cents? Sam hadn't actually bought anything over the counter of a shop—let alone a pushcart—for at least a decade. What was more, he didn't have any money in his pockets. How could he? It would upset the line of those perfectly creased trousers.

Telling the shop-owner he was Sam Goldwyn didn't do much good, when at the same time he was unable to find the price of an apple. It took a hasty call to Laurel Lane and an equally hasty return trip by the chauffeur to extricate Mr Goldwyn from a situation more serious than any since he had first 'shlepped' his suitcase of glove samples.

He didn't always use a chauffeur, however. Sometimes, Frances drove for him. He never learned to drive himself. It was an unnecessary hassle, although he didn't always admit the fact. Once he berated an underling who tried to prove he knew more about the film business than he did: 'Look,' he said, 'you drive a Ford and I drive a Rolls-Royce—and you argue with me?'

His partners at United Artists argued with him a lot, even though they had no say in the films he made. Samuel Goldwyn Productions were now the mainstay of the outfit, and besides, he did own much of the real estate, a fact that continued to make him less than the best friend of Mary Pickford. They hated each other, barely gave a nodding time of day when they met—which both contrived to do as little as possible.

The relationship with the other directors—Alexander Korda was now part of the outfit, too—was no better. In fact, each one hated the other so much that they refused to meet face to face, and when meetings were held they sent their lawyers to represent them. This worried Sam less than his colleagues. At least, he was putting out his own films, albeit under United Artists' releasing arrangements.

Besides, on the whole, he was making highly prestigious pictures that made a great deal of money. Handing Samuel Goldwyn the idea for a film was like presenting a Savile Row tailor with a bolt of cloth. He looked at the material, felt it with fingers that had experienced the finest yarns ever made, imagined the kind of lapels, the button-holes, the buttons that would adorn it, and decided if it could be made up to standards he had himself set. Once having gone past that part of the operation, things were able to move more smoothly.

His 1936 movie *Dodsworth* fitted perfectly, a bespoke movie if ever there had been one. It photographed beautifully, its sound quality was just about the best yet heard from an American studio and Walter Huston was exactly right in the title part of the businessman who on holiday in Europe changes his whole life-style. The story by Sinclair Lewis was superbly adapted for the screen by Sidney Howard, and directed by William Wyler, both of whom received Academy Award nominations.

There were, naturally, the usual disputes with others working on the film. One man ventured that parts of the story were 'too caustic'. 'To hell with the cost,' said Sam, 'we're going ahead.'

The cost to Hollywood, however, seemed excessive when considering what may be called the sub-plot concerning Miss Mary Astor, Walter Huston's co-star.

It just so happened that while the seemingly prim and very proper Miss Astor was working at Formosa Avenue, a totally different lady of the same name and identical appearance was appearing in a very different show—at the Los Angeles Superior Court. Of course, she wasn't a different lady at all, but her movie audiences would find it very difficult indeed to recognize their heroine from the tales being told to the judge.

A short while before, Mary had agreed to a divorce from her husband, Dr Franklyn Thorpe. Now, though, she had changed her mind. She didn't want to stay married to him, but she wanted the marriage annulled—so that she could be granted custody of her daughter Marilyn. She also had it in mind to claim a great deal of the doctor's fortune.

Now, Hollywood divorces always made news and this one would have had the usual treatment, since Miss Astor was a very big star. Sam, like any other mogul, wouldn't have liked it one bit. He still believed in the necessity of showing his stars to be nice, clean individuals who never got involved in scandals—and, in the 1930s, divorces were always scandalous.

That would have been the case had this been any ordinary domestic court case. However, it wasn't.

Miss Astor, who, it should be repeated, few would have thought to be particularly sexy (although pretty enough to co-star with John Barrymore in *Don Juan*, the first movie with synchronized music and sound effects) turned out to have a pedigree that made her Hollywood's Number One Jezebel.

Many people knew of her affair with George F. Kaufman, the writer, and this was the original cause of Dr Thorpe's divorce action—even though it was now all over and Kaufman had gone back to his wife.

The real problem was that Miss Astor had many of the characteristics of a nymphomaniac and had a diary to prove it. In this, she not only referred to her love-making with Kaufman—allegedly twenty times in one night—but detailed all her affairs. She listed, it seemed, every male in the film community—detailing the bodily attributes and sexual capabilities of each and every one of them (including the size of the vital parts of one man with whom she was travelling in a car).

She also made another list—of her Top Ten lovers (again, all Hollywood names), and wrote of the 'thrilling ecstasy' of love-making with one of them.

Now, in opposing his wife's action, Dr Thorpe was producing the diaries in court—and the Press was prepared for a feast, the like of which they had not enjoyed since Fatty Arbuckle's party.

The only people, it appeared, who did not like the fun the diaries were provoking—apart from Miss Astor herself, that is—were the studio heads. For once, and perhaps for the only time on record, the hard-headed bosses were as one. The diaries had to be suppressed. And Sam was saying Include Me In with the support of all his colleagues.

Had it just been Sam's problem—and perhaps Jack Warner's, too, for he had loaned Astor to Goldwyn—Mayer, Zukor, Cohn and the others would have had as much excitement as finding out that Mr Hays ran a brothel from his 'decency' office. But there was a lot more to it than that. Every one of their business operations was threatened by the publication of those books—because the 'Top Ten' were apparently scattered among every studio in Hollywood.

For instance, discovering that Clark Gable was great at a kind of sexual activity nice people were not supposed to know about could kill his appeal at the box-office—especially if he were not as well endowed as women might like to think. Was she saying anything about him? Mayer shuddered to think.

And then could she have been saying something unpleasant about Robert Taylor? (Mr Taylor, it would turn out after his death, had a totally different kind of 'problem'. He was a homosexual, but no one knew that at the time.)

As one voice the moguls decided to ask the court not to allow the diaries to be produced and to demand that Miss Astor withdraw her suit—to ensure that there would be no reason for the books to be brought in.

To complicate matters, newspapers had already started speculating about her list. They all had George Kaufman in front. Mary said it was a load of twaddle and they shouldn't worry. The film men didn't believe her and did worry.

The Judge finally said that the diaries were not admissable—some pages had been torn out and so they could not be produced. It was not the end of the matter, however.

A warrant was issued for Kaufman to come to court to give evidence—and this, the moguls agreed, would be as damaging as having the diaries published, mutilated or not.

Kaufman disappeared, smuggled by MGM aboard Irving Thalberg's yacht. Meanwhile, the Goldwyn studios were involved in the kind of invasion that was about to be organized by other members of the Press at Buckingham Palace and King Edward VIII's country home Fort Belvedere.

Everything that Mrs Wallis Simpson was shortly to be subjected to, Mary Astor was having now—while she took refuge in the studio dressing-room which had been hastily converted by Sam's carpenters and designers into an apartment.

In the end Sam and Mary and everyone else in the Hollywood community—apart from the newspapers and their readers—drew breath and welcomed the end of the case. No scandalous incidents were revealed and the judge divided the custody of the child among both parents.

It seemed to put years on Sam, but then that was how he liked things. Miss Astor was not the only problem in his life.

David Niven had a supporting role in *Dodsworth*, the best he had had to date. Sam didn't object to what he did in the film; in fact, he was pleasantly surprised. What he did object to was that Niven was in the midst of a steamy affair with Merle Oberon. It was practically a case of pistols at dawn. Sam ordered the romance to cease—at once. He couldn't afford his principal leading lady to be sullied in this way.

It was all part of Sam's concern for the image of his stars. As far as Oberon was concerned, it was an image he was busily remaking.

In an article in *Esquire* Gilbert Soldes told about the time a pile of photographs of the star were brought into Sam's office at North Formosa Avenue. Goldwyn waved them aside. He said he was fed up with 'all that slant-eyed stuff'. As Soldes said, 'Miss Oberon had made her name as an oriental. . . . Actually, he gave her a new movie life.'

Sam was in the business of giving people new lives. Not least of all the writers whom he continued to cosset.

He had a love-hate relationship with Lillian Hellman, whom he took on as a staff writer, and then proceeded to create into a lifelong adversary. He lunched with her regularly and admired the way this far from beautiful woman was able to conjure words in conversation quite as well as she could on paper.

When her play *The Children's Hour* opened on Broadway to smash notices, he seemed as pleased about it as she was. He told his executives he was going to buy the rights.

'You can't do that,' one of them told him. 'Well never get it through. It's about Lesbians.'

'That's all right,' said Sam, 'We'll make them Americans.'

At least, that is the legend. Another story has it that he said it in relation to the book *The Well of Loneliness*, which did not become a Goldwyn film. Nor did *The Captive*, yet another story to which the rejoinder has been attributed. That was the trouble with Goldwynisms. Too many people were taking the credit for having heard them the first time. Others are more definitely attributable.

Sam took the risk with *The Children's Hour*—and, as usual, began to wish that he had not. His actresses—Miriam Hopkins and Merle Oberon—were not getting on. In desperation, he cornered his male lead Joel McCrea.

'Can't you straighten the girls out?' he asked. 'I'm having more trouble with those people than Mussolini with Utopia.'

Since it was the time of Italy's invasion of Ethiopia that story can be more firmly fixed to that film and Joel McCrea has always insisted it happened.

Again, the Hays Office, that organization for which Sam had nothing but contempt, reared its far from pretty head and indicated that if he did dare attempt to make a film about Lesbianism, they would have him blacklisted throughout the United States. The result was that the picture was cleaned up—with considerable help from the director, William Wyler—and now became the story of a schoolgirl spreading rumours of an illicit heterosexual love affair involving one of her teachers.

The picture was called *These Three*.

Sam remembered that title. Some other names in the industry came harder to him. He was always getting people's names wrong. Shirley Temple was to be Anne Shirley for ever after. He called Henry King, King Vidor. And then there was Anatole France. 'How are the affairs of Anatole?' he asked after a trip to Paris. He knew he made those mistakes, which was probably why he respected the words of professional writers who didn't make them.

Joel McCrea, who was to star in *Dead End*, was a member of the Goldwyn stable for years, but eventually decided to go freelance. Sam gave a farewell lunch in his honour, and made a speech paying great tribute to his friend 'Joe McCrail.'

In a stage whisper, an executive corrected him. 'Sam,' he said, 'it's McCrea. . . .'

Goldwyn was not impressed. 'Listen,' he said, speaking even louder than his employee, 'for seven years, I've been paying this man $5,000 a week. And you're trying to tell me I don't know his name?'

There were others who just couldn't register their names with Sam—like the writer Everett Freeman. Every time Sam met him, he'd say, 'Hey . . .

Whatshisname.' On one occasion, he introduced him to a visitor to the lot. 'I'd like you to meet Everett Whatshisname,' he said.

Which Groucho Marx might have thought preferable to the way *he* was treated by Goldwyn. Every time they met, Sam would say, 'And how's your brother, Harpo?'

Eventually, Groucho said, 'You always ask me about Harpo. Why don't you one day ask me how I am?'

'Next time I will,' said Sam. 'But for the moment, how's your brother, Harpo?'

For the story rights of *These Three* alone Sam paid $160,000—which was $5,000 less than he had given for *Dead End*. In that film, incidentally, third billing went to an actor called Humphrey Bogart. The stars were Joel McCrea again and Sylvia Sidney and a group of youngsters who became the Dead End Kids (a few years later they had a life of their own as the Bowery Boys).

Sam's relationship with Lillian Hellman was probably the most difficult part of making that picture. They were constantly squabbling—and if Sam hadn't had that innate respect for her, she would have been out of the Formosa Avenue studio long before.

It was Frances who realized the writer and her husband had to make peace. She invited Hellman for tea, so that they could have a nice woman-to-woman conversation. Unfortunately, Sam walked in—and then joined in. Before long, they were arguing. Eventually, Frances called to her husband: 'Sam, would you go upstairs?'

He went and the argument was over for a time and Lillian was prepared to write *Dead End* for her hostess's husband.

The story was about a group of slum kids living almost cheek-by-jowel with the people in New York's most fashionable area, a situation that non-New Yorkers always find difficult to understand.

Sam understood it perfectly. He also understood it was a good film. That was not a commodity too much in evidence. And again, he realized that spending money wasn't the panacea to create more like it.

He bought the rights to Edna Ferber's (she wrote *Show Boat*) novel *Come and Get It*, and then disliked the finished film so much the he ordered it to be remade—after spending $800,000 on the first completed picture.

The new version was only made after a heated row with William Wyler—which, in turn, followed a row with Howard Hawks.

Hawks had made the film in the first place. The first half seemed to go splendidly, but then on, Hawks himself was dissatisfied and rewrote the script without consulting anyone, least of all Sam, who was furious when he found out. He sent for Hawks and told him: 'You're paid to direct, not write.' Since the film was now finished, and Hawks's commitment over, there was nothing more he could do, but that was never enough for Sam Goldwyn. He fired him just the same.

He then summoned Wyler and asked him to reshoot the second half. Wyler refused. He said he couldn't rework another man's picture. Since one didn't refuse a request from Samuel Goldwyn, that was not an easy thing to do—especially when Sam was in bed when in the early hours of the morning the request turned into a demand.

The shouting from Sam's bedroom the night that Wyler answered the call was like the wrath of some god descending from the Hollywood Hills—smashing two cans of film on the way.

Frances was so disturbed that she rushed into the room and started hitting her husband on the legs with a fly swatter. In the end, for the sake of a quiet life and a not inconsiderable fee, Wyler agreed to bury his integrity and reshoot the second half of the picture, which was about a wood merchant living in Wisconsin in the nineteenth century.

Sam approved what Wyler did with the picture—at a cost of a further $900,000—and ordered that his name appear on the credits as the sole director. Wyler refused and eventually both his and Hawks's names were credited with directing the movie. It didn't stop the picture being one of the worst flops in Sam's entire career.

Goldwyn was never able to understand Wyler's objections or the constant rows that their relationship produced—even though the director was under contract and there was no legal way he could object to any work Sam gave him. Once more a director had threatened to bite the hand that laid the golden egg.

Some of Sam's eggs were more golden than others. *The Goldwyn Follies*, which finally went before the cameras in 1937, was better for its music than for its girls—possibly because Frances, now firmly established as an unofficial senior executive of Goldwyn Productions, insisted on vetting each young lady presented for Sam's attention.

She may have been merely trying to help, or in a more serious way aiming to steer Sam from the paths of temptation. The days of the casting couch were past, but he still enjoyed looking at beautiful women and she was not prepared for a reprise of some of the escapades rumour had it preceded the selection of girls who went into the *Ziegfeld Follies*. (She may have heard that Sam had just had a somewhat unproductive afternoon chasing the beautiful actress Madeleine Carroll around his desk.)

Since beauty had the reputation of being only skin-deep, the producer of those shows claimed a need to dig at least that far. The girls needed the work and allowed him to make the examinations. Frances was not going to give Sam that headache.

That did not mean he was easy in his selections. Girls came for his approval fully-dressed, made up and with their hair beautifully done. He looked them over—and then demanded they all let their hair down. That done, he made his choice of the Goldwyn Girls.

There was less trouble in the score written for *The Goldwyn Follies*. Since Sam always wanted the best, there was no reason why he shouldn't have the best music—which was why he chose George Gershwin.

It turned out to be the most memorable score Gershwin ever wrote. Not the best, but the most memorable, for it was also Gershwin's last. *Love Walked In*, the best song in the film, was the last thing the composer ever wrote.

It was while working on the film that Gershwin complained of incessant headaches, found he was unable to co-ordinate his fingers with the piano keys and complained of a constant smell of burnt rubber—all finally, but much too late, diagnosed as symptoms of a brain tumour. He died on the operating table soon after reaching hospital.

Sam was deeply shocked. Gershwin was still in his thirties and everyone was speculating just how much he could have produced in a normal life span. The industry mourned a man they couldn't afford to lose. Good music wasn't the only thing not sufficiently available.

'The trouble with this business,' said Sam, 'is the dearth of bad pictures.'

13
Wuthering Heights

As one would have gathered by now, it wasn't the easiest thing satisfying Sam Goldwyn—or understanding whether or not he really *was* satisfied. He once told an executive: 'If I don't say a thing's bad, it's good.' Sometimes, it would have been nicer to get some outright praise, but that wasn't his way.

Alva Johnston in that *Saturday Evening Post* piece suggested that Sam feared contentment. That must surely be an over-simplification. Certainly, he was wary of resting on his laurels, but the smile on Goldwyn's face when he saw something had paid off, like a successful film première, was a joy to behold.

In his private life he revelled in his contentment. Frances continued to dote and he continued to sit back and admire her—sometimes in the way other men admired fine paintings or beautiful sculpture. Their son Sammy was introduced to the film business from the moment he could talk.

He told me of the times his father took him on to the set watching Goldwyn films being shot. He remembered the scripts piling up at home and Sam sitting in his chair reading them, sometimes digesting Frances's first summary of the plots and her assessment of them.

The senior Goldwyn didn't suffer fools gladly, Sam Junior told me in our magazine interview. That was also why he didn't like yes-men.

He even took on one particular executive simply because he *wasn't* likely to say yes. In a moment of sheer bloody mindedness he gave the man a very exciting contract. Then he warned he was going to find a way to cancel the agreement—because the executive did, after all, agree with him.

Contracts were Sam's Ten Commandments—except that every now and again he searched for a Revised Version. They worried him. When he wanted a man badly enough, he treated him like a king, provided superb lunches with the finest wines. Finally, for dessert, he offered a contract and a fountain pen.

One man said: 'I'd like my lawyer to see it first.'

'I'll be your lawyer,' said Sam, almost guiding the man's hand on the dotted line. Later, he said, he felt mesmerized by this Goldwyn touch. Of course, he signed.

Sam knew his power. He also knew his faults. Once, in another argument with a producer he told him: 'You know your trouble, don't you? You're a bigger egoist than I am.'

Not that he always thought he was right. There are witnesses to a story conference at which he said, 'I had a monumental idea last night. But I didn't like it.'

As Sam Junior said, his father's trouble was that his brain worked faster than his lips. In Hollywood that was like undressing in front of a television camera.

Sam hoped for an Oscar for *Dead End*. It didn't come, but by then he was so engrossed in his next picture that it didn't matter—and Frances was always around to help him put things into perspective.

People still talked about the Goldwyns almost as though their romance was new and they were part of a fairy story. Seeing them together at that time was quite memorable.

But, back in the world of reality, Sam's main obligation now was to make sure that his films were memorable too.

And that also went for the people working for him. There was a lot of talk early in 1937 of banning foreign actors from working in America—a restrictive measure on behalf of the American acting community to be sure, but something that didn't exactly help Sam's campaign for bringing European Jews to work in the States. The answer was that they were merely trying to restrict 'ham' actors from working on their side of the Atlantic, which perhaps was not a good term when referring to Jews.

'It's ridiculous,' proclaimed Sam in one of those stentorian statements he expected people to take not only seriously but as a declaration of faith.

'We cannot place tariffs on talent as we would on ploughshares'. (Nice one that; a Biblical touch, yet.)

'It is exactly as if we would ban H. G. Wells and Noel Coward because they are foreign authors.'

The Bill currently before Congress 'would add a menace to American films and jeopardize one of the greatest industries of the nation . . . . If they are indeed hams, they must be very enjoyable hams as the public seems to enjoy them.'

Naturally, they were not hams that Sam was sending back to Warsaw, but he was still sending money to a city now reeling under an anti-Jewish boycott declared by the country's Government, two-and-a-half years before Hitler's invasion.

His brother Benjamin had by then joined him in America, changing his name to Bernard Fish (he died in 1946, a follower of Christian Science, which might be considered an even greater change from the life in Warsaw than Sam's).

Four or five relatives of various closeness were being given monthly allowances of up to $100; some really distant cousins automatically received Chanucah gifts from him—one of his only demonstrations of religious observance. His sister Nettie used to benefit from his advice as well as from his bank balance. When she wrote to inform him of her n'er-do'well husband, he replied: 'Please stop crying. I didn't marry your husband, you did.'

Relationships closer at hand were sometimes even tougher. Eventually, Sam's daughter Ruth discovered her link with the movie producer. When she married and had a child, she wrote to Sam to tell him about it. He scribbled a note to his secretary at the top of this: 'Ignore this letter.'

He felt threatened by it—as he did by many of the people who worked for him. He once asked an employee: 'I'd like your word of honour that you'll never work for anyone else.' The man said he couldn't possibly do any such thing.

'Right,' said Sam. 'If you can't give me your word of honour, will you give me a promise?'

What he still wasn't going to allow was for people to ignore him. Having patently missed the first voyage of the boat that floated talking pictures, he wasn't going to be caught in any backward stance as far as colour movies were concerned. He said that he hoped all his 1937–38 production would be in colour. Of course, it wasn't, but the papers were still noting practically everything he said.

So, indeed, were most people—like film producer Arthur Hornblow, who told him of the new baby born to his wife and who like himself and his father before him would be named Arthur. Sam didn't like that and lost no time in telling Hornblow of his misgivings. 'Don't,' he implored and, as though he had as much right to dictate such things as the script for a film, added 'every Tom, Dick and Harry is called Arthur.' You couldn't easily argue with that.

It was about this time that Sir Cedric Hardwicke, the expatriate British actor—who doubtless would not have been excluded by the Congressional Bill—wrote to *The New York Times* complaining about the Hollywood preview system—when studios decided whether their pictures had been successes or failures by the reaction of out-of-town audiences. He hated them. Without them, Sam would have been deprived of one of his greatest ways of intimidating underlings. After one preview, he was heard to demand of an executive, 'And how did you love my picture?'

For a time in 1937 it seemed that Sam was going to have a special love for all United Artists' pictures. Suddenly, in May of that year, it was announced that he and Alexander Korda, head of London Films and as such Britain's only real film mogul, were taking control of UA.

They had a deal all bottled up to wrest the business entirely from Mary Pickford, Douglas Fairbanks and Charlie Chaplin. They were granted jointly an option to buy up all the shares owned by the three super-stars for what was estimated as $10 million.

(Two other independent producers, Selznick International and Walter Wanger Productions, would not be affected by the sale.)

It would make Sam the undisputed boss of the UA operation—the head of a major studio once again and no longer the independent he spent so much time saying he enjoyed being (which he undoubtedly did, although financing all his own output was a headache even to him). The idea occurred to him, he said, because of the comparative lack of activity of his partners as producers.

Matters were confirmed when Sam's banker friend Dr Giannini, who was now President of UA, confirmed the sale—although the figure involved had now been reduced to a mere $5,930,000. Meanwhile, Mr E. H. Lever—the head of the Prudential Assurance Company of London who were the financial backers of Korda's British operations—arrived in California to provide the guarantees of security to the deal.

More and more statements appeared in the Press, confirming the deal, speaking of ten-year contracts with outside organizations for distributing their films and of arrangements for utilizing the magnificent United Artists studios to the full.

Then, quite suddenly, it was all off. Completely.

And it was Korda and Goldwyn who ended the courtship. All the financial arrangements had been sorted out, it seemed to everyone's satisfaction.

Then, Sam said, Pickford and Fairbanks started making demands for a say in what was being produced by the studios. And that, neither Goldwyn nor Korda was prepared to accept. As Sam said, they were having to take all the risks while the other two wanted to enjoy the fruits of their speculation and work.

It took more than seven months, to December 1937, for the dream—for that indeed was what it now was—to come to an abrupt, final end.

The statement they issued declared: 'Owing to insurmountable legal complications, we have decided not to exercise our option for purchase of three units of United Artists Corporation stock held by Mary Pickford, Douglas Fairbanks and Charles Chaplin and, accordingly, are returning the option today.'

It all seemed straightforward and businesslike, but the statement hid the bitterness. If the five directors had found it difficult to talk to each other before, now it would be impossible. Between Sam and Mary Pickford in particular, an intense feud was in progress.

But that was only part of the story, as David Rose now revealed to me. Rose had been principal 'marriage broker' in the affair and had arranged the financial deal with the Prudential.

Bosses from the insurance company had dinner with Sam and Korda in Sam's suite at the Waldorf Astoria in New York.

'Then Sam got on one of his sprees,' Rose remembered. 'He started saying that Korda's pictures weren't worth a damn in America—right in front of the guy who was backing him and in Korda's presence too.

'Korda got mad, turned the whole table of food over and broke that up. We were actually getting the papers drawn up. It took three days with lawyers to get the two together again.'

They came back to Beverly Hills. Rose told him not to discuss the matter with Korda privately. But he did—and they had another row.

When it was all over, but with the dust of the negotiations still unswept, Sam left for Honolulu—and what looked very much like a wide-screen sulk (if only wide screen had yet been in general use).

He said he had no plans to produce more films under the United Artists banner. If most Goldwyn films now cost $1,500,000 on average to make, he needed at least $2,250,000 to be taken in rentals before he himself started showing a profit. (As he pointed out, he was paying three-fifths of his profits to non-producing partners simply for the privilege of having them distribute his films for him. The studio space didn't bother him, since he was paying rent that would have been dearer elsewhere and some of the money was coming back to him anyway.)

Soon afterwards, there were plans for merging United Artists with RKO—with Sam at the head of the new empire. He was once more in New York to settle the deal, staying at his suite at the Waldorf. David Rose was at the Sherry-Netherland.

The deal was set. Sam alone would earn $18 million from the arrangement, more than he had ever gained from a single deal before. It is a story never previously told.

At one o'clock in the morning Sam phoned his old friend and business adviser. 'Can we have a walk?' Goldwyn asked. Rose dressed and they met at the Waldorf.

'He said he had had a talk with Frances and he didn't want to get involved in it.' Being head of a new company like that would be taking partners again.

'He was probably right. We told him he would handle the fine pictures and someone else would be responsible for the others. But it wasn't enough.'

Not all of this was a matter of personalities alone. Everyone was talking of war. The old days of international markets were over and most hopes of expansion overseas were being shattered every time Adolf Hitler opened his mouth and demanded more 'concessions'. Neither Goldwyn nor Korda felt he could take on any additional risks at that time.

Sam, in particular, felt that pressures like these would only serve to blunt enthusiasm, and without that, there was no picture business. That was why he agreed to allow producer Merrit Hulburd to leave the company and go back to his former job on the *Saturday Evening Post*, even though his contract had three-and-a-half years to run. Sam was 'astounded' anyone could give up the big money of Hollywood to work in journalism. But he said: 'Enthusiasm is necessary to success and, if a man wants to do something else, no contract will force him to show enthusiasm in a job he is holding against his will.' The decision may, however, have inspired Sam to institute a profit-sharing scheme among his top 'creative employees'.

Then he laid it on the line: 'The making of good motion pictures is so personal an endeavour that I feel that better pictures can be accomplished by having my fellow-workers feel and have a real interest in the profits of my pictures.'

(It wasn't a totally original idea, even for Hollywood. Only the previous week David O. Selznick's brother Myron had announced a similar scheme for their own company.)

But *was* this the end of the United Artists story? It was not. Quite suddenly, in April 1938, it was announced that a deal had, after all, been concluded for Goldwyn and Korda to take over UA—and on substantially different terms from those previously discussed. Now the finance was coming from a British banking syndicate and not the Prudential. And, more significantly, *all* production companies being distributed by United Artists would in future share in the profits—which may have been Sam's plan in profit-sharing in his own company all the time.

It all seemed cut and dried—except that it didn't happen. A year later, Sam was suing the company and his supposed partners. He was charging breach of contract—because, as he said again, none of his other partners was producing films.

The day after the suit was announced Sam withdrew his charges—and asked to withdraw from the company.

The End at last? Not quite. The very next week he was renewing his suit. And so it went on, week in, week out. One minute Sam was withdrawing, the next he was suing. One week he was still part of the distribution team, the next he was looking for new outlets.

But in the motion-picture business, one expected that sort of thing to happen. There was no way of living a nice quiet life in Beverly Hills and simply guiding the affairs of the studio from a telephone.

When he bought an original story from Leo McCarey and Frank R. Adams, nothing seemed simpler than to put it into operation. The story was called *The Cowboy And The Lady*.

McCarey told it to him lying on a couch in Goldwyn's office. Sam ordered his story editors to take notes, 'but quietly' as McCarey seemed to doze off in mid-flow. Eventually, Sam wasn't so sure he liked it. 'It's only a treatment,' said the writer. 'Well,' said Sam, 'let's have a treatment of the treatment.'

Eventually, Sam was sold on the treatment of the treatment.

The problem was there had already been a story of that name by Clyde Fitch and the writer's estate was claiming proprietory rights to the tale. Sam then had a typical Goldwyn brainwave. He would call his story *The Lady And The Cowboy*.

The estate was not having any, however—until Sam coughed up what they demanded in compensation. He liked the title so much that he offered to buy the original. No deal was concluded—except that no other studio would be able to use that title without Sam's permission.

Later that same year the McCarey-Adams story was made into a Merle Oberon-Gary Cooper film. And under its original title. David Niven was given a supporting role in the movie, but all his scenes were excised before it was released.

It was the usual story, treated like an extra at his 'home' studio but loaned out to the competition for huge amounts. Warners reputedly paid $175,000 for his services—unwittingly. A Warner executive casually asked Sam how much he wanted for Niven. Goldwyn told him $175,000 and they shook hands. When Jack Warner heard about it he was livid. He phoned Sam, said the man had no authority to negotiate and the deal was off. Sam wouldn't allow the deal to be off. A handshake was a handshake and Warner paid his $175,000. But Niven himself didn't get any of it, and being cut out of Sam's own film was finally too much.

Both David and his agent, the renowned Leland Hayward, protested—with the result that the actor was put on suspension (a familiar Hollywood treatment) and the agent was banned from the Goldwyn lot.

Sam was so angry that he ordered his publicity office—that extraordinarily sophisticated and over-worked operation—to put out anti-Niven stories, just as they had been instructed to blacken the character of Ronald Colman.

Quite suddenly, the people who were in business to extol the virtues of stars were now releasing details of how every other actor in Hollywood detested the upstart Englishman.

Eventually, a new contract was negotiated which promised David up to $1,000 a week by the time the agreement's seven years were up. He also starred him—in a remake of Ronald Colman's *Raffles*.

There were, however, to be certain complications in this which none of the parties had anticipated. Britain declared war on Germany in September 1939 and Niven, without Goldwyn's permission—but he knew that Sam could never, publicly at least, protest—took off to volunteer for military service. (The publicity boys were put to work again. This time, writing about Raffles going to war. Sam agreed to pay Niven while he was away, although not as much as his Hollywood salary, and issued an order 'to that bum Hitler to shoot around him'. But that was still in the future.)

Before that, the row over Cooper's affiliation to the Goldwyn organization was finally sorted out. The agreement called for the star to still make one, and possibly two, pictures for Paramount each year while under contract to Sam.

He said he might now remake *The Winning of Barbara Worth*, which had, of course, been a silent, and this time with Cooper boosted as the principal star. It didn't happen. But a lot more did. Including opportunities to ingratiate himself with the mighty in the land. Mayors, governors, presidents. They all came into the Goldwyn orbit. In fact, Sam wouldn't allow any figure of major importance to come to Hollywood without calling on his studio first.

All the big picture companies strove for the same target. Some made it, some didn't. Jack L. Warner liked to entertain the mighty to lunch in his private dining-room and then waylay them with speeches which inevitably turned into a series of dirty jokes, or if not dirty jokes then unseemly repartee—like the time he told Albert Einstein, 'I have a theory about relatives, too. Don't employ 'em'. Or telling Mme Chiang Kai-chek, 'That reminds me, I have to take my laundry in.'

Sam liked them to see the films he made and the degree of technical excellence he brought into play. When the Mayor of New York, Fiorello La Guardia, came Sam took full advantage of the Mayor's known love of music. He was there in time to see and hear Jascha Heifetz play on the set of *The Reckless Age*.

When Heifetz finished playing on the otherwise empty sound-stage there was an overwhelming response of applause. La Guardia was dumbstruck. Where did it all come from?

'Oh, from a phonograph record,' Sam explained, feeling, he believed, justly proud of the advances of motion-picture science achieved in the past ten or so years. 'Remarkable!' said La Guardia. 'I think I could do with one of those records when I finish my speeches.'

'Right,' said Sam. 'Send three of those records to Mayor La Guardia immediately.' He had no idea that the Mayor was joking.

Sam simply believed it was good public relations—as it was taking on James Roosevelt 'in an executive position'. Roosevelt had been secretary to his father, the President, but had to resign because of ill health. Sam couldn't use him in his employ at all. But he wasn't wrong in thinking that it couldn't possibly do either him or his studio any harm.

Soon the front pages of America's papers were emblazoned with the news that there was now a Vice-President Roosevelt—for that was what James's position had become. It was to be the thirty-year-old man's third stab at a career. Before working for his father he had been an executive with a yeast company. Nobody accused Sam of taking the rise out of the media or of the rest of Hollywood, but that assuredly was what Sam was doing. It was a shame for Mr Roosevelt, but Sam Goldwyn was enjoying it thoroughly.

It all looked terribly patronizing. James said he didn't know what his duties would be. 'I'll do whatever Mr Goldwyn says,' he told reporters. 'That,' said Sam, 'would be the best he can.'

Later, it became obvious that some sort of modification of that wide scope was necessary. Both Goldwyn and James agreed with the Government's policy that there should be a separation between studios and theatres—but since the only theatre in which Sam had an interest was the Capitol in New York he was not being named in any of the suits before the courts at that time. Besides, James would not be involved in any negotiations with the Government.

Eventually, it was worked out that James's role would be as a kind of trouble-shooter. Now, that sounded important—until it worked out that if you saw a Sam Goldwyn film you didn't like, Roosevelt was the man you wrote to to complain. Not much of a deal, New or otherwise, for him.

: first Goldwyn film, and the first made in Hollywood — *The Squaw Man.* Elliot Dexter makes a point

ı's favourite relaxation. Cards with Frances. She is *not* one of his partners who accused him of cheating. Plenty ːthers did

Louis B. Mayer. He and Metro were never Goldwyn's partners. Their closest contact was when he and Sam had a punch-up in the locker room

ney Poitier, Dorothy Dandridge and Pearl Bailey. They agreed to do *Porgy and Bess.* Harry Belafonte and ck organizations wished they had not

n discovered Gary Cooper when he was featured in *The Winning of Barbara Worth.* Here with Vilma Banky

Frances and Sam at the time of *Porgy and Bess*. His last film. He would have been lost without her

(opposite) The tempestuous Bette Davis — in *The Little Foxes*

LFD- A

Mabel Normand was Sam's protégé — and his casting couch companion

ı wanted the Goldwyn Girls to be seen — a publicity picture for *Whoopee*

Danny Kaye's first film role. With Dinah Shore in *Up in Arms*

None of this, of course, really mattered. Sam ran a good, efficient shop and was a perfect window-dresser. James sitting in front of the glass gave him the clout he wanted without writing a single note to the White House. One shouldn't imagine that the Democratic Party, a year away from the next Presidential election, were very upset by it either, not least of all having Samuel Goldwyn support them. It had been no secret that Sam, like most of the moguls, was a dedicated Republican supporter, but he saw the wisdom of having a man like Franklin Roosevelt on the same side.

Then another new job was found for James—to go to England to help plug *Wuthering Heights*.

This was to prove one of the great milestones of the Goldwyn career, a picture that not only made money but brought a not considerable amount of glory to his name—which was more than Sam did to the title of the picture. For ever afterwards, he insisted on calling it *Withering Heights*. (And would say that his proudest moment was when the head of English at an Oxford college invited him to lunch and told him that the film was the best way he knew of interesting students in a work of literature.)

The idea for the movie was brought to him by director William Wyler, who was unquestionably the blue-eyed boy of the outfit. It was Sylvia Sidney who first attracted him to the idea of filming Emily Bronte's Yorkshire love-story, but she was not alone in thinking of it.

By then the book had long been in public domain and producer Walter Wanger had the idea it had the germ of an exciting film in it. He it was who engaged Ben Hecht and Charles MacArthur to hone out a screen-play. They handed him their work and he didn't like it. No humour, said Wanger, who really should have thought of that earlier.

So they turned to Wyler who prepared a synopsis for Sam's benefit. That very night Sam phoned him back. 'Let's do it,' he said. Frances was later to say: 'It was the only time Sam ever made that kind of decision quickly; he tortured and fussed over all the others.'

He did his share of torturing and fussing over this one, too, it must be said. He may have been quick in saying Yes. He was fairly quick the next day in changing his mind.

He was U-turning again. Despite his long-ago statements about final embraces, he now said he liked happy endings.

This one ended tragically. 'It's a great love-story,' Wyler insisted. Sam still said No. And a firm No at that.

Later Sam was convinced. But he still wanted a change in the ending. 'I don't want a corpse in the fade-out,' he declared.

As Hecht said: 'Sam treated writers like an irritated man shaking a slot machine.' But this was a time he hit the jackpot.

He was helped in agreeing to do the film by the thought that Hecht and MacArthur could write it. Gregg Toland would be in charge of photography.

It would be a movie with international appeal. After all, as he liked to say: 'Goldwyn films griddle the earth.'

Between them, they decided that it would be a good idea to bring in the new British matinée idol Laurence Olivier to play the lead role of Heathcliff.

He had no doubt that the female lead of Cathy had to go to Merle Oberon. Olivier came to America, didn't like Hollywood one bit but took something of a shine to Goldwyn—the kind of affection, it must be said, that cultured young people frequently have for 'rough diamonds', the uneducated family retainers whom they suddenly discover have a lot more money than they do themselves.

There was just one thing that Olivier insisted upon—that the girl with whom he was madly in love should have the Cathy part. Her name was Vivien Leigh.

Together they had just starred in *Fire Over England*. Sam had seen the film and had been taken by Olivier to see her latest, *St Martin's Lane*, in which she appeared with Charles Laughton.

But he still wasn't budging. He had Merle Oberon under contract and saw no reason not to use her. She was English, wasn't she? (Well, actually no. She was half Burmese, which was why there had been those 'slant-eyed' pictures Sam hated so much. She had actually been born in Burma, but in films she sounded English and that was why he wanted her for *Wuthering Heights*.)

Wyler was prepared to offer her the supporting role of Isabella. But it wasn't what he wanted.

If Myron Selznick hadn't come on the scene at this time and suggested Miss Leigh to his brother David for a certain movie he was also making, there might have been a bigger crisis on Sam's hands than he had. As it was, Vivien became Scarlett O'Hara in *Gone With The Wind* and Sam was allowed his choice for Cathy.

As for Olivier, Sam knew his reputation as a great actor with even greater promise. But he wasn't going to allow himself to be intimidated.

He thought that the Englishman was hamming it up. Olivier said he was merely being 'flamboyant' in the tradition to which he had been bred.

Sam declared he was stopping the entire film. Olivier asked for a private audience. He got it and explained what he was aiming for—the role as he sincerely saw it. Sam said he appreciated sincerity but Olivier wasn't making *Potash and Perlmutter* (since it was more than forty years away from his appearance as the cantor in the 1980 remake of *The Jazz Singer*, the idea at the time was quite ridiculous) and the work on the picture went on.

He appreciated, too, Wyler's contribution—although it wasn't always obvious. There was, for instance, the time that a journalist began a sentence, 'When William Wyler made *Wuthering Heights* . . .' Goldwyn corrected him: '*I* made *Wuthering Heights*. Wyler only directed it.' Maybe the reason was that Goldwyn always called the picture his favourite film, even though Wyler was to say it took him two years to persuade Sam to make it—whatever Frances claimed.

There were other casting problems. David Niven wasn't happy with the supporting role of Edgar—but mainly because after working with Wyler on *Dodsworth* he considered him a 'sonofabitch' to have as a director.

And then there were the rows between Merle and Olivier—no doubt owing not a little to the still blistering feeling at having had Vivien Leigh ruled out for the role. Olivier spluttered on camera. Miss Oberon asked him to stop spitting at her. It was a trivial incident, but they both walked off the set in apparent disgust.

Sam wasn't all that happy about Olivier's appearance for that matter. He had dirt on his face—and he didn't bring a handsome English actor to Hollywood to look dirty. 'But he's a stable boy,' Wyler protested. Sam still said he liked people to look beautiful. 'Don't worry, Sam,' Wyler insisted. 'He'll look great later on when he's rich.'

Goldwyn went away muttering about the money he was spending on getting beautiful people who were made to look ugly. Later, he told Wyler: 'If this actor continues to look dirty I'm shutting it all down.' He meant it—but since Olivier would be rich in the next scene to go before the cameras (and Sam would be invited down to see it) the director wasn't going to worry too much.

Sam was living up to his reputation of now getting-it-right-at-any-price. He sent a camera team to Yorkshire to film the genuine moors in which Bronte set her story. He also imported thousands of heather plants for the scenes to be shot at the Formosa Avenue studios. It totally contravened the Californian health and agriculture regulations, which prohibited the importation of any plant or vegetable matter, but the Goldwyn motion-picture budget was not going to be limited by such minor matters. A certain customs officer was made to feel a little happier that week.

Sam was equally extravagant when it came to the costumes. He updated the period forty years so that the dresses worn by Miss Oberon suited her more—he also had her taking a bath because it gave him a chance to show her shoulders (you couldn't be more daring than that in 1939).

And he decided, after all, to shoot a new ending—even though that might mean the corpse at the fade-out being Wyler's. The director refused. Olivier refused. So Sam got another cameraman to superimpose on to a cloud a shot of Olivier's stand-in and an unknown girl, walking hand in hand.

Wyler hated it. But it didn't stop him getting an Oscar nomination for his direction—would he have got the Oscar itself without that ending? Gregg Toland did get an Award and there were nominations too for the script, the music (by Alfred Newman) to say nothing of one for Laurence Olivier in the best actor category and for Geraldine Fitzgerald as best supporting actress. Sam also had to content himself with a nomination—for best picture.

Everybody treated it as a Very Important Picture. It couldn't have been anything else with a premiere attended by Mrs Roosevelt (did James have anything to do with that?), by Irving Berlin and his wife Ellin. The only one of any note who wasn't there was Wyler. Sam had banned him after their latest row. Even so, he went on record saying he had the greatest of respect for Goldwyn. That had to be respect indeed.

The critics liked it well enough. It took the New York Critics Award for best picture and in England, the magazine *Punch*'s critic Richard Mallett said it was a 'strong and sombre film, poetically written as the novel not always was, sinister and wild as it was meant to be, far more compact dramatically than Miss Bronte had made it'.

None of that made it too difficult for young Mr Roosevelt to sell when he arrived in Britain, although it would be more than twenty years before it made a profit in the United States.

In December 1939 it was announced that James was to be promoted—to President of the Samuel Goldwyn Studio Company.

Other Goldwyn endeavours would prove less successful. He hadn't bid very seriously for *Gone With The Wind* and he had failed to make *The Wizard of Oz*—even though he owned the rights to Frank Baum's stories. For $50,000 MGM bought them from him.

Mervyn LeRoy has described that as a sale which 'must go down alongside the Louisiana Purchase as one of the biggest bargains of all times.' LeRoy produced the Judy Garland classic.

'Why Sam didn't want it I really cannot guess,' LeRoy told me. 'Perhaps for once he didn't see the potential. We all make mistakes.'

Sam tried to give the impression that he was concerned above all with the welfare and the morals of the nation—which was why he 'wrote' an article ('Reading time ten minutes fifteen seconds', declared the strapline to the feature) demanding a drive for clean pictures. 'Who,' he asked, 'except the Hollywood moral hit-and-run drivers, can object to the drive for clean pictures?'

Not the people who went to Sam's home to see his own movies. They sat in splendid comfort; deep armchairs, rugs over their knees on chilly evenings. Sam controlled the sound himself, but the real sound control was of the conversation. The man who didn't encourage yes-men asked comments at the movies' end. But if you wanted to keep your host happy, you didn't criticize too loudly.

People went to movies as families—even though girls sometimes read stories they didn't want their mothers to see. It all helped illustrate just how long ago 1939 was. 'As long as pictures are made for family interest, not on moral grounds, but because that is the audience for pictures, I don't think that it will ever be a sin to attend a film.' And that was despite reading that a little girl had said she was giving up Ronald Colman for Lent.

Sam was no prude. But he had his standards. What he did to the English language was one thing; what others did to it with their four-letter words was another. On one celebrated occasion he walked out of a dinner-party at the home of Harry Cohn, boss of Columbia Pictures, because he just couldn't stand the language Cohn was using.

He almost felt the same way about illicit sex. Now that he was older and had found and loved Frances, his sessions with girls in his locked office were, most of the time, things of the past. But he remembered what it had all been about. One day, he heard the ribald chatter of a group of aides. They were talking about a colleague who had gone into an otherwise deserted sound-stage with a starlet.

Sam walked round to take a look. He got there just as the man was removing the last vestige of clothing from the girl and was about to mount her.

'Not on my time, please,' Sam scolded—and walked out. Nothing more was said about it.

He might have wished that some of his gambling companions were equally generous; the stories of Sam's cheating were now jumping through the town. When he installed a croquet lawn at Laurel Lane he played the game with the intensity of a varsity football match. Not everybody said he was terribly scrupulous about the methods he used to get the ball to go where he wanted it.

In his alleged writings, no one had to think that Sam was courting respectability. He certainly had that to the point where there was even a town in Arizona named after him. Goldwyn it was called, and Sam immediately said it would be used as a permanent set for all the Westerns he was going to make. It was a duplicate for the early Texan towns and would be perfect.

The first production to be shot there would be *The Westerner*.

It was a film which again had William Wyler directing and starred Gary Cooper and Walter Brennan in a post-Civil War story about a refugee from Kentucky taking over a Texan town. It was another opportunity for a row between producer and director.

Wyler wanted a part for his wife Margaret Tallichet (whom he called Talli) but Sam refused. He didn't want wives involved in the business. Frances was the exception, but, then, he was the boss. Sam insisted on Doris Davenport having the part of Mary-Ellen. It was not a good move, but, again, Sam was the boss.

In making *The Westerner* Sam took in Frances's suggestions as ever. Her influence was always, but always there. Sam would sit in the midst of a story conference, but Frances was there hovering in the background, taking notes. Afterwards, she would tell him what she thought—usually soon after picking him up from the office after 5.30.

He spent a million dollars on the production and was now going to let the world see how much he had spent. It had its premiere in the autumn of 1940 in Fort Worth, Texas—could there be a better spot (after the shindig for *Gone With The Wind* in Atlanta, a suitable town outside Hollywood for a premiere was now *de rigueur*). As it turned out, and as we shall soon see, it was spectacular in its own way and for entirely unexpected reasons.

On the way to the theatre Sam's men organized a full-scale parade reminiscent of the minstrel and circus processions which had been so much part of American life. Nearly 100 locally-bred cowgirls led an assembly of Hollywood life flown in specially for the occasion.

Once having had the ballyhoo, there was the question of bringing people into their local picture-houses. The film was sold to Loews for an amount that Sam thought was insufficient.

He asked his former PR man Howard Dietz to do something for him. 'How well do you stand with Joe Schenck?' he asked. Schenck was now head of Loews.

Dietz told him they got on very well. Then came the request for the favour. *The Westerner*, said Sam, was even better than *Gone With The Wind*—only not as long.

The trouble was that they had sold the film to the circuit for 25 per cent of the gross—whereas *Gone With The Wind* was guaranteed 75 per cent. He wanted Dietz to persuade Schenck to tear up the contract—and up the amount he would get to 50 per cent.

As he told him, it was only now that he realized how good *The Westerner* really was.

But the deal had already been signed, Dietz protested.

'Yes,' said Sam, 'and I want you to change it.'

Dietz then had the temerity to suggest that Mr Schenck might ask him for whom he was working.

'I guess', said Sam, 'you don't know him all that well after all.'

At about that time Sam was a guest on the Jack Benny radio programme. Charles Farrell, who had starred with Janet Gaynor in *Seventh Heaven* for Twentieth Century-Fox, was in the programme too.

The script had it that Sam was to say to Benny: 'Well, I'm sorry I didn't produce that.'

Benny was then to reply: 'Produce what?'

'*Seventh Heaven*,' said the script and Sam went along with that idea enthusiastically. The show went on the air—live—and Sam was perfect. At the end of the programme he said to Benny: 'Well, I'm sorry I didn't produce that.'

'Produce what?' asked the comedian.

'*Gone With The Wind*,' replied Sam.

Afterwards he explained that *Gone With The Wind* just slipped out. 'If you want to know something,' he added, 'it made a fortune.'

The significant thing about *The Westerner* was that it was not to be distributed by United Artists. Or so Sam said. The contract was virtually at an end and that meant he had to go elsewhere.

For the first time Warner Bros. were distributing a film made by an outside company. When *The Westerner* was completed Sam sacked all but a couple of his executives—which movie-industry watchers determined was a further sign that he was moving out of the United Artists' story and looking for studio space elsewhere.

Except. . . . The Goldwyn seesaw was still riding and the suit was still continuing. Meanwhile, after all, United Artists released the picture.

Even so, he was still going ahead with plans for other films. The $750,000 he still had tied up in *The Westerner* wasn't going to kick him out of his business.

Kick Sam Goldwyn out of business? Pickford and Fairbanks would have liked nothing better. He was the only factor still keeping them together—to say nothing of Chaplin. But he wasn't interested in them.

He was by now such a household name in America that he was being nagged to write an autobiography—a ghosted book had been written years before but no one took that seriously. 'My autobiography', he declared majestically, 'should only be written after I'm dead.'

There were, though, plenty of people ready to make assessments of him and he had plenty to be proud of.

Now he had something in his lair called *The Little Foxes*, for which he had just paid Lillian Hellman $100,000.

But he wasn't going to do anything about it just yet. The film had all the potential hallmarks of a great success. Bette Davis was going to repeat her success in *Jezebel*; at a time when everyone was clamouring for more Southern stories following that picture's success—to say nothing of a little thing called *Gone With The Wind*. This one had the Deep South etched into its very fabric. The screen-play that Miss Hellman had written was brilliant and the viciousness of the family she portrayed in her original play seeped into every word of the revised film-script.

Everybody knew it was going to be a scorcher. But Sam also knew it was likely to make a lot of money for United Artists and he wasn't in a mood to help them out in any way.

In a fit of pique he took off for a cruise to Hawaii with Frances. He enjoyed himself. So much, in fact, that he indulged in small talk, which was not a usual Goldwyn characteristic.

One of his fellow-passengers was Howard Dietz, who recalled the incident for me shortly before his final illness: 'Sam and I were on deck when we met. He looked at me and said: "Dietz, where are *you* going?" I said, "Same place as you, Sam"' Short of jumping independently into a lifeboat, there really wasn't much else he could do.

Which might also have summed up the deal that Sam initiated to bring Miss Davis to work at his lot in *Little Foxes*.

Both he and William Wyler—by now reconciled to the point of agreeing to work with each other—wanted Davis in preference to Tallulah Bankhead, who had starred on Broadway in the role but whom few audiences knew.

Fortunately, it was a time that Warner Bros. wanted Gary Cooper. Jesse Lasky had now joined the company as a senior producer and needed Cooper for the lead in *Sergeant York*. With great trepidation he approached Sam for a loan out.

The man who had spent the last few years foul-mouthing the mogul who had married, deserted and then divorced his own sister wasn't looking forward to having to ask the question. But he summoned up the necessary courage, blurted the request out in a sudden stream of words like a small boy asking for a new penknife and was amazed when Sam answered with equal economy of words: 'Sure you can.'

Later, as the deal was finalized, Lasky said how much he appreciated Sam's generosity and asked if there was anything he could do in return. 'Yes,' said Goldwyn, bandying no more words than before. 'You can lend me Bette Davis for *The Little Foxes*.' The horse-trading between one stable and another had never before been accomplished with such ease.

And it was as something like a horse that most actors felt, as they nearly always did, when they were sold off in this way.

Davis didn't have any great desire to work for Goldwyn. He had first seen her in a test made in New York for the supporting role in Ronald Colman's *Raffles* film. Sam's reaction to the film he was viewing was: 'Who did this to me?'

Partly with that memory in mind, she had no desire to work for Sam in *Little Foxes*. As she wrote in her autobiography *Mother Goddam*: 'Miss Bankhead gave a great performance of Regina Giddens. I begged Samuel Goldwyn to ask her to play it on the screen, as Tallulah played it the way the playwright Lillian Hellman wrote it.'

Then, she went on: 'There was no *new* Regina—and we have always resembled each other facially, hair, etc. So what could poor little me do?'

Miss Bankhead herself said of Bette Davis fifteen years after the film was made: 'Speaking of imitations. . . .'

Goldwyn insisted that Bette see the Bankhead performance on stage—which was a mistake, and she said so at the time. She didn't want to see another performance which could influence her. Influence her? As she wrote: 'William Wyler wanted me to play it differently, but I could only see it Tallulah's way.'

Once signed for the film, Bette recalled Sam's 'Who did this to me?' line. Now she and Warner Bros. were doing a lot to him—costing Samuel Goldwyn a great deal of his own money.

But he was anxious to get his money's-worth—even if that involved spending even more cash. Instead of relying on publicity pictures from unit cameramen, Sam hired five highly prestigious photographers to take portraits that appeared in magazines ranging from *Esquire* to *Ladies Home Journal*.

Sam didn't worry about problems in hiring Miss Davis. He should have been more concerned, because if he had, the shock of some of the difficulties might have been less.

She was known as the spitfire of the Warner lot and Jack threatened to fire her—although never to her face; he was sweetness and light whenever they met—on practically every picture they made together.

This time her dispute was essentially with Wyler, to whom she played prima donna most of the time she was on the set. One day he was infuriated when she appeared with her face smothered in something looking rather like calamine lotion. 'It's to make me look older,' she said.

According to the Teutonic Wyler the only way she was going to look older was by suffering under his direction. He ordered her to take it off. She, in turn, took herself off to her beach-house and said she wasn't going to return.

All the hell of Hollywood on a bad day was unleashed—by everyone, except Sam. He remembered a clause he had had inserted in Miss Davis's contract. This said that if she caused a break in filming for any reason other than her state of health, she would be responsible for the entire cost of the picture. Needless to say it wasn't long before she was back at work and contributing to what became a brilliant film.

It was notable, too, for a magnificent supporting performance by another of Goldwyn's discoveries to add to the stable of finds of Cooper, Colman—in a way, even Olivier—and McCrea. Her name was Teresa Wright.

Otis Ferguson was to describe it as 'One of the really beautiful jobs in the whole range of movie-making'.

Bosley Crowther—or Crowtherly Bos, as Sam was wont to call him—wrote in *The New York Times*:

> *The Little Foxes* leaps to the front as the most bitingly sinister picture of the year and as one of the most cruelly realistic character-studies yet shown on the screen.

It didn't win any Oscars, but there were nominations for Wyler, Bette Davis, Teresa Wright, Lillian Hellman, Meredith Willson, Patricia Collinge and another for best picture.

The Goldwyn Touch was still there.

14
Pride Of The Yankies

Even with *The Little Foxes*—a stunning story of the days immediately after the Civil War—the film industry was in something of a crisis, said Samuel Goldwyn.

It was mostly Sam enjoying the bad health of the movie business, as ever. If it had been much better he would have gone out of his mind.

As it was, he couldn't really predict that the war situation was going to make for a very healthy time indeed for the motion-picture industry. True a huge swathe of business was going to be lost because of the war—with all the Nazi-occupied territories banned to him and the rest of the studios, but, just as in the days of the Depression, people were going to spend money going to the cinema while they may have had to do without much else.

As for America itself, its own war was not to begin until December 1941. But Sam was worried by the writing he had seen scrawled on the studio walls. He said it again—there were too many films being made and the theatres were charging too low admission prices.

As he told *The New York Times*: 'Hollywood produced 600 pictures last year (1939) . . . yet there are not brains enough in Hollywood to produce more than 200 good ones. In this lies the real and honest answer to what is wrong with the motion-picture industry.'

And because there were so many bad pictures it was totally wrong to charge the same admission prices for those bad movies as were demanded for the good ones.

He said he was going to organize a nation-wide survey to try to work out just what *was* wrong with the films being offered to the public.

He was also against the number of double-feature programmes—he, of course, didn't make 'B' pictures and, therefore, couldn't understand why other people should, either.

He believed they spoilt an evening's entertainment in the cinema—as did raffles and the holding of bingo games, which were a couple of the things happening in American theatres at the time.

The Times took him up on his philosophy in their editorial columns.

They mentioned the number of films that Hollywood didn't make for fear of upsetting the dictators of Europe. Films, the paper declared, could make enough money from the American market alone.

> Now no one cares what the dictators like. It is no use caring. Appeasement has proved futile in art as in politics. Films can be, and indeed have been, made for the American public alone. Maybe a few trillion dollars can be shaved off the original cost, so that our motion-picture lovers can pay for them. Maybe, as Mr Goldwyn suggests, fewer and better pictures will do the trick. Here, at any rate, is a challenge—superbly met in some screen dramas already released, capable of inspiring a still more vigorous answer. Mr Goldwyn is quoted as wishing to 'give 'em romance'. One hopes for romance, but also for a more robust expression of our varied American life.

It wasn't totally complimentary; but it was a tremendous compliment in itself that a paper of that standing should take up one of Sam's themes—so often dismissed as publicity stunts—so seriously.

Not many people were dismissing his rows over United Artists as such. By then, anyway, the subject must have started to turn people off Goldwyn rather than attract them. Even the lawyers were getting bored—retrieved from that situation by the stimulation of the cheques that kept flooding in. It was obvious that they were the only ones gaining from the feud.

By 1941 Sam was rowing with his erstwhile partner Alexander Korda. The Hungarian-born British studio-owner had been the only member of the group allowed to distribute his product, using other studios. Sam claimed that this invalidated his partnership. Finally, Goldwyn himself dissolved his partnership. Korda would continue to use the studios, but would no longer have any other connection with the outfit.

By 1942, with America at war, Sam was making a conscious effort to reduce personal hostilities with other people—although sessions at the Hillcrest Country Club were inclined to be difficult if Goldwyn and Mayer happened to be in the same room.

And there were others for whom the name Sam Goldwyn didn't provoke unmitigated thoughts of joy.

Relations between Sam and that other notable independent producer David O. Selznick were, to say the least, complicated.

In 1943 Selznick wrote Goldwyn a letter in which he took Sam up on his oft-repeated claim to be a 'frank man' and told him in one of his famous letters; 'Sometimes, Sam, I am frank to say that I don't understand you.'

What Selznick objected to was Sam's calling for Alfred Hitchcock—'one of my people'—and talking with him 'without so much as either asking us or even letting us know after the fact. I wonder just how you would behave if I reciprocated in kind—or if any of the big companies did it with your people.'

Since Hitchcock had a contract with a minimum of two years to go, he felt rightly offended. And Selznick added: 'By contrast with your own behaviour, I have for months met criticisms of you with praise for your work and for your contributions to the business, and for your integrity of production. I have said to literally dozens of people in important positions that you have never received as much recognition in the industry as is your due.'

The letter was written in January. Selznick concluded his letter with 'best wishes for a fine and reformed New Year'.

It's precisely what Sam might have wished the industry.

At the same time, his public pronouncements now tended to be on important national issues—like the one in 1942 following President Roosevelt's call for a maximum wage of $25,000 a year.

Now this either meant wholesale opposition or another of his celebrated U-turns. (Remember what Sam had said about premiums on talent?) But now it was politic to back the White House.

The President's declaration was, of course, sweet music to the ears of any employer of expensive labour, and labour came no more expensive than it did in Hollywood.

One could almost see the expressions of relief on Sam's face as he declared: 'I agree with the President that incomes should be limited for the duration. While the boys in the front lines are sacrificing their lives, the least we can do is limit our incomes.'

The words were not just patriotic, they were also articulate. If one began to analyse the dichotomy between Sam's genuine 'Goldwynisms' and his official statements—even crisp two-sentence jobs like this—a picture emerges. Sam, with his suits made of the finest Swiss silk, was making a serious effort to show that he was a man to be admired and respected by people who knew that a command of the English language was a passport to that very respectability. He gave the impression of being a dolt. 'That's not really me,' he was saying, and those official statements were more in the way of being pleas from the heart.

No one at the time dared publish Sam's personal income, but it was in the region of a million dollars.

His statement was, however, prompted purely by patriotic motives. He was considering the public. So he was when he supported the Government's efforts to ban block booking of films.

Block booking meant that theatre chains bought films in blocks of up to a dozen at a time, sometimes—very often—before they were even made. It suited the big studios perfectly, providing them with a ready market—often in their own chains of theatres—before a penny had been spent on them. Since Sam didn't own a theatre chain, and rarely made more than two or at the most three films a year, the proposed ban was very good indeed.

Naturally, the theatres were opposing the move. Sam told them what he thought of their efforts in a letter to *The New York Times*. The opposition, he said, 'constitutes a long step backward toward (even though the letter was ghost-written some Goldwyn syntax inevitably spilled through) the shooting-gallery days of the movies'.

He concluded: 'Hollywood is anxious to make fewer and better pictures. The producer wants only a fair share of the returns on pictures. But he has a right to expect the exhibitor to devote as much energy and thought to selling them to the public as he, the producer, does to making them.'

It was a good time for Sam to make his protests. He didn't like double features or too many pictures being made. Now he could say it was in the national interest to conserve film stock. That was being patriotic and a good businessman at the same time.

He was flying his flag very high now. All actors were having their salaries pegged—but at a maximum of $67,000 a year and not the $25,000 Roosevelt had suggested.

Hollywood was, after all, a very patriotic community. As Sam said at the time: 'The band tours, the salary donations to war charities, the enlistments and the unselfish services rendered are widely known . . .

'I am sure that already a few stars have baulked [what a marvellous opportunity this was to attack the stars, the hands that fed the hand that fed them!] at the thought of no further remuneration for the year, but this sort of revolt must be short-lived when the star realizes that the subsequent benefits will accrue not only to himself but to his picture following and that his further appearances in films will be considered part of his duty to his country. At the same time, the star, realizing that his income is cut, nevertheless will seek out better pictures in which to display his talents.'

There it was: All Sam's philosophies summed up in one somewhat lengthy paragraph.

As he also said: 'Many splendid things are arising out of current circumstances. For one thing, we in Hollywood, as well as the rest of the nation, will learn to conserve resources frequently squandered. For another, the importance of doing work without accent on profit will level us to a point of solidarity that will be a beneficial unifying experience for Hollywood . . . You can rest assured that Hollywood now, as before, will arise magnificently to meet the occasion.'

To a studio there were principally three aspects of being at war: a blatant flag-waving kind of patriotism (whether on behalf of America itself or of its allies); telling a story that told of personal gallantry to which any fighting man or the family of any man in uniform could instantly relate; or pure escapism—which in its way could be judged the most important job of a film industry at that time, providing entertainment into which an already war-weary nation (from the moment war was declared, lists of casualities came streaming in and the morale of the country was at risk of being sapped) could flee.

Sam had all three under his belt. His first, *Ball of Fire*, turned into a highly entertaining vehicle for Gary Cooper and Barbara Stanwyck. It was equally highly improbable—which served to make it more entertaining still.

If one could imagine the highly athletic and incredibly handsome Gary Cooper playing an English language professor locked in a large house with a group of other unworldly professors, then you were on the way to accepting the premise of the film. Imagining Miss Stanwyck as a stripper was also stretching things somewhat. But it became highly entertaining and the gangster sub-plot—the girl was on the run from the gang—made it even more so.

Also entertaining to recall is the sub-plot of the making of the picture. In one scene Gary Cooper goes to Miss Stanwyck's night-club where he hears the jive talk of a number played by a band. It was suggested that the routine—by Phil Silvers and Saul Chaplin—should be included in the movie. It added a new dimension. Cooper, the wordsmith, discovers words he has never heard before and intends to use in the encyclopaedia he and his fellow-professors are producing.

The trouble is that the routine included the song *I Can't Get Started*.

'He buys it,' Chaplin told me. 'Then he decides that Phil Silvers would do it with Barbara Stanwyck. They need a name band to play it. Gene Krupa is playing here at the Palladium, so they ask Gene Krupa to play it. They try to clear the song and discover they have to pay $15,000 for it. That's too much, Sam decides. So we offer to write a new one, with jive talk in it. He says OK.

'Sammy Cahn and I write one. There's not a word in it anyone could understand if they don't know jive talk.'

The song was taken to Sam's office, where it was played for him on his grand piano. He was not thrilled. 'I don't understand it,' said Sam.

'That's the whole point,' said Chaplin. 'You have to know this jive talk.'

'Not one word,' said Sam.

The song was called 'Coppin A Plea'—jive talk for 'making excuses'.

'Mr Goldwyn,' said Chaplin, 'everyone understands "coppin a plea".' It was a term well known in gangster circles.

'They do?' said Sam. At which point he pressed every number on his intercom. People streamed in. One after the other was asked whether they knew what 'coppin a plea' meant. They all said No.

Finally, a little grey-haired old lady came in. He asked her. Chaplin begged him not to do so. He knew she wouldn't know.

But Sam persisted.

'What does "coppin a plea" mean?' he asked.

She replied: 'Making excuses'.

At that point, Chaplin remembered, Sam said: 'What does she know—a little old lady!'

Sam sold the film with all the enthusiasm of a war bonds rally—in fact as if there were no war on at all. His publicity department were deputed to make it one of the biggest exercises of its kind. They did not let him down.

One of the publicists involved on the project was Irving Fein, later to be the manager of Jack Benny and finally fulfilling the same role—as well as producing his film and TV shows—for nonagenarian George Burns.

He started with Sam in 1941 and *Ball of Fire* became his first big project after leaving Warner Bros. What happened in getting him there showed a very nice perception of what it was to be courted by Goldwyn. 'I was secure at Warner Bros., making big money there. In fact, I'd just got a $25 a week raise, which *was* big money in those days. About a month or two later, Goldwyn asked me to come over there as associate publicity director.

'I was reluctant. But the more reluctant I became the more Goldwyn wanted me to join him, selling me on the idea of coming over. He was a very tough man with employees, but that wasn't why I wanted to stay at Warners. He finally offered me $50 more than I was getting at Warner Bros. Before I had this sudden $25 raise. Now, I was, in effect, doubling my salary in two months. I took a chance and came over to Goldwyn, who kept saying "Mr Fein. You'll like it here."

'I had only been there three days when I met Goldwyn on the lot. He said, "Mr Fein how do you like it here?" I said, "very much, Mr Goldwyn".'

That was when he was put on to *Ball of Fire*, which had been partly written by Billy Wilder (in partnership with Charles Brackett). Howard Hawks directed the picture, but it is generally regarded as the film in which Wilder learned how to be a director. As Fein told me: 'Howard Hawks allowed Wilder to sit on the set with him all day long and explained to him why he was doing all his shots.'

Goldwyn asked him again that day: 'How do you like it here, Mr Fein?' And Fein again told him he liked it fine. 'Do you like it better than Warner Bros.?' Fein told him he had only been there three days. But from then on, every time they met, he kept asking: 'Do you like it better than Warner Bros?'

'That went on for a whole year. And I never did give him the satisfaction of saying that I liked it better than Warner Bros. He was always very sweet with me. He shouted and argued with a lot of people.'

Ball of Fire didn't give him any reason to shout or argue with Fein. Because it was a film about a stripper, Fein dreamed up the idea of paying the girls from the local burlesque theatre to picket the studio. Day after day they formed a circle around the studio gates carrying large placards (made in the studio art room, but nobody had to know that) reading UNFAIR TO STRIPPERS. WHY NOT HIRE REAL STRIPPERS FOR THEIR FILM?

When Fein heard that a girl, Betty Rowland, billed herself as 'The Ball of Fire Girl' and played at the Follies Theatre in town, it was a publicist's ration of manna from a movie heaven.

The girl was known as the Gipsy Rose Lee of Los Angeles so there was a chance of making a great deal of fun out of her.

Until that moment *Ball of Fire* had been no more than a working title.

'Nobody considered using it permanently', said Fein, 'Most of the people on the Goldwyn lot considered it to be a "B" picture title'.

But suddenly it was realized that the 'B' picture working title could now become the real name of a Goldwyn film.

'Fire' had already been used in a dozen different ways to promote a picture nobody would see for at least six months. Fire Prevention Week was linked up with the film—using, too, Betty Rowland on front pages of magazines. If both girl and film used the same title, why not exploit the fact? But it went further than that.

It was Fein's idea to get the Ball of Fire Girl to sue Goldwyn Productions for using her own title without permission. 'I figured I'd give her five hundred bucks for doing this. And we'd get lawyers to arrange the suit; after all the publicity, of course, we'd get her to withdraw it.'

He told Goldwyn about it. He loved it. 'Or at least he didn't say it was a bad idea.'

So he phoned Betty Rowland. Her reaction wasn't as expected. 'She was very off-hand with me and I couldn't figure why. But I explained the idea to her. It was then she said: "I *am* suing you." There was a long silence. She said: "I saw my lawyers this morning and filed suit then." '

Telling Goldwyn was even more difficult. After all, she was now really asking for $100,000. The lawyers had to get busy and arrange a suitable sum for which she would settle. It *was* all good publicity after all. The picture was an artistic success as well as a commercial hit.

It was Fein's job—and those of everyone at the studio—to make up Goldwynisms. This was the time when Sam thought that the more people spoke about him the better—if it was for business. His sensitivity on the subject of his command of the English language would come a bit later.

To Sam Goldwyn was attributed–although the phrase was invented by Fein at the Goldwyn lot— 'He was quick like a flashlight.'

Did anyone care? The columnists didn't. They knew Fein had made up the phrase, but they were willing to put a paragraph in their papers, just for old time's sake—and the promise of a real story later on.

Their relationship with the Goldwyn studios and Sam himself was somewhat better than that between Sam and his writers—those demi-gods whom he also called his racketeers, out of the same sense of frustration an inadequate child feels in the company of a young genius. He was feeling so piqued at this time by another script dispute over some long-forgotten picture that he declared unequivocally: 'From now on, there will be no writers at story conferences.' It made the very notion of a story conference totally ridiculous, but Sam had rules and standards and if you worked for him, you kept to them.

Pride of the Yankees fulfilled the second requirement of movie patriotism—glorified personal courage. This was the story of Lou Gehrig, the baseball champ whose name gave a title to a disease, the same muscle-wasting syndrome that was to kill David Niven forty years later.

Sam was intrigued by the personal bravery of Gehrig, and truly believed his story, if told properly, would not only make a lot of money but also stir the nation's pride and emotions.

It was a role made in heaven, it seemed, for Gary Cooper—even though Cooper, educated in England, had never played baseball in his life.

Nothing was left out and a certain amount was put in—the pretty wife played by Teresa Wright owed more to script-writers Jo Swerling and Herman J.Mankiewicz than to reality.

Miss Wright had had an unconventional introduction to Goldwyn, who discovered her in the Broadway play *Life With Father*.

Sam liked her and came round backstage after the play to say so—which was quite a daunting thing for a young actress who tried to protest that she had no plans or even desire to go to Hollywood.

She insisted, on signing the document, that she would not be required to do what the business euphemistically called 'leg art', be guaranteed that no one would try to invent romances for her and, as she said, 'no orchid and ermine setting for my background'.

She had already appeared in *The Little Foxes* and been out on loan to MGM—somehow she didn't get any prohibition of that into her contract—for a small part in *Mrs Miniver*. But the role of Mrs Gehrig was her biggest to date and she was playing it the way she wanted to, as a very pretty girl with a lot of heart.

The real Mrs Gehrig liked the role. So much so that she allowed a copy of her personal scrapbook of her husband's career which was used in the making of the film to be presented to the National Baseball Museum Hall of Fame.

That wasn't the only part of the picture that *was* based on reality. There was the famous farewell speech that Gehrig made on the baseball ground and even an appearance by Babe Ruth, the best-known baseball player in history.

Only one real problem seemed insurmountable: the way Cooper, as Gehrig, handled a bat. It wasn't how the real one did. The star, who despite his drawl would have been happier with a cricket bat in his hands—he was a wicket-keeper too at Dunstable during his schooldays—had to have the most elementary training in the game. But one of his coaches, Lefty O'Doul (that name is important, as we shall see), said at the time: 'I'll either make Coop look like a first baseman or I'll break his leg.'

O'Doul was a former National League batting champion. And, as his name indicates, left-handed. Gehrig was left-handed, too—and the way he played with that left hand had a great deal to do with the mystique of his command of the game. But Cooper was right-handed and nothing could be done to make him use his left with anything like the same effectiveness.

It was Sam himself—possibly using that experience from his glove-selling days—who came up with the answer: reverse the film when printing it. So that that could be done properly, the numbers and lettering that Cooper wore on the baseball ground set and everything else in view were reversed, too.

Irving Fein worked on this picture, as well. He suggested hiring Babe Ruth and the other real baseball players—including the entire New York Yankees team. Fees of $500 each were paid, plus travel expenses and the cost of their hotel accommodation. One man insisted on receiving $1,500 because it would entail him giving up his full-time job. Sam's reaction was predictable: 'Robbery!' shouted Goldwyn. 'All that money for a third baseman. Doesn't he know I can get a first baseman for only $500.'

Fein remembered for me being in the projection theatre one day when Sam was looking at the rushes of *Pride of the Yankees*—which was no happier an experience now than with any other film.

Sam was shuffling in his seat. He didn't like what he saw and he told director Sam Wood so. Wood was annoyed: 'I think it's great,' he said.'

'No,' said Sam, finding it difficult as usual to express himself but, also as usual, knowing that something was wrong, insisting on it. 'It hasn't got the mood somehow,' he said. 'We've got to shoot it again.'

Since, once more, it was Sam's language that was being paid for, Wood had to agree to make the change. The rushes of *this* work were played over for him and, this time, he liked it. 'Much better,' he said. 'You're right,' said Sam Wood. 'I take my hat off to you.'

Sam had just demonstrated a natural instinct. It wasn't something you could learn at a film school.

Wendell Willkie, who had been the Republican candidate in the 1940 Presidential election, told Sam after seeing the film: 'You have done something important here. You help democracy everywhere by showing what opportunities there are in America. I like it because I can think of the influence it will have when people all around the world see it.'

The film came out at about the same time as Warners' *Yankee Doodle Dandy*, with James Cagney. There was an unwritten agreement between studios that they let their competitors have advanced copies of their work and Sam rang Jack Warner asking for a favour.

'What is it?' asked Warner.

'I want you to send me over *Pride of the Yankees*,'

'Right,' said Jack, 'providing you let *me* have a copy of *Yankee Doodle Dandy*.'

'It's a deal,' Sam agreed, not realizing for a minute he had asked for a copy of his own film.

Musicians who worked on Goldwyn pictures seemed to feel they were as important as anyone else. 'He had as great respect for musicians as he did for writers. He was smart, he knew he needed these people,' Saul Chaplin told me. (Saul later became a top musical director of films like *The Sound of Music*; he was also producer of *That's Entertainment, Part Two*.)

There were Oscar nominations—but again no Award—for best picture and best script and for Gary Cooper and Teresa Wright.

Out of that sense of patriotism, the pictures Goldwyn was going to make for the rest of the war were, on the whole, going to show the same American spirit—even if, sometimes, that spirit was displayed by writers.

The North Star, written by Lillian Hellman, was one of these—although to Sam's taste it got a little near the mark.

Sam, as we have now more than established, considered himself above all an American. For nearly all the time he had lived in America it was the epitome of patriotism to be anti-Communist (for which read anti-Russian).

Now, however, the Soviets were America's allies and Sam's friend Franklin Delano Roosevelt made no secret of the fact that he wanted the Hollywood studios to drum up a little enthusiasm for the Russian cause.

Warner Bros. were responding magnificently to the call with their picture *Mission to Moscow*, a movie which Jack Warner would later regret making and which would involve questions from Red-baiting congressmen and senators soon after the war was over.

Sam's own answer was *North Star*, which told, supposedly, the story of a Russian village defending itself against the German invader.

The film was directed by Lewis Milestone, who had been responsible for that archetype First World War drama, *All Quiet On The Western Front*. (What Sam called *that* boggles the imagination.)

The trouble was that Milestone didn't get on with Lillian Hellman and Goldwyn didn't get on with Milestone.

He told him to come to his house for dinner to discuss his problems. The director refused—although Sam insisted that as an employee he had to do as he was told.

'There's nothing in my contract Mr Goldwyn,' Milestone was to tell me he replied, 'nothing at all that says I have to have dinner with you.'

'Right,' said Sam, knowing when he was almost beaten. 'Come round to the house *after* dinner.'

They talked and Sam sided with him—so much so that Hellman walked off the Formosa Avenue studio lot in tears and demanded the return of her contract. She got it—and was to say terrible things about the film (in fairness, almost everyone else said terrible things about it, too) until she died.

Sam was to admit at one stage that there were things in the picture that he didn't understand. Milestone turned to Sam Junior, then fifteen years old. 'Did you understand it?' he asked the boy. 'Yes, I did' he replied. His father was not to be swayed. 'What are we doing now,' he demanded, 'making pictures for fifteen-year-olds?'

It had a half-star cast, including Anne Baxter, Dana Andrews, Dean Jagger, Walter Huston and Erich von Stroheim. And it didn't come off. Critic Richard Winnington commented that it was one of those films that 'steps out of its scope.' Perhaps he meant that it Steppes out to create an image of Russia that was more in the mind of the director Lewis Milestone and his cameraman James Wong Howe than in reality. As James Agate remarked: 'Putting American villagers into Russian costumes and calling them by Russian names is never going to deceive this old bird.'

Sam, meanwhile, was trying to apologize for his previous shortcomings: 'Americans sold Russia short because the Hollywood screen had never presented in entertainment form a true picture of contemporary Russia, while Soviet films had only a limited audience because they were dismissed as "arty" or "propaganda".

'The more we delved into research for the picture, the more amazing it became that Americans had never previously been educated to their kinship with the Russian people. Russian and America and the peoples of the two countries are alike in many ways. Both are peace-loving, both love their land. The pioneering in Russia, as its vast resources were opened to development by the people, resembles closely the development of our own west. In telling the story of the Russian people we can't help but feel that we are telling the story of a people who think and act as do Americans.'

They were words calculated to make a man want to wash out his mouth with salt—if you were the Samuel Goldwyn of, say, 1946. But this was only 1943, a time when—despite the war—Hollywood and its moguls were still regarded as some kind of super race. (After all, how many people, like Sam, had an office with a grand piano, deep carpet and its own bedroom and kitchen?)

Sam as always, whenever he wanted it, could get the headlines in the Hollywood newspaper columns.

'One day, we got every column in every paper,' Irving Fein recalled.

'We used to clip the stuff and every day send in the papers to Goldwyn. After about four days we had piles of clips coming in. On the fifth day there was nothing. Goldwyn came in and said, "Fellows, what's going on here—there's nothing in the papers today?" He wanted that stuff out all that time.'

Like the other moguls, Sam would sometimes invite his favourite employees to join him for lunch in the executive dining-room—only while they *were* his favourites (a situation that didn't usually last for long).

One day a treasured writer was given the invitation.

It was a marvellous meal, the best cooked food (at least outside Warner Bros., who were renowned for having the finest cuisine in California) elegantly served; the finest wines. And, above all, Sam in a mellow mood.

'You know what I do?' Sam told his guest. 'I have a dressing-room here. I have an hour for my lunch, which I always enjoy. Then, I go in for another hour, take a nap and then get up, have a wash, put my clothes back on and feel very refreshed.'

The next day, he met the writer again. The man told him: 'I've been thinking about what you said about having a sleep in the afternoon,' he said. 'I'm going to do the same.'

'Good,' said Sam. 'We give you an hour for lunch. Take half-an-hour for your meal and half-an-hour for a sleep.'

The year 1943 was an important one for him—the thirtieth anniversary of his entry into the film industry. He tried to give the impression now of being a benign editor—leaving the detailed work on a picture to his director and underlings, sitting in on the rushes and other preliminary work and fondly giving advice when it was called for.

That wasn't him at all—any more now in 1943 than it had been in 1913. Pictures were made at his behest, always only with his approval. It was still his language that was being bought with his money.

But he wasn't letting it be known to the general public. He was even denying that he made stars—what a perfect world it would be if he didn't need them!

'God makes stars,' he said—no doubt, not including *The North Star*, but religious fervour was part of the mood of the time and it seemed the right thing to say.

'The public recognizes His handiwork. What counts is personality. In the entertainment field there are three types of personality—radio, stage and screen. Some few people have all three. This is rare, and that's the reason many successful stage actors fail on the screen and many screen favourites are flops on the stage.'

That was Sam's serious side, or at least the side that seemed serious to the public. He was serious most of the time, although so much of what he said now seems if not funny, at least bizarre.

There was, for instance, the publicist who did an extremely valuable job for Goldwyn and then had the temerity to ask what was in it for him. 'I'll tell you,' said Sam, quick as a flashlight, 'if you ever need a prostate operation it's on me.'

At about this time Sam was desperate to get hold of Tyrone Power, then, as for most of his career, under contract to Twentieth Century-Fox. Sam wanted to borrow him for a part, and as always wanted him the easiest, cheapest way.

He rang up Darryl F. Zanuck—on his direct line.

'This is Mr Goldwyn,' he told the secretary, 'I want to talk to Mr Zanuck.'

'I'm sorry,' she replied, 'Mr Zanuck is all tied up at the moment.'

'I must speak to Mr Zanuck,' he replied.

'I would like to put you through,' said the secretary. 'But I've been given strict instructions not to disturb him.'

'You *must* disturb him,' said Goldwyn using that high voice of his to its greatest, most threatening effect. 'It's a matter of life or death.'

At that, the secretary decided to take if not her life then her job in her hands and disturb her boss. He came to the phone.

'Hello . . .', Zanuck began.

At that point, a tired and somewhat flustered-sounding Sam Goldwyn responded: 'Yes Darryl, what can I do for you?'

'But you're calling me . . .', protested Zanuck.

'Am I?' asked Sam. 'Well, I can't remember who called whom. But while I've got you on the phone, how about lending me Tyrone Power . . .?' He never got him.

Neither did he really succeed in making comedy films. The days of the Eddie Cantor blockbusters were now over. Yet he still felt a need to have a niche in a market in which he never really felt comfortable.

The question to ask himself now was simply: who is the new Eddie Cantor? And he came to the not unlikely conclusion that the man must be Bob Hope, who was fairly firmly ensconced at Paramount, home of the various *Road* pictures with Bing Crosby.

In his usual cunning pose, Sam won Hope over to Formosa Avenue for two Goldwyn movies.

The first was *They Got Me Covered*, in which he—of course—was the innocent abroad in the midst of a Nazi spy ring. Dorothy Lamour and Otto Preminger (as actor) were in their usual roles, suitably adapted for the kind of movie that seemed to be playing at every neighbourhood picture theatre in 1943.

Years later Bob Hope told me about the trouble Goldwyn had in getting him for the role. 'I was offered $100,000,' he recalled. 'My agent wanted another $25,000.'

Hardly surprisingly, Sam said No and equally not unexpectedly, later said, 'Come back, let's talk.'

It wasn't until the premiere of another film that the deal was settled—on stage.

Hope was the master of ceremonies at the opening. But, that night, Sam did a very unexpected thing. Before the comedian was due to go on, he button-holed him and asked: 'Bob. Can I make an announcement?'

It was very unusual for Sam to want to make any public appearances of any kind. But this looked more unusual than ever. And if Sam Goldwyn made a request, no one in his right mind would think of saying no.

No one—certainly not even Hope—knew what he was going to say. But he went to the centre of the stage, slightly shaking, took hold of the microphone and then that high, unsteady voice announced: 'I haven't made a comedy since the great Eddie Cantor. Now I'm going to make a movie with Bob Hope.'

'I thought that was wonderful,' Hope recalled. 'We'd done a deal and I didn't know about it.'

Just as the audience thundered its whistles and claps, Hope kidded him: 'Wait, Sam,' he said. 'We haven't done a deal yet. What I suggest is that we lie down right now and talk money.' They did. They lay down on the stage—and discussed the extra $25,000—which Goldwyn now agreed.

His second Hope vehicle, *The Princess and the Pirate* had the same director, David Butler, and an equally predictable story—this time about, you guessed it, pirates—and introduced a young lady who had been brought out to make a different comedy film. Her name was Virginia Mayo, but before she was allowed to do the picture he had other plans for her. Meanwhile he was seeking methods of getting his own way in more serious directions. Like in law.

One of the writers of *The Princess and the Pirate*—with Don Hartman—was Melville Shavelson.

'I always respected him,' Shavelson told me. 'He always thought he was speaking for America—which was perhaps unfortunate because he didn't speak very well and that was why he tried to avoid public appearances where possible.

'Of course, we were always having rows over scripts and it was usually a pretty good bet to sue him—because he wouldn't go to court. So I was always resigning and he was always bringing me back.

'He really wanted to make very special films. But he also made comedy films—because he also wanted to make money.'

Either fortunately or unfortunately—depending solely on the state of your relationship with Sam at any one time—anyone working at the Goldwyn studios saw a great deal of him. 'We had almost daily contact with each other,' Shavelson recalls.

'You'd talk to him about a project he dreamed up and say: "What do you want?" The answer would usually be "I don't know". All Sam knew was that he wanted it good and if it wasn't he'd tell you.'

The frustrating thing was that he would have several strings of writers working on the same project. 'That was terrible because you never knew where you were with him. There were plenty of writers who because of this took his money and didn't do anything for it. They didn't respect his intelligence as much as he respected theirs—and there is no doubt that he respected writers more than any of the other Hollywood bosses.' But staying a Goldwyn writer could be tiring.

'If you wanted to talk to Sam, you had to walk with him. We had to take constitutionals to get anything talked through.'

Shavelson, too, made up Goldwynisms. His favourite was 'Everything he says you take with a dose of salts.'

But doing that, too, implied a sense of respect. 'Oh,' said Shavelson, 'he was a shark in a sea of whales.'

David Rose—another David Rose, this; one of the most important names in Hollywood music—was musical director on *Princess and the Pirate*. Rose told me:

'He was involved in every stage of the work. I think he was the most knowledgeable man among all the moguls; more knowledgeable even than L. B. Mayer and Zanuck.'

Sam was still complaining in the summer of 1944 of too many pictures being made too badly. The industry had become 'slipshod and neglectful at a time when it should be building goodwill for the leaner years to come'. That was more to the point: when the captive audiences of the war years—those with nothing better to do while loved ones were overseas, or stationed in lonely outposts—wouldn't necessarily be there when it was all over. Sam was the only one admitting that. He was to be proved right.

He was thinking about the audiences for his pictures all the time—and his latest film had an opening announcement that servicemen were being admitted free of charge.

It was called *Up In Arms*.

15
The Kid From Brooklyn

This was going to be yet another example of the quality which made Sam Goldwyn so exceptional—a finger on the pulse of a market which welcomed the notion that what he was offering was likely to be brilliant.

And it had all the necessary requirements, a story that was going to see things from the soldier's point of view. Not an attractive young officer with medals on his chest and the suggestion of scrambled egg on his cap—as braid was known in those days—but a gawky looking redhead whose nose was a little too big, but who was going to be the greatest clown of the decade, and some would say the best who ever made a movie.

Sam had seen *Let's Face It*, a show about soldiers finding it difficult adjusting to military life in wartime. What really made that show was what jazzmen have always called 'scat singing'—Ella Fitzgerald does it all the time—but of a highly original kind from the star, a man named Danny Kaye.

Kaye stood in the middle of a barrack-room and lamented on the day he had his call-up papers. You couldn't understand the words—for, in Kaye's fashion—there really weren't any. Just an odd syllable that was recognizable—'Mailman', 'fine specimen', 'KP' and a host of grimaces, flexing of legs and the movement of a pair of hands which had they been transferred to his feet would have been called ballet.

That was Danny Kaye, a comic who had begun in the 'Borscht Belt' circuit of the Catskill Mountain resorts, had done a highly successful tour of the Far East before the war and then played opposite Gertrude Lawrence in *Lady In The Dark*.

He was undoubtedly a great talent—with one superb advantage: a wife called Sylvia Fine, who wrote all his material, including that scat number which was called *Melody In Four-F*, about a meek little fellow who suddenly finds himself inducted into the United States Army against his will (and probably that of the Army, too).

Let's Face It had been bought for the movies and filmed by Paramount. But instead of Danny Kaye it starred Bob Hope—and, needless to say, there was no *Melody In Four-F*, either. Those two details, to say nothing of a constant feeling of being miffed because of Hope's less than brilliant results with his own outfit, decided Sam on the need to bring Danny Kaye to Formosa Avenue.

Kaye was not over eager to come. He had had a number of movie offers before, but was afraid that he would be lost in the Hollywood machine. What he did required his own very personal approach, and that was likely to get swallowed up in a film studio. He like to 'busk' things, to do them his way according to the mood he was in at any one time; that was why performances varied from show to show. He wasn't the only stage entertainer to feel that way and Sam, a man of Hollywood and the entertainment business if nothing else, understood him completely.

But he persuaded, he cajoled, he flattered—and Frances added her two-cents'-worth to the persuasion, the cajoling and the flattery. They were taking risks, because Kaye wasn't known outside of Broadway and he was fairly new there too.

What was more, Sam with his inbred reluctance to feature Jewish stars, wasn't totally happy with the image presented by the Brooklyn-born David Daniel Kaminsky either. As he went into his persuasion act he looked at Kaye's nose and worried about the problems he might bring. But the more he spoke to Danny, the more convinced he became that he would be the choice he wanted.

Kaye was still reluctant. He had just turned down an offer from MGM worth $3,000 for every week he was in any way working on their pictures, either as an actor performing or as one being consulted on the parts he would play.

But he had said no. 'I would work for much less, believe me,' he said at the time, 'if they would give me character roles and let me learn how to act. But I know they would just put me into a speciality spot here and there and one bum picture would put me back two or three years. I'm very young. I've got lots of time.

He was now thirty-one and was finally convinced that what Goldwyn was offering was nothing like a 'bum' picture at all. So he accepted. He would not be sorry—at first, at least. Goldwyn was making him an international super-star, perhaps the biggest of the kind he had ever created, a man who if only he had wanted to, would be just as big today more than forty years later. But that really is another story.

Back in 1944 when the film was being made he was known only to a very limited section of the American population. Those who had known him in Japan before the days of Pearl Harbour and all that followed were not encouraged to remember him at all.

So he and Sylvia went to Hollywood and he sat in front of a camera at Formosa Avenue. By the time the tests were completed every one concerned wished that he hadn't and had been left to the relatively simple life of an actor, with a suite at the Sherry-Netherland Hotel in New York City, waiting for the next offer of a starring role on Broadway.

Again the scene in the projection-room at the Goldwyn studios was not one for small children or those of a sensitive disposition. Sam didn't like it, but as usual didn't know what it *was* he didn't like. The film went home with him to Laurel Lane and Frances—with Sam Junior peering in at it—and he sat and wondered; firstly at what had gone wrong and secondly at how they could have been so stupid to offer a starring part to this unknown who—putting it plainly, for that was the only way it could be put—was not just unattractive but so darn ugly.

There was, for one thing, his nose. Frances was to describe it as 'like Pinocchio's'. That was being very gentle or perhaps gentile about it. What worried Sam so much was that it was a very Jewish-looking nose—and what would hiring someone like that do to his image as an American? Such thoughts seem strange in these perhaps—in this regard, at least—more enlightened times. But even when America was fighting a war against the Nazis, the most barbaric anti-Semites in history, Jewish Americans were frightened of having their own characteristics viewed on the cinema screens—as though, by doing so, their own loyalties were being compromised or at least put in doubt.

Other executives came to see the rushes and came to the same conclusion. Several of them pressed Sam to forget the film—which was to be a wartime remake of *Whoopee*, featuring the man he was already planning to build up as the next Eddie Cantor, about a hypochondriac drafted into the Army. Cut your losses, they said. Either that, or you cut your throat.

A man who a generation before could discard almost a million dollars on reshooting half a film wasn't going to be easily swayed and persuaded to give up.

He was up all night, with Frances fussing round him trying to sooth his nerves, supplying endless hot drinks in an attempt at getting him off to sleep. They didn't work. Any of them.

The film went with him in the Rolls-Royce back to Formosa Avenue the next morning. There was a 'Do Not Disturb' notice on his office door and he paced the floor seeking an answer.

Could they afford to cancel the movie? After all, even the Goldwyn Girls had been selected with Frances's help. All the sets had been built. The script was not only written—by Don Hartman, Robert Pirosh and Allen Boretz—but was supposedly in its final, edited form.

He had another look at the tests and sank back into his morass of misery. Frances was in an outer room, knowing what he was feeling, worrying about him and hardly daring to go through to ask. She knew the sort of reaction she would get and the idea of an additional flea in either of her ears had lost its attraction.

Suddenly, there was a loud shout from Sam's room, the kind that Frances recognized as the one he uttered when he had stubbed his toe. This time, it was an idea that stubbed through his mind.

Like Archimedes shouting 'Eureka' in his bath, Sam revealed that he had had it—the idea, that is, that would solve most of his problems.

At last, the phone in his office was allowed to be used and he demanded to be put through instantly to the studio hairdresser. 'Expect Kaye in ten minutes,' he barked. 'He's having his hair dyed blond.'

The vagaries of the studio system being what they were, Kaye was not expected to protest—or, indeed, have any say at all in the matter.

The dying of his hair blond tended, Sam believed, to soften Kaye's Semitic face. Of course, he would have been much happier still had there been time to give him a nose operation—but that would take at least a month or more for bruising to die down. And Danny himself promised he would have something to say about that. As he told Goldwyn once they were on less formal terms: 'Tell you what Sam, you shorten your nose and I'll shorten mine.'

Whether that peroxide dose did have very much to do with it, and there is considerable reason to doubt that it did more than satisfy Sam Goldwyn, *Up In Arms* launched Danny Kaye on a tremendous career.

The story about the draftee who took his medicine chest into the jungles of the South Pacific was a superb vehicle for a couple of the 'speciality' numbers that Danny had said he was frightened of being limited to by other studios. In addition to *Melody in Four-F*—now transferred to the deck of a huge troopship which miraculously had the acoustics of a concert-hall and where no one seemed to notice that the young soldier was a wanted man (for secreting on board the Army nurse with whom he was in love), there was the *Lobby Number*—otherwise known as *Manic Depressive Pictures Presents . . .*,

This, too, was by Sylvia Fine—'I'm a wife-made man,' Kaye only partly joked; 'She has a wonderful head on my shoulders,' and captured perfectly the mood of many people sitting in the theatre watching at that precise moment.

Danny, with his friends Dana Andrews, Dinah Shore and Constance Dowling were waiting in a line in the spacious lobby of a cinema. Danny suddenly went into a whimsical mood and provided the perfect illustration of all the frustrations felt by movie audiences as they wait for a film to begin—the credits for the studio, Manic Depressive Pictures, the title and everyone who ever had anything to do with it, including 'Terpsichory by Dachery and Dickery by Dock'.

For years afterwards—until they got to know him for *Minnie the Moocher* and *Ballin' The Jack*, to say nothing of *Tubby the Tuba*—it was this number that people associated with Danny Kaye and for which they begged him when he appeared to sensationally successful results at the Palace, New York or the London Palladium. There is not the slightest doubt that *Up In Arms* created Danny Kaye the film star—thanks to the inspiration of Sam Goldwyn, who would, of course, put it all down to dyeing his hair blond.

Virginia Mayo had equal hopes of being made a top star as a result of *Up In*

Arms. Instead, she is simply one of the Goldwyn Girls, seen climbing a ladder on to the troopship and then sunning herself, painting her nails on deck.

Whether Frances had anything to do with this cannot be firmly established, but since she vetted all the Goldwyn Girls—with and without capital 'G's—it may be assumed that the veto on Miss Mayo doing any more work in the film had something at least to do with her.

Miss Mayo told me: 'Mrs Goldwyn was always around a lot of the time, although I didn't see a lot of her. Goldwyn himself always seemed to be interested in making me a star. It was his perception of me and why, he told me, he was going to keep sending me off to dramatic coaches.'

As she said: 'He was constantly on my neck.' And on the phone day and night. 'He'd ring me and say: "I want you to come in. I've got a new coach for you." It was a bee in his bonnet, and once he had one of those bees it was difficult to get it to go away. I was a very eager student and didn't need all that. But he would occasionally say: "Look you were very good in that." He gave me the same coach who had been teaching Ingrid Bergman, so I guess that was a compliment.'

It wasn't a compliment not to use her in *Up In Arms*. 'He said he didn't think I was ready for it, which disappointed me I can tell you.'

Sam certainly thought that by doing the picture at all he was helping the war effort, making the Japanese out to be dangerous idiots and at the same time aiding morale in America and the other allied countries.

It was this sense of patriotism he would have welcomed from the movie exhibitors of America. Instead, it provided him with one of his not infrequent opportunities to declare war on the theatre owners.

He had had enough of these men paying a flat rental for his pictures. He wanted a percentage of what a film took. Since they wouldn't play ball, he decided that *Up In Arms* wouldn't be offered to any of them. It was part, he declared, of his 'long fight against monopolistic policies'.

He had announced a war with the McNeil-Naify Company, which ran 100 theatres in and around San Francisco, where they were based, and other parts of California and Nevada—in Reno they controlled all five cinemas.

Sam decided that opening his own theatre was the answer. He knew he was playing Don Quixote, but he thought he should at least tilt towards the big screen windmill and its sails (sales).

He tried to hire the State Auditorium, but since it was State property, it was declared out of bounds to a private commercial organization.

So he hired the El Patio Ballroom in Reno—immediately adjoining the railway tracks.

He had trouble there. The owners were got at by the theatre monopoly who managed to persuade the local fire chief that Sam's portable projection-box didn't meet with his own fire regulations.

Sam then planned to show the film through a window. McNeil-Naify got an order ruling that this would cause obstruction—as would building

America's first drive-in cinema on a parking lot, which was another one of Sam's plans.

In case he could still get away with showing *Up In Arms* at the ballroom, the exhibitors took full-page advertisements in local newspapers—reminding prospective patrons that, if they did go there, they would be seeing a film 'sitting on uncarpeted floors' with 'the whistle of freight trains' in the background and having to endure the 'static in the sound system'.

But in this fight, for a change, Sam had the support of his former partners in United Artists, who, despite the old problems, were distributing the film for him.

With Mary Pickford by his side Sam personally nailed the last spike that held the 400th chair to its position on the false floor fitted to the ballroom, and hoped that the baiting would end. It wouldn't. More and more obstacles were put in his way.

The exhibitors retorted that it was not that they wouldn't buy Sam's films. It was more that he wasn't willing to sell them at other than exorbitant rates.

The movie had cost him $2 million and he was determined not to give it away—even if for the moment he appeared to be simply throwing away more money by renting ballrooms. Of course, he couldn't do that all over America, but he was hoping that his protest would register.

Mary Pickford spoke out loud and clear on his behalf—which the former silent star rarely did on anyone's behalf, not even her own.

'To produce *Up In Arms*', she said, 'Mr Goldwyn spent a whole year of intensive work and $2 million of his own money. This is a lot of time and a great deal of money. But to what avail? Only to be told upon completion that he shall not be permitted to show his picture except as dictated by monopoly. I would prefer to sit on a wooden chair, bench or even on the floor to see a fine film than to rest upon plush-covered opera chairs and be forced to witness a dull, stupid and boring film in the finest movie-palace in the country.

'We are making history here tonight—you, Mr Goldwyn and I—for we are taking our stand for the inalienable rights for free enterprise and as free Americans, to see to it that no one man, group, combine or monopoly shall dictate how and when.

'So I say it is not merely the question as to whether this one or dozens of Goldwyn's pictures do or do not play in Reno or the entire State of Nevada. It's rather the question of whether he or I, or other Americans, are to be given opportunity to carry on our lives and businesses openly and honestly.'

The trouble was that independent producers without theatres of their own were always forced to offer their products to chains on a take-it-or-leave-it basis—70 per cent of the theatres in America at the time were controlled by the major studios. He was, therefore, not only fighting for his own rights—which had to be his major consideration—but was also becoming largely responsible for having studio control of theatres outlawed.

By nailing in the seat at the Nevada ballroom, he was also hammering in the first nail in the coffin of studio monopolies—and, by so doing, of the whole studio system, for without the theatres taking ticket money from patrons and paying income to the big film companies, there was no longer a ready market for their products. Without that market the studio could no longer be guaranteed full employment fifty-two weeks of the year. They would no longer be able to sell blocks of a dozen films to exhibitors outside their own control before those films were made. It was all going to change and Sam Goldwyn was the one who was changing it.

But could he beat the Establishment? If he couldn't then, of course, nobody could. But he could. He announced that he wasn't going to take a penny from the sale of tickets at the El Patio ballroom. All the receipts would be handed to the local Camp and Hospital Service Committee. Could the theatre owners object to that? Inwardly they did, but outwardly their opposition had to be stilled. And it was.

They allowed him to bring in his portable projection booth—but stipulated that he had to have a special print made on non-inflammable film. That alone cost him another $1,000. In fact, it was reckoned he had spent about $25,000 on his campaign and had only earned $1,000 in return.

But he made a great deal more—if only in publicity throughout the country for *Up In Arms*. There was, though, more.

At the time he was waging his war, the US Department of Justice filed a court application aimed at forcing the big distributors to get out of the theatre business within three years. It would take a little longer than that, but eventually America's anti-trust laws put paid to the kind of monopoly Sam had so assiduously been campaigning against himself.

He wasn't doing so badly by Danny Kaye either. The following year he was starring him in *Wonder Man*—which was even more successful for both star and producer. Kaye played a double part—a night-club performer and his twin brother, a studious 'schlemeil' who somehow became a brilliant entertainer when forced to enter his dead brother's body and perform numbers like Sylvia Fine's routine about the Russian singer who sneezed every time he was faced with a vase of flowers. He did a wonderful sneeze, did Danny Kaye.

The Kid From Brooklyn wasn't anything like as good, but Danny still had his contract and both he and his boss concluded that you couldn't win them all, all the time. Danny Kaye as a milkman who became a boxer took a little believing. But there was better to come. Including a remarkable piece of movie magic called *The Secret Life of Walter Mitty*.

Between these films, Sam had a new mission. And one again, it was Sam the patriot.

16
The Best Years of Our Lives

The first news was simply that Sam was going to England. That didn't surprise many people. He had been going to England for years, selling his products, telling people how great American films were and having the satisfaction that most people truly believed him. It was still wartime and most private flying overseas had long been curtailed. However, he *was* Sam Goldwyn and February 1945 was to everybody's mind near the end of the fighting.

All anyone was told was that this was going to be a 'special mission'—the details of which were being held back by the Foreign Economic Administration. Presumably, thought those who bothered to think at all, this was an attempt to find new ways of selling Goldwyn movies when the war was over—after all, it would bring in foreign dollars and that couldn't be bad.

Later, it appeared that the US Embassy in Grosvenor Square had put an office at his disposal. Could that mean that he wasn't simply helping Goldwyn Productions?

It could and it did. His visit, when he did finally agree to talk to newsmen, had 'nothing whatsover' to do with the movies. One was also able to assume that it had nothing whatsoever to do with gloves. Therefore, the 63-year-old (give or take a year or two) Mr Goldwyn was going into a totally new undertaking. Suddenly, the man who most people thought couldn't speak English properly was to be a fully accredited diplomat.

While in London he had dinner with Churchill. Lord Beaverbrook entertained him royally. After a few minutes they ignored his accent, accepted the Goldwynisms which assuredly were dropped as frequently on these occasions as any other and accepted him for what he was, a sometimes brilliant man with a tremendous command of the situation and a perfect charm. 'But he was as tough as nails,' producer David Rose, who was with him, recalled.

Then it began to be clearer. 'I am here', he said, 'on a fact finding mission on reverse lend-lease.' Lend-lease being the method by which America provided ships, aircraft and other wartime equipment in exchange for bases in Britain and the sharing of intelligence; but now the idea was that to put Europe on its feet, it would have to start making and selling things—particularly to the United States.

But he couldn't totally ignore movies.

Suddenly, he was declaring that Hollywood wasn't just the centre of the American film industry, it represented the pictures of the world. 'To those in Great Britain who argue against the importation of Hollywood talent, I say: You are short-sighted. They don't take jobs. They make jobs. The sooner we forget the idea of British stars or American stars, the better we will be. I don't like this idea of Britain and America. I resent it. I think after this war we should live together.'

That comment couldn't have pleased America better had it been written personally by President Roosevelt sitting by his own fireside in the White House. As it was, the President was sick—no one officially knew he was dying—but still in control, and he did like it. So did Churchill. He sent off a cable to Roosevelt commending him on his choice of diplomat.

Sam revelled in the role. No longer did he have to be, if not ashamed, then wary of his lack of education, the ability to stand in the company of the wise and the worldly. Nothing made him prouder than to accept the invitation of the Master of Balliol College, Oxford, to talk to the dons and their students.

Everyone had passed a lot of water since they had last seen Sam Goldwyn so happy.

'For years', he told them in what seemed like an impromptu speech, 'I've been known for saying "include me out". But today I'm giving it up for ever. From now on, let me say, "Oxford and Balliol include me in".' The Gelbfisz family in Warsaw, if any of them were still alive— and it soon became obvious that they had all perished in death camps—would have been very proud. Frances was, too. And so was Sam Junior, who was still Sammy to his parents.

'Understanding alone can save our world from future wars,' he told his audience. 'Only information and learning can create that necessary understanding. The newspapers, films and radio of Great Britain and the United States of America have done an outstanding job in giving our free peoples truthful information.

'Germany burned the books and, as a result, she herself is now burning.' It was a profound statement and you couldn't help go along with this new kind of Goldwyn philosophy.

In that same spirit of truth he was to say before long that America's films were ten times as good as Voice of America broadcasts. Well, it was difficult to argue with that.

And he thought the delegates to the first United Nations conference to be held in San Francisco should go to England and to Europe to see what the Germans had done while burning people and buildings as well as books.

He—or rather his current ghost-writer—wrote a feature for *The New York Times* magazine. He wrote of 'The Future Challenge of the Movies' and repeated his gospel of the responsibility of the movie-makers.

The cinema was the world's best educator. 'There will be a better place if the soldiers who come back understand the European viewpoint as well as the

American.' In that spirit he was given permission to make a film biography of General Eisenhower who led the Allied troops from Normandy to the final victory in Germany. It didn't happen as a feature film, which is perhaps fortunate. Within seven years Eisenhower would be President.

Sam was embarking on a personal crusade to make the film business useful and decent. And for once one didn't have to be cynical about it. He really showed every sign now of taking his responsibilities seriously without having a personal axe to grind.

After all, the world was changing. A war had been fought and was being won using totally new methods. As he declared in August 1945: 'This atom bomb is dynamite.'

He was warning about the possibility of a new gangster era. Did the film industry want to follow the First World War pattern and show more and more glorifications of a different kind of battle—the Gang War? He pleaded for a different approach as 1945 melted into 1946.

He was addressing his remarks to the man who now ran what was still called the Hays Office, Eric Johnston, the new President of the Motion Picture Producers and Distributors of America.

'Since the return of peace,' he said, ' . . . dangerous symptoms have appeared on to the American scene. Juvenile delinquency has risen sharply. Violence and bloodshed are not laid aside and quickly forgotten in the days of peace and plenty, for not everyone *has* peace and plenty.'

Some studios were already making new gangster pictures. 'Hollywood,' he went on, 'can exploit it, glorify it, help bring about another gangster era and reproduce another jazz age. It has the alternative, however, of fighting it and helping lead young women and men to normal, decent standards. The answer is in industry self-regulation. I am sure that if the case were properly presented and kept before the film industry, a unanimous support would back you in finding a solution to this great problem.'

Whatever he did now seemed to have some bearing on what he had seen in England. No one would suggest that he wasn't interested in making money any more. Certainly no one with any sense at all would think that he had stopped loving the movie business or even knowing what went into a good film. But the priorities looked as though they were changing.

And that was how he came to produce what many regard as the most important film of his career.

The Best Years of Our Lives was so real that today it stands up as as good an idea of what life was like for families in the United States in 1945–46 as a local weekly newspaper.

The idea for it was Frances's. According to Sam Junior she saw a photograph in a magazine which showed homecoming troops and started wondering what sort of life they had in store for themselves.

The magazine was probably the 7 August 1944 issue of *Time*. On the train in which they were travelling, a group of Marines had chalked the message

'Home Again'. The magazine had suggested in its caption that it might not be all happiness for the men once the war was over and they had settled themselves in front of their own fireplaces. It was that notion which had got Frances thinking.

How indeed would they settle down? Would the adjustment period with their families be too difficult for them? Would romances that budded before the war or during it now bloom? Would marriages that were shaky when the man was called up now crash? And what about careers? Would the promise shown to be so remarkable before Pearl Harbour now materialize? But hardest of all was the question of the men who had been wounded and maimed by serving their country. Could they settle in? Would their families and loved ones accept them?

They were questions that people were asking themselves but which no one ostensibly involved in the entertainment industry dared to ask. Frances suggested the idea to Sam and he agreed to ask them.

A story was commissioned in true Goldwyn style. He didn't go to a hack screen-play writer. He asked for a story treatment from Mackinlay Kantor, who wrote a great deal of fiction based on historical fact. War and its aftermath—notably the Civil War—were his speciality.

Kantor wrote well and incisively. Instead of merely coming forward with a treatment, he produced a novel with a title called *Glory For Me*. Sam had the film rights option before it was sent to a publisher. Not that he liked it all that much. The book was written in blank verse, which he didn't pretend to understand. As he might have said, he paid a man $12,000 to produce a treatment, instead of which he gave him a poem.

And it didn't even rhyme. It was Frances who persuaded Sam to take a second look at it.

Within nine months a director and a screen-play writer were retained.

Glory For Me was about three homecoming war veterans and the problems they faced. Sam thought it was right to have his picture directed by a man who had just returned from the war himself. He chose William Wyler, who had done just that.

He thought someone who had gone through the pressures of wearing an Army uniform—albeit a well-tailored officer's suit—and was now taking up where he had left off in civilian life would do a better job than one who had spent his war doing little more than complaining about food shortages and fuel rationing.

Wyler had actually lost the hearing in his left ear from being too close to a gun on the aircraft *Memphis Belle*. He made a highly -praised film (President Roosevelt sat with him at a preview and declared it should be required viewing for the nation) about the last mission of that Flying Fortress called *Memphis Belle*.

His war-time experiences made him more than ready to deal with the painful transition from war to peace.

Wyler liked *Glory For Me*, but thought another writer should do the screen-play, which was a different art altogether. He chose Robert E. Sherwood. It was now clear that such a high-powered team were being brought in to produce an extremely important movie.

It would be bascally the same story as Kantor's—about three men on the same plane home, an Air Force officer who was born in poverty, two-timed by the cheap girl he married and who now falls for the daughter of the sergeant on the plane with him—a bank official in civilian life. No matter how hard either of these two will find their adjustment, for both of them it will be extremely easy compared with the third member of their party—war-wounded Homer.

Very little of this was changed. The officer is no longer divorced by his wife from the wrong side of the tracks. Instead, he wants something more from love than the girl he had originally had. The biggest change would be in Homer. Both Wyler and Sherwood agreed that he couldn't be the man made a virtual spastic by his wounds—totally unable to co-ordinate his movements. Having an actor playing a man like that would inevitably look false and probably insulting. Instead, they thought they would have an amputee—such people were easy to impersonate on screen. For years, actors had walked around sets with arms or legs fastened behind them. Laurence Olivier had done a splendid job just five years before playing Horatio Nelson.

They went round the wards of military hospitals. The men knew why they were there. They saw the amputees and were not surprised by the reactions they got. Here were the successful, virtually unscathed millionaires from Hollywood who were going to make even more money out of someone else's tragedy.

They tried to show that what they were doing was honouring these people, but few of them were convinced.

It was Wyler who remembered seeing a documentary about the use of artificial limbs. The Army itself had made the film, featuring a man called Harold Russell.

Russell had himself lost both hands, dealing with some dynamite that exploded too soon. He hadn't even had the satisfaction of losing those limbs in action. It had happened on manoeuvres while still in the States.

The director found him—thanks to one of the patients in the ward he and Sherwood had visited. 'He's lucky,' the man told him.

That seemed a strange judgement on a young fellow without hands. But the amputee stood by it. 'He's got his elbows.' As he said, with elbows you can have 'claws' fitted.

They met Russell and talked to him. They thought he could act. Wyler said he was chosen not simply because he had those 'claws' which were strapped on by ugly leather thongs but because he had adapted so well to his enforced life-style.

For the banker they picked Fredric March, who was looking for something new after having been rejected in favour of William Powell for the lead in *Life*

With Father. His role in *The Best Years of Our Lives* was to prove considerably more satisfactory, both for him and for the picture.

Dana Andrews was chosen for the officer and Virginia Mayo—now obviously having passed the Goldwyn acting tests—played the cheap wife, who he for the moment didn't know was two-timing him.

There were other problems selecting the banker's wife and daughter. Both Sam and Wyler wanted Teresa Wright for the daughter's role—she had acquitted herself so well in *Pride of the Yankees*, that she seemed an obvious choice.

But who could play her mother? They wanted an attractive actress, not a stereotyped mother image. But would such a woman want to play the mother of Teresa Wright?

They plumped for Myrna Loy, but for the reason they anticipated, she wasn't keen. So the Goldwyn charm was brought in. She was invited to dinner by Frances at which both she and her husband told her how important the part was—and how young Teresa Wright was and how it could be assumed that she, too, had married early.

Myrna was more easily convinced than either of the Goldwyns expected. But she wasn't that happy about having Wyler direct. 'I hear he's a sadist,' she told them.

It was a moment for Goldwyn loyalty. 'Of course not,' he said soothingly, smiling to disarm her. 'He's just a very mean fellow.'

The final casting was in the part of Wilma, the girl to whom Homer comes home and marries. She was the one who had to share his future, while at the same time getting used to what must have begun as the horror of seeing him take off his 'claws'.

Cathy O'Donnell was cast. No one could be sure that her initial wincing at seeing Homer remove those artificial 'hands' was just good acting. She had to see it actually happen, not in a clinical way but in what was presumed to be a moment of intimacy.

There was one other piece of 'casting' that had to be settled—of an aircraft 'graveyard' in which a collection of bombers and fighters built for the war, but prepared too late for use, were lying and decaying, minus engines. Wyler had spotted the graveyard—with literally hundreds of these planes falling to pieces, covered in ever-deeper layers of dust—in Ontario. He reported his find to Sherwood with the instruction: 'We've got to use this.'

The use was made when Dana Andrews goes back there, in search of what had been his own glory—the plane which made this former soda jerk into an officer and a gentleman.

It was extremely symbolic.

Writing in the magazine *Screen Writer*, Wyler said: 'We did nothing in the interior of the B–17 except show Fred Derry (Andrews) seated and staring out through the dusty plexiglass. Then, we went to a long exterior shot of the plane, in which we could see the engine nacelles, stripped of engines and propellers. As we panned from nacelle to nacelle you heard motors starting up as though there really were engines in them, and the plane was starting up for a take-off . . . .'

The Best Years of Our Lives was to prove not just the best film of Goldwyn's life, but also the best to date with which either Wyler or Sherwood had had any contact.

The music by Hugo Friedhofer was appropriately stirring for a picture that lasted more than three hours (*Gone With The Wind* apart—it was three hours, forty minutes—an almost unheard of length).

Goldwyn didn't like the score at first—although he was finally convinced it was so good it would win him an Academy Award.

Emile Newman, head of the music department, was constantly bombarded with calls from Goldwyn about the music. Every day there would be at least one from him, asking when it would be ready, when it was going to be scored, how would it fit into the final picture.

Finally, there was a call in which Goldwyn sounded hesitant. 'What's the matter Mr Goldwyn?' Newman asked him, pressing the phone closer to the mouthpiece.

'Nothing,' said Sam.

'Are you sure?' pressed the musician.

'Sure, I'm sure,' said Sam into the phone. 'What's the matter? Do I look bad?'

The film was ready for release in January 1947. Wyler begged Goldwyn to get it out the previous month—so that it could qualify for the Academy Awards to be presented for 1946 movies. 'Do you think it'll win anything?' Sam asked him. Wyler said he thought it might.

Sam was by now so excited that he was telling people: 'I don't care if it doesn't make a cent—just so long as every man, woman and child in the country sees it.'

The January booking was cancelled and the picture opened at the Astor in New York on 22 November 1946.

Because it was a long film, special 'road show' prices had to be charged. In addition, a massive advertising campaign was initiated, with huge posters going up all over the country and abroad, too. It became the most talked of film since, in fact, *Gone With The Wind*.

Also the most appreciated. General Omar Bradley liked it so much that, in his capacity as head of the Government's Veterans Administration, he wrote to Sam telling him he was making it compulsory viewing for his subordinates in Washington.

It would help them, he said, 'to realize what these veterans mean to the people of this country. I cannot thank you too much for bringing this story to the American people . . .you are not only helping us to do our job, but you are helping the American people to build an even better democracy out of the tragic experiences of this war.'

At the same time, the War Department announced it was using the film to 're-educate' Germans.

Wyler's optimism was justified. Entering the movie for the 1946 awards, instead of waiting for 1947 when later films would have been more clear in the minds of the judging panel, proved a wise move.

Sam went on the Bob Hope radio show, fully primed to give his new film the best plug possible—after all, the Hope ratings were practically the highest on radio.

The script said that Bob was to ask him—calling him 'Mr Goldwyn' to emphasize his importance—how business was at Formosa Avenue since his own two Goldwyn films had been completed. To this, Sam was supposed to reply: 'I'll tell you Bob—since you left, we've had the best years of our lives.'

Bob asked the question. And Sam replied: 'Since you've left, things are better than ever.'

The audience thought it was a simple interview question and answer, but Hope, realizing the throwing away of a marvellous plug, was doubled up.

Sam himself won his own first Oscar—as producer of the best film of the year. It was just one of a clutch of Academy Awards for what everyone in the industry now simply called *Best Years*.

Sam was also presented with the Irving Thalberg Memorial Award. It was given for his 'creativity over the years (which) reflects consistently high quality of motion-picture production'.

Among those with smaller roles in the picture had been pianist-songwriter Hoagy Carmichael. As Sam wound up his speech of thanks to all those involved in the film he said he had to mention that great artist 'Hugo Carmichael'. By Goldwyn standards that was practically accurate.

Oscars also went to William Wyler, Robert Sherwood, Fredric March, Hugo Friedhofer and to Harold Russell for best supporting actor. It was his first and only acting part (apart from the documentary) but this recognition of his brilliant performance was not done for sentimental reasons.

Most of the people concerned made a lot of money from the picture, too—it would take more than a million dollars in its first year and, it was claimed, more at the box-office than *Gone With The Wind*.

The salaries paid to the stars and the senior technicians were high and for Wyler and Sherwood a share of the profits—20 per cent for the director and 5 per cent for the writer. But Wyler wasn't satisfied, and more than ten years after the movie was first shown, he sued for $408,356 which he claimed was owed to him.

He said, in effect, that Goldwyn had 'cooked the books'. And that, indeed, was how it looked. What Sam's very clever accountants had done was to add the percentages already paid, to the expenses of the operation, and since the money to be paid was based on profits, the point at which these occurred was seen to get more and more remote as the taking piled up.

Eventually, the matter was sorted out without bringing in a judge and jury—with Sam saying his director made a total of $1,400,000 from the film.

It left a sour taste from a film that suited most people's palates.

Sam tried not to have his rows with directors and other exhibitors on the set. He was always there, watching things going on, but he left the fights to his room with its grand piano and with his always-smart ('smart not pretty', says David Rose) secretaries out of the way.

He didn't always care about audiences for his rows, though. 'He flared up at Wyler with me in the room', Rose told me. 'I just walked away. He had a hell of a temper. But he was a great, great man in my book.'

With *Best Years* completed, Sam settled down for something audiences might consider entertainment.

17
Come And Get It

If Sam *was* having The Best Years of His Life—and the box office reports and the Press reviews seemed to say so—he wasn't so sure about the rest of the film industry. He had a number of lighter projects up his sleeve, including the new Danny Kaye film, but he thought the rest of Hollywood ought to get busy and produce more 'significant' films.

It continued to be an amazing fact of film life that whatever Samuel Goldwyn chose to say the papers were there, with notebooks metaphorically poised at the ready, to listen to him and tell their readers what they'd heard. It was a situation that irked his competitors who were free with their back-handed, or perhaps it should be back-projected, compliments.

Darryl Zanuck took his hat off to his 'genius' rival.

He didn't like Sam's suggestion that the other Hollywood studios had 'run dry' of ideas and were 'living on borrowed ideas of the past'. As Zanuck said: 'There is nothing wrong with Hollywood that cannot be cured by the liquidation of self-appointed oracles.' That was playing it very tough indeed.

But it was true Sam did like to pontificate.

The Best Years of Our Lives had gone a long way to promote the kind of America Sam wanted to see—he described it as a 'kind of love song in this country of ours, in war or out of it, it doesn't matter'.

But there hadn't been enough movies showing the 'real' America. The country was being distorted by Hollywood. No one doubted that, but when Sam Goldwyn said it in a *New York Times* magazine piece again people took notice.

Zanuck's view had not been universal. One man wrote to *The Times* saying that Sam's views represented a 'kind of statesmanship'. By all accounts, he was not a Goldwyn employee.

'America is not the Cinderella land which Hollywood has too often portrayed it to be. It is not the racket-ridden private domain of the Scarfaces and the Little Caesars which Hollywood once pictured. America is not a land composed almost exclusively of neurotics and psychoanalysts as a recent cycle of pictures might lead one to believe. It is only true that we have given currency to the impression that Americans are luxury loving, law-defying and self-satisfied.'

And he went on: 'The American film has not often enough turned the spotlight on imperfections in our system which need correction.'

Of course there was more carping. But it didn't bother Sam. On the contrary, since they always spelt his name right, he liked just to hear and read about people quoting what he said.

Mind you, sometimes it was difficult to quite understand what he meant. As he told *Life* magazine, too many did misinterpret his motives. 'Every time I don't agree with somebody, they call it a disagreement.'

It was difficult to argue with that, but most people took his meaning.

Zanuck, however, did not.

'It is remarkable that Sam Goldwyn has only now discovered that the screen is a medium of enlightenment as well as entertainment. Most Hollywood producers dicovered this long ago and practised it both during and before the war.'

As for 'significant' films turned out by the studios, 'If he doesn't have any significant pictures to release, if he's putting out some little musical comedy or other, he will issue a statement that it's Hollywood's job to brighten the lives of the people and not worry them about serious issues. And then, when he has a significant picture to release and he knows its going to be praised for its significance—something like *The Best Years of Our Lives*—he will wait until just a day before it comes out and issue a statement saying that Hollywood isn't producing enough significant pictures.'

Zanuck was still admiring Goldwyn's 'chutzpah' although it was not a word he used. 'It's chemically impossible for Sam ever to see any other viewpoint than his own. There's nothing intellectual about it. It isn't a matter of arguing, or logic. It's just chem-i-cally im-possible.'

The Twentieth Century-Fox boss had more than one encounter with Sam, not including his appeal for Tyrone Power those years before. Once Sam rang him complaining about a certain company. He said he was never going to deal with them again.

Zanuck asked for details and after Goldwyn had spilled out his heart he said he thought Sam was wrong. The company had been totally right. His rival hit the roof. 'That's the trouble with this industry,' he said. 'They never stick together.'

Sam then put down the phone.

But, said Zunuck, Goldwyn 'is one of the really great successes of Hollywood. You just cannot argue with that fact. This is a very tough business and anyone who has stuck with it the way Sam has, and stayed close to the top from the beginning, is entitled to a bit of sunshine now.'

David O. Selznick suffered a similar kind of Goldwyn relationship as Zunuck. Sam had suggested that they use the same studio—and both could thereby save a lot of money on office rentals and other financial headaches.

Selznick was frightened this might affect his independence and said No. He wasn't interested. Goldwyn was furious.

Despite everything, Selznick and Goldwyn had a great deal of mutual admiration for each other. Selznick called Sam 'a superb constructionist'. Now a different kind of construction was coming into question.

Fifteen minutes after having made the phone call, Sam was in Selznick's office, 'You're afraid of me, aren't you?' he charged.

Selznick had nothing to gain or to lose. So he admitted it. 'Yes, I am,' he said. 'Why should you think I'm the only man in Hollywood who can live with you?'

Goldwyn wasn't sure how to take that. 'I'll tell you what I'll do,' he said, offering the kind of consolation that makes antagonists want to accept the first proposition they had turned down, 'If you or any of your people ever think you're not getting a fair deal, you can come direct to me—and I will prove to you how wrong you are.'

'That's what I'm afraid of,' said Selznick.

As Zanuck said, nobody else would dare do it. But Sam dared.

'It doesn't faze Sam. He doesn't bat an eye.'

The critics weren't batting many eyes either. To The *Los Angeles Times* the picture stood for 'the better American spirit. It deserves to be seen by people throughout today's chaotic world. It typifies the kind of life most people know and understand in this country.'

But for all that, it was equally true that if a nation fighting for its life wanted escape, those coming back home and facing the problems those in *Best Years* faced wanted it too.

Danny Kaye's *The Secret Life of Walter Mitty* hasn't always been seen as such, but looking back now with the hindsight advantage of close to forty years, it is undoubtedly the best of all his movies and perhaps the funniest comedy film the Goldwyn organization ever produced.

Sam wasn't keen on filming the James Thurber story—about a timid little man who dreams of glorious adventures. He didn't think that, to the sophisticated Thurber fans who may have picked it up in an anthology or read it in *The New Yorker* apart, it had much appeal.

Sam read *Mitty* in synopsis—which is a little strange since the whole tale only occupies four pages in its original printed form.

He finally agreed to having a script done. But afterwards he said it wasn't his cup of coffee at all. 'Could you be more specific?' Kenneth Englund, who with Everett Freeman wrote the piece, asked. 'Yes, I'll be more specific,' Sam consented. 'I don't like the last sixty pages.'

Englund was sent off to New York to talk the matter over with Thurber. Sam said he knew he would be able to handle it, 'because Ken, you are charming'.

But not so charming as to be able to solve the problems overnight.

Englund was to write that Goldwyn ordered him by telegram to phone immediately he got into his Manhattan hotel.

That was when he told him:

'You've got ten days at the most! I've set the shooting date for 15 March. Goodbye, Ken.'

Changes *were* made, reasonably to Thurber's own satisfaction. He then wrote Sam a note, with thanks for sending Englund to him. He said:

'I feel that I have learned a great deal in a short time about some of the problems that face a motion-picture producer and motion-picture writer.'

The completed film was as close to genius time a comedy has ever achieved, mostly due to Danny Kaye, who has always been more than something of a Walter Mitty himself—after all, he is a frustrated surgeon, has a commercial jet pilot's licence, conducts symphony orchestras and is reputed to be the finest Chinese chef in the United States.

In this film he was the meek and mild magazine ideas man who imagines, in a series of beautiful tableaux, he is a Western hero, a Mississippi river-boat gambler, a sailing-ship captain, an IRA gunman on the run, a RAF Battle of Britain hero, a designer of women's hats (a superb opportunity for him to perform his speciality, *Anatole of Paris*) and, of course, a surgeon. These were many more than in the original story—in which Mitty only dreamed of being a lawyer, a surgeon and a US Naval pilot. But Sam knew it had to be a stage for which Danny could be Danny, again a *schlemiel* who has the most sophisticated dreams—and always to the sound of 'ta-pocket, ta pocket, ta-pocket' racing through his mind as he mends an anaesthetic machine with his fountain-pen or tells Virginia Mayo—again—not to worry as he stands at the helm of a storm tossed sailing-ship with an injured arm: 'Don't worry. It's only broken.'

The IRA scene was later dropped, ostensibly because of lack of time, but it could easily have caused a great deal of trouble, particularly in the United Kingdom.

Threaded between them all was a story about Nazi spies and the killing of an innocent old man, supposedly Virginia Mayo's uncle.

There were constant rows throughout production. One, which Ken Englund later reported was over the alleged over-abundance of satire in the picture. He was constantly reminded, said Englund, of George Kaufman's dictum that 'satire in the theatre is something that closes Saturday night'.

Sam worried about that, too. Sophistication, even to Quality Goldwyn, wasn't good for business. He told Englund, the writer remembered: 'Ken . . . let me tell you something for your own good as a writer in Hollywood, outside of a few thousand people, you are the only one in the rest of America who ever reads that *New Yorker* magazine.'

Englund pointed out that the story had been reprinted in *Reader's Digest*. Goldwyn said that that still wasn't as many as would see the movie.

In the end, there were additional changes made. Instead of having a hen-pecking wife, Walter was unmarried with a devilishly spoiled fiancée who had a harridan of a mother. His own mother had all the pacifity of Benito Mussolini.

Thurber worried about the humour in the story—his tale *had* been sophisticated and intensely psychological. He wasn't sure that he liked the idea of Danny interposing his German music teacher routine in the midst of his RAF flyer dream—when he is welcomed to the officers' mess by his adoring fellow-pilots. But it was a sure-fire Kaye act and Sylvia Fine persuaded Sam to allow it to stay.

Sam was even told by his commercial advisers that a film called *The Secret Life of Walter Mitty* wouldn't sell. Goldwyn himself wasn't sure—so he commissioned a public opinion organization to test the views of men and women in the Los Angeles streets. *The New York Time*, however, got to hear that *Mitty* was being filmed and said so. Changing the title after that would have undone all the value Goldwyn got from the advance publicity and so *The Secret Life of Walter Mitty* it stayed.

Sam heard that Thurber thought there was too much violence in the picture and sent his own regrets that the great writer might have believed it to be 'too blood and thirsty'. To which the writer replied that, more than that, he was also 'horror and struck'.

(Which was precisely what Michael Powell and Emeric Pressburger, the writers of the British film *Black Narcissus* might have thought. Sam said they had written one of the best pictures he had ever seen—*Black Neurosis*.)

Sam wasn't difficult to everybody. He liked what David Raksin (who had become a respected Hollywood name after writing the theme song for *Laura* four years earlier—the only case where a picture's music is better known than the movie itself) had done with the score for *Mitty*. Sam wanted the beguine sequence Raksin had written for the *Anatole of Paris* scene to become the main title theme.

Raksin tried to talk him out of it, but all Goldwyn did was tap him lightly on the cheek and say: 'I think this'll be better.' As Raksin told me: 'He could have tried twisting my arm and been difficult. But he was very nice—a remarkable guy. He *was* right. It *was* better for the picture.'

Sam had the finest musical talents on the picture—Sylvia, who wrote the numbers, Raksin, who arranged them and Gene Rose, who orchestrated them. Either of the last two could have done both jobs; both were established names, but there wasn't time for them to do so. 'While you are putting all your efforts into orchestrating a piece, you could be working on composing the next sequence,' Raksin told me.

Even the music men made up Goldwynisms—pretending they were feeding lines to newspapermen. 'Did you hear what Mr. Goldwyn said about . . . .'

At Raksin's suggestion, Goldwyn bought the rights to a Broadway show called *Billion Dollar Baby*. Raksin was given Gary Cooper's old dressing room—a living-room, bedroom, bathroom and music suite—to work on it.

Goldwyn wanted a completed treatment in twenty-four hours. The writers and the music men worked all night—'and I do mean all night'. Robert Russell did the initial screen-play, based on the Broadway story of gangsters and their molls.

Goldwyn sent for him to discuss it, 'champing at the bit', said Raksin, 'because he had to leave for New York at that moment'.

The first thing Sam said when Russell walked in was, 'Well, I hope it's not about gangsters.' Which was a strange thing to say—considering that the story he had bought was precisely about gangsters and nothing but gangsters and it was writing about gangsters that Russell had been doing all night.

But as Raksin said: 'He was the most impressive producer I ever met. He had class.'

Other people might not always have thought so. He still loved London. On one occasion he was royally entertained by the former cabinet minister Sir Samuel Hoare. 'Thank you,' he told him at the visit's end. 'And please come some time to Hollywood. You must visit me—and bring Mrs W. with you.'

Parties were frequently problematical when Sam was involved. Writer Harry Kurnitz gave one and the Goldwyns were treated as honoured guests. As they got ready to go, Kurnitz went up to Sam, shook his hand and said how pleased he had been to entertain him. 'Thank you,' said Sam. 'Can we drop you any place?'

After *The Secret Life of Walter Mitty* Danny was told he was to make *A Song Is Born*, which by Goldwyn standards was a cheapie. Not only would he have Danny Kaye starring as a music professor, but Virginia Mayo was conveniently on hand to play a singer running away from a gang . . . .

Did it all sound slightly familiar? Well, there was a clue in that the director was Howard Hawks—who just six years before had directed *Ball of Fire*. This was *Ball of Fire* remade—without the fire. And no one seemed to be having anything like a ball. But Sam didn't have to buy any story rights and the cast were under contract.

It was in colour, there were various famous musicians taking part, like Louis Armstrong, Benny Goodman, Charlie Barnet, Lionel Hampton and Tommy Dorsey. But that aside, the story was practically the same—the professors living with Kaye looked exactly like those residing (in exactly the same house) with Gary Cooper, except that now their speciality was music, rather than English.

Since the film followed on Kaye's triumphant appearance at the London Palladium it lost a lot of his enthusiasm. Now—having already temporarily left his wife Sylvia—Danny announced he was leaving Goldwyn. Sam wouldn't give him a clause in his contract that allowed him to work for other film companies, too. So he was getting out.

Danny admitted that might sound ungrateful. But that wasn't how he felt—as he noted at the time:

'Let me say that I consider Sam to be a great producer and to admit that he has been wonderful to me. No matter what he does, Goldwyn has a certain ever-present dignity that commands admiration and respect. I think it's because we all know how much he lives and loves pictures. He doesn't want the Goldwyn name attached to anything mediocre. But however much I like and admire Goldwyn, I have my own career to think about.'

But he didn't believe Sam was being entirely generous in his motives. 'I don't think Sam gave me my first break out of charity. He took a gamble with me and the dice came up eleven. We both profited by our relationship. And I'm sure that if my picture had lost money, he wouldn't have kept picking up my options. He's a realist, too. I belive that Goldwyn made an honest attempt to find something different for me in every picture we made. But there was a certain sameness about them and I felt that if I continued to do similar films people would get wise to my tricks and to my mannerisms.'

Sam for one had got used to Danny's tricks and mannerisms—a number of which were making fun of his own tricks and mannerisms. It may have seemed that he was biting the hand that laid the golden egg, but at parties he would imitate Goldwyn at the slightest chance and Sam laughed the loudest. It got so he could impersonate him on the phone so effectively that even Frances was taken in.

He would imitate Sam and make everyone who had ever had a single dealing with Goldwyn practically helpless. He could even do it by telepathy. Once, he phoned Sam at home in Laurel Lane from New York, 'Sam,' he told him, 'I'm doing the fish face'—and Goldwyn fell down, pounding the floor.

Now he was pounding that floor in anger. He didn't like his stars to leave him, especially those for whose success he took a share of credit.

He claimed to be a great believer in helping staff—though he still believed that a happy studio made poor pictures. A variation on this is that he was once worried by the fact that his story conferences were very quiet affairs. ('From quiet conferences come quiet pictures,' he said; not sure whether or not he liked them that way.)

He had formed a new company in which his employees owned half the stock. 'I believe the future trend is going to be towards co-operative effort.' Which might have sounded even communistic, if one didn't know Sam Goldwyn better.

It was a new business organization taking over from the firm he had headed for twenty-two years.

Samuel Goldwyn Production Inc., capitalized at $10 million, would produce four pictures a year. Sam himself would own half the stock; his employees would be able to buy in to the other half.

He explained his move as giving a chance to those who had given 'long years of service'. It would also recognize 'the contributions which individuals made towards the good of the company'.

The first to receive stock was Gregg Toland, head cameraman for Goldwyn who had worked at Formosa Avenue for twenty years.

As a gesture of thanks to people like Toland they could buy stock worth $100 a share for $1 each. But they would have to hold on to them for at least five years.

He explained: 'Our stockholders will consist of executives, creative talents, technicians and administrative experts—and no one else. Without their combined talents working together for a common purpose, ownership means little or nothing.'

It was indeed something of a revolution—and Sam recognized it. 'Up to now I have always owned my companies 100 per cent. But I believe this move will provide a greater incentive for individual initiative. This way all of the important people in the company will have a voice in its affairs. I don't want to have a lot of yes-men working for me. I never did like the idea of having yes-men around.'

Significantly, he was not offering shares to his stars—and that included Teresa Wright to whom he had just signed to a new seven-year contract—or to writers or directors. These were the people who were likely to disagree with him and he didn't want them turning up to company meetings. As things turned out, Sam owned a great deal more than half the shares, but those who had them really did feel as though they were taking their places in the business.

The real partner, though, was Frances. Sam is reputed to have told William Wyler at the time of their row over money from *Best Years* that he didn't make a penny from the film. Wyler asked him where his own profits had gone—'To Frances and Sammy,' he replied, not thinking he was saying anything untoward.

Everyone with even the remotest connection with the business knew how strong Frances's influence was.

As his friend and U.A. colleague David Rose told me:

'Frances was the greatest wife I've ever known for a fellow and worked in every way she could—particularly on things like costumes. But Sam's was the last word. There was no way of changing his mind when it was made up.'

She was also a superb hostess—complementing Sam, who entertained generously himself.

'He had people up at the house all the time, actors like Jimmy Stewart and some of the very important people who were very dear friends of his like Averell Harriman and Lord McGowan, head of Imperial Chemicals. He was the most charming host.'

The strange thing was that he was able to converse with people like them on an equal basis; Sam the uneducated immigrant and the products of the finest schools and universities in the world.

'Oh,' said Rose, 'but he was so well read. He could speak on any subject, on world affairs. He read every newspaper that was important.'

Relations between Sam and Sam Junior—'Sammy'—tended to be fraught when it came to business.

Goldwyn loved his only son as perhaps only a Jewish father could love a son, but he assumed he would follow in the business.

Ever since Sam had brought home scripts to read, Sammy had inevitably been involved. He picked up the business by osmosis. He knew what stories his father had in his script 'bank', knew what he was doing to them.

There was a huge bust-up when he discovered that Sam senior was about to dispose of a script which he thought would make a great movie—it was called *Hans Andersen* (the *Christian* part of the title was added later). That was a fight he won. His father held on to the script.

In others the youngster—he was still in his early twenties—was not so fortunate.

Years afterwards Sam Junior told about a discussion 'with another man who happens to have the same name as mine and who has produced some pretty fine pictures over the past forty years'.

That man told him—with some justice—the question everyone would ask would be 'How will he stack up against the old man?'

Frances had begged Sam not to bring him into the operation—she forecast it would create friction. She was right. After one spirited row, Sammy ran out of the house in a rage.

For a time he worked in London for the Rank Organization.

But always there was the spectre of what his father thought. As he said, his father told him:

'A name on the door doesn't make a producer. Better make a picture before you join my organization.'

Sam persuaded him to be an independent producer himself and make a film with Alan Ladd. Sammy lost everything he put into it—of his own money.

Of course, dealing with the older Sam outside the family was no easier—although it could be amusing, and usually was.

John Green, at one time head of the music department at MGM but who knew Sam socially, tells of one occasion when the welfare of his staff may not have been the consideration uppermost in the Goldwyn mind.

Green and he used to meet for breakfast at Sam's office—'and great breakfasts they were, too; wonderful coffee, brewed tea and great blueberry muffins and Danish pastries and things like that'—when they sat on the same film industry committee together.

They were interesting meetings, Green told me, because everyone there was always amazed at the man's punctuality—'considering that he walked most of the way with his chauffeur driving slowly behind'.

Because of his reputation, everyone else always came on time, too: 'You didn't come late for Sam Goldwyn,' as Green pointed out. But one day, it was Sam who wasn't on time.

'He finally got there about ten minutes late. There was no explanation or anything, but in that high, accented voice of his he announced: "Gentlemen, for your information I'd like to ask you a question . . . .'"'

On another day when Green was visiting that office on the north side of Formosa Avenue, a sound of fire-engine sirens penetrated the second-floor room.

As Green remembers it, that was a moment to cherish. Sam's windows commanded a view of that street. He sat with his back to that window with its Venetian blinds cutting out the light, and on that day the view was spectacular, to say the least. So was the sound penetrating the glass.

'You can't go a half hour without hearing sirens so close to Santa Monica Boulevard,' Green mused. And, as he recalled that was what happened that day as any other.

'So no one took much notice of these, except that they got closer—well sirens do get closer and then they go away . . . .'

These got closer, too; ever closer, 'Only they didn't go away.'

'Before long, one realized that they were so close, they were almost in Goldwyn's office—and for very good reason. Now you could see bellowing black smoke covering the windows, cutting out the light and even, it seemed, coming through the Venetian blind.'

At that point someone shouted: 'Sam, the fire's here. It's coming from the sound stage below.'

As Green remembers it, what happened next should one day form part of a Hollywood movie:

'His studio's burning down . . . Sam opens up the Venetian blind, opens the window and gives a holler to the people running below: "Go back to your desks, I do not pay you to run!" His studio was burning down, but all he could think of was that they weren't at their desks.'

Despite that, he remembers Sam with affection: 'He was a glove salesman, but you only had to meet him to realize that he had a very great sensitivity.'

There were those, on the other hand, who thought that perhaps he was a little too sensitive.

When his name was linked with a list of Hollywood personalities reputed to have been bilked of a total of millions of dollars by a card sharp, Sam retorted: 'The statement in the papers to the effect that I am reported to have lost a large sum of money to card sharps is a shocking falsehood made out of whole cloth . . . .'

No one was going to cheat him out of anything. That was why he formed the Samuel Goldwyn Music Publishing Corporation, in association with Chappell and Co. The concern would publish sheet music for future Goldwyn musicals.

It all helped swell the coffers of the Goldwyn organization and might aid, it was thought, a dozen good causes.

At about this time it was revealed that Sam had personally donated $5,000 to the Democratic cause at the 1945 Presidential election (He was not alone:

Ronald Reagan was among those listed as having helped the Democrats; in his case to the tune of $1,000).

But now he seemed to be indicating a certain leaning towards the right. If not entirely so. For instance, the menace of what would soon be called McCarthyism was hovering over much of Hollywood at that time.

J. Parnell Thomas was Chairman of the House Committee on Un-American Activities. He revealed the names of ten Hollywood writers whom he accused of aiding the Communist cause in their work. The 'Hollywood Ten' were victimized for years afterwards.

When Sam heard that Robert Sherwood was being accused of using *The Best Years of Our Lives* for propaganda purposes, he was incensed.

Sam wasn't going to allow that to happen to the man who had written his most successful movie ever.

He sent a detailed telegram to Thomas and asked all his fellow-moguls—including Louis B. Mayer, who was one of the most vociferous protagonists backing the committee's charges—to look to their own responsibilities in the matter. As he said, the studio heads like himself approved every line of every script. If Communist propaganda slipped in, it was up to the moguls to make sure that it was removed.

At one stage, Sam was subpoenaed. He then demanded, as *The New York Times* put it, that he be 'included in' and called to give evidence. It was preventing him leaving for Europe, he said. But he wasn't called.

Later, Sam visited President Harry S. Truman at the White House and told him how disturbed he was at the Un-American Activities Committee's behaviour. He said:

'Mr Thomas is looking at the movie industry through pink-coloured glasses.' Rather than Hollywood, it was the committee itself which was un-American. 'The movies are the greatest medium in the world for showing democracy at work and our way of life. It is one of the best ways to fight communism'.

The investigations, said Goldwyn, were a 'flop' and a 'disgraceful performance'. 'What is the matter?' he asked 'Are they afraid to call me?'

Just the same, it would be difficult to brand Sam as a fellow-traveller. By no stretch of the imagination was he a Communist sympathizer. Indeed for a long time he served as California Chairman of the Committee on the Present Danger, an organization set up by prominent American businessmen to 'guard against Soviet aggression'. Nor could it possibly be argued that politics were becoming more important to Goldwyn than his films.

While this was all going on, Sam had produced *The Bishop's Wife*. It starred Cary Grant and, in his best role to date, David Niven. Grant played an angel visiting a bishop (Niven) who was having trouble with his wife (Loretta Young).

It was not one of Sam's most successful pictures and certainly not the easiest to either get under way or then make, even though it was to be selected in Britain as the Royal Command film.

Grant—whom Sam insisted on having—wasn't available. Goldwyn kept ringing his MCA agent and offering more and more money. MCA kept saying no—until quite unexpectedly a film Grant was about to make was cancelled and so he fitted *The Bishop's Wife* in its place.

It has been suggested that Grant was originally cast as the bishop and Niven as the angel, but all the evidence points to Sam having had a Cary Grant angel in his plans all along.

Yet Sam didn't like his performance. It wasn't sexy enough, not manly. Grant said he liked playing it that way.

'You want me to be happy don't you?' asked the British-born star.

'I don't give a damn if you're happy,' said Sam. 'You are going to be here for only a few weeks and this picture will be out for a long time. I would rather you should be unhappy here, then we can all be happy later.' There were others who had heard that before.

By all accounts Grant played things Sam's way and was miserable most of the time he was on the set.

Goldwyn didn't care how a mere actor wanted to play it.

Robert Sherwood was commissioned to write the script. He did, but nobody liked it. What should have been a frothy piece of gossamer (wasn't that how angels were supposed to be clothed?) seemed plodding and heavy.

But the man he blamed was the director William Seiter.

'I was with Sam watching the dailies,' David Rose recalled for me. 'He hated them. So he fired Seiter. It cost him $900,000; paid him his full salary and brought in Henry Koster in his place. Then he started all over again. That's the sort of man Sam was.'

Goldwyn was to say about that—in an interview in *Life*—'I am a lone wolf. I am a rebel. I defy every convention. I make a picture to please me. If it pleases me there is a good chance it will please other people. But it has to please me first. Yes, I am difficult. I must be—other people say so. There was a lot of criticism because I threw away nearly $900,000-worth of work on *The Bishop's Wife*. I can't help that. That's the way I make pictures.'

It wasn't his only problem once the film had been made. Loretta Young hated him—because he said she was too pretty. 'A bishop's wife is not a glamour girl,' he told her, using the 'in' phrase of the moment. 'I don't like those layers of make-up.'

Sam was proud to say that she came over and kissed him after seeing the rushes.

He wasn't always sure, however, *who* his leading lady was. In his usual manner, he kept getting her name wrong and constantly called her Laurette Taylor. It was Henry Koster who put him right. He pointed out that Laurette had been dead for months.

'That's funny,' Miss Young remembered for me Goldwyn saying, 'I was talking to her only a few moments ago.'

Goldwyn still wasn't satisfied after the first preview. He rang up Billy Wilder and asked him to come and see it. Wilder brought his then partner Charles Brackett. Neither of them had been connected with the movie, but they agreed to provide three more scenes that Koster could shoot three days later. The scenes were made and Sam said he'd pay the writers $25,000.

Billy Wilder told me what happened next: 'We were invited to dinner with Sam. We thought about that $25,000. With taxes the way they were, we wouldn't have been able to keep much of it, so we thought it would be in our future interest to be magnanimous and say we didn't want it. We told Sam that. He replied: "That's funny. I've come to the same conclusion".'

Other conclusions to which he came were more, shall we say, unilateral. Sam's help toward Black causes made him politically suspect in some quarters. When he accepted the chairmanship of the film division of the Urban League Service Fund, he said: 'I have undertaken this task because I am convinced that the Urban League economical and social service programme is indispensable in the alleviation of the obstacles facing the Negro people.'

His support of Sherwood continued to dog him.

Sam had threatened to publish the text of his telegram should Sherwood be further investigated—to say nothing of prosecuted. But nothing more was heard of the matter and the Un-American Activities Committee—among whose members was a certain Congressman, Richard M. Nixon—went on with their Hollywood baiting in other directions.

All in all, it was a very brave step for Goldwyn to have taken; another way in which he was showing himself to be apart from the other Hollywood moguls.

He was not apart from them in another political cause that some might have thought to be much closer to home—Zionism.

At first, particularly in the early days of the war, Sam's reluctance to get involved in the campaign to establish a Jewish State was seen as yet another symptom of his super Americanism. Like Louis B. Mayer and the rest—David O. Selznick once got himself into a tremendous controversy over whether people regarded him primarily as an American or as a Jew—he thought very carefully before associating himself. Identification with Zionism could be seen as yet another question mark on their loyalty to Uncle Sam and the Stars and Stripes.

In the early days of the war Sam had even gone public in saying that he believed stories of the concentration camps and the preliminary stages of a holocaust were 'probably exaggerated'.

Yet when Selznick apparently had a change of heart and allowed his name to go forward supporting the idea of a Jewish Brigade fighting side by side with the Allies—something that would take until 1944 to get under way—Sam offered his full support and attended a rally addressed by a retired British officer, Colonel John H. Patterson, who had commanded the Jewish Legion—a forerunner of what this rally wanted to establish now—in the First World War.

The trouble was that Patterson over-played his hand. Instead of positively fighting for a Jewish Brigade in the British Army, he attacked his own country as being anti-Semitic. That was not the sort of thing to say in Hollywood, particularly a Hollywood that was pledging support for Britain's war effort.

In the end, Sam stood up and ordered Patterson to 'sit down, sit down'.

A total of $130,000 was pledged—very little of which was ever actually donated.

It would take the eve of the actual establishment of Israel for Sam and his fellow-moguls to offer real financial support.

In 1947 he called for the support of 'every creed and race' for the United Jewish Welfare Fund of Los Angeles and said that Los Angeles's target of $8,500,000 would be set off with a sizeable donation from himself—towards 'relief and rehabilitation in Palestine and the carrying of Jews to Palestine'. Immigration to Palestine at that time was strictly illegal, but American Jews had finally decided to fight the British Labour Government's anti-Zionist policy. In the forefront of the campaign was Ben Hecht—who upset Britain (and so the British market for his films) by saying that his heart did a little dance every time a British soldier was killed in Palestine. Sam didn't back that, but he knew that American public opinion was definitely swinging in favour of the establishment of a Jewish State.

'History', Sam declared, 'holds Hitler guilty of the murder of six million Jews. History will also hold us accountable for our negligence if we refuse to alleviate the plight of the surviving 1,500,000.'

Sam's problem was that he didn't always do it on his own account.

Writer Norman Panama told me: 'I was working at Goldwyn's studio at the time and there was a big fund-raising affair for Israel. All the writers and executives were there. In public, in front of everyone, Goldwyn looked down the list and told me how much he wanted me to give. It was embarrassing because it was more than I could really afford.'

Sam was, however, giving a lot to a whole host of different charities. He gave $50,000 in 1947 for a model rehabilitiation centre being built at New York's Bellevue Hospital. As he said, it was rehabilitation that had led to the success of Harold Russell in *Best Years*.

What more people were interested in was the state of the film industry. For all Darryl Zanuck's protests, when Samuel Goldwyn took off on a theme, people did sit up and listen. At this time, he was putting himself in the prediction business.

'By 1952', he said, 'ninety-five per cent of American films will be in colour.' He was perhaps ten years too early, but of course it would happen. He also suggested that some would be in three-dimension. There, he was spot on. By the time 1952 came, Hollywood had woken up to the threat, as they saw it, of television and was searching desperately for something that the small screen couldn't do. They took up 3-D—and then promptly dropped it again. (Jack L Warner was the mogul who principally came unstuck with his worship of the special two-colour glasses one needed to wear to watch 3-D films.)

Sam wasn't predicting the end of censorship—but once more he was fighting it. And this time not, apparently, for his own purposes.

He returned from England in 1947 to hear that both Catholic and Protestant groups were assailing unmercifully *Duel In The Sun*, a David O. Selznick picture starring Jennifer Jones and Gregory Peck—termed *Lust In The Dust* locally. Sam thought that was a bad sign.

'I personally oppose censorship,' he declared after pointing out that he had not actually seen the film. 'I feel that the public should be its own censor.'

In that, he was being even braver than some people were prepared to realize. Later that year, in an interview with Hedda Hopper, he once again was attacking the colour bar and condemning anti-Black feeling in the country.

Lloyd Binford, the self-appointed censor of movies in Memphis, Tennessee, had attacked a film called *Curley* because he said it glorified a Black actor.

'In the last war,' said Sam—and in the process angering a legion of Goldwyn customers in the Deep South—'a million Negro soldiers fought and many died right beside the white soldiers. Was there any thought of racial discrimination on the battlefields?'

(The answer that Sam didn't choose to recognize was that yes, there was. There were separate Black and White battalions.)

'As far as I'm concerned, any Negro with talent has just as much right to work in pictures as he had to bear arms in defence of our country.

'How can people of Memphis tolerate such a man as Binford? Why doesn't he go the whole way and ban from the public libraries the works of Joel Chandler Harris, Stephen Foster and other sympathetic delineators of the spirit of the American Negro?'

Now, the word Negro would itself be considered offensive in the 1980s, but there were many worse epithets in common circulation in 1947 and very few people were saying what Sam Goldwyn was. And even if so much of the so-called interview was so obviously ghost-written, letting it go out under his own name was extraordinarily courageous at that time.

'If Mr Binford and his associates attack my pictures and bar them simply because they contain Negro artists they will find that I won't back down. If necessary we'll take a little trip together to the Supreme Court.'

That really was saying it. Signing Black artists like Lionel Hampton and

Louis Armstrong had begun a slew of protest that would linger on now.

As he added, the censor ought to 'start calling in his attorneys. He'll need them.'

He was also taking the unusual step of praising another studio's films. It was good PR on his part, though.

Soon after attacking Britain's new quota system which would cut down on movie imports from America, Sam was saying the nicest things about Laurence Olivier's *Hamlet*; It was, he said, 'the highest spot in the drama of our day—perhaps any day'.

Olivier had just been knighted by King George VI, but Sam thought it worth while paying his own tribute.

Then he added the supreme compliment: 'I think I have seen every great actor of our time play the part from Beerbohm Tree, Forbes-Robertson . . .and the unforgettable John Barrymore. Great as they were, they do not equal what Sir Laurence Olivier does on the screen.'

The way he said it sounded like the tribute of a headmaster to one of his old boys—which was precisely how Sam saw the man who had starred in *Wuthering Heights*, the picture which he still said was, in fact, Olivier's discovery by Hollywood.

Meanwhile, Sam was concerned about his own countrymen's prosperity. If America was feeling the pinch economically—and losing the British market wasn't doing Hollywood much good—he was once more going to set an example. He was going to slash his salary 'considerably'.

On the surface that was a generous thing to do—until it was realized that the people who benefited from salary cuts were the stockholders—and, in Goldwyn Productions, the biggest stockholder of all was Samuel Goldwyn.

18
My Foolish Heart

There was still something of the romantic in Sam—despite what his opponents said, despite the hard-nosed businessman who softened only to explain to people why they were wrong.

Frances saw it even if no one else did.

He was always telling her about his early days, when things were much harder than she could possibly imagine. But they were just stories. Gloversville was a place in Sam's history and on a map.

But now she had an opportunity to see for herself. They were on holiday in Saratoga, very close to Gloversville. It didn't occur to Sam to suggest visiting the scene of those heady early days—or if it did, he didn't think it opportune to suggest to Frances doing so.

Now, though, the matter was taken out of his hands. When they returned to their their Saratoga hotel suite, a letter was awaiting them. Would Mr Goldwyn care to address a meeting of the local businessmen's club?

Secretly, of course, he was flattered—in a way that any old boy who had made good was flattered to be asked back to his school. but he didn't want to make any speeches and that was final. He told Frances so and she accepted it—until the phone rang. It was Albert Aaron, his old boss in the glove business.

For his sake, would Sam go to talk to the businessmen? For his sake? How could he possibly refuse? Without Aaron there may well have been no Sam Goldwyn Productions, to say nothing of no Famous Players-Lasky, no MGM, perhaps no Paramount . . . .

He was so nervous when the evening arrived that he couldn't decide what suit or tie to put on, what Frances should wear, whether she should put on any jewellery. He was making the whole thing a huge production number—as they were inclined to say in the Hollywood of the day.

He couldn't eat. When he had finally chosen his tie, he was constantly tying and retying it, rearranging the handkerchief in his breast pocket.

Things got even worse on the journey to the Kingsborough Hotel, the same Kingsborough on which he had cast those envious eyes so many years before. He told the chauffeur they had retained for the evening to stop the car as it journeyed along a dark, tree-lined road. He rushed out—and Frances followed. She didn't know what it was all about. All that she did know was that he seemed to be ill. Not ill. Just so nervous that he couldn't wait to relieve himself at the nearest secluded spot. It happened twice more on the same journey before reaching the Kingsborough.

As Frances later recalled, they and the chauffeur had got to know each other so well as a result of those stops, they were on first name terms with each other.

And, predictably, that was as nothing compared with the relationship between Sam and his audience at the club that night.

The marble floors were mobbed for the arrival of the celebrity. No product of Gloversville had ever done so well and they were going to let him know how proud they were of his achievements; all of them brought more credit on the town than the gloves which gave it its name could ever do.

They still made good gloves there—as the presentation of a box of them to Frances made clear.

He was surrounded and had one of the must successful evenings of his life. But nothing else that night could compare with the moment when someone tapped his shoulder and introduced himself.

The man said his name was Jacob Libglid. Libglid was a familiar name, but why? Libglid? Then he stared at the face of the person in front of him—it was vaguely familiar, the face of a man perhaps just a little older than he was himself.

'You don't remember me?' the man asked.

'Yes,' Sam said, he did remember. But from where?

Then the man said Hamburg—and it all came back. Libglid was the fellow who made the collection for him, called him 'landsman' on the day he roamed the port's streets looking for a boat to England. They embraced. They talked gloves—at which point a crowd of other glove men gathered round. At that moment, he was Sam Goldfish, glove salesman again. He talked about skins, about designs, about sizes. In fact it was strange that a glove expert like him also seemed to know a little about the movie business.

Nervously, throughout the evening he was carrying his hat. No one quite knew why. He kept dropping it.

They asked him to make a speech. Sam stood up, wiped his brow and that high voice of his hadn't sounded quite as high since it broke at the age of fourteen. 'I've always been honest,' he said, a statement nobody at that evening was prepared to doubt. 'I've . . .' he couldn't finish his sentence. His throat was choked and there were tears rolling down his cheek. He sat down. Everyone stood up, clapped and cheered.

Other gatherings were not always so successful.

Jack Warner gave a party for Field Marshal Lord Montgomery of Alamein at about this time and Sam, with all the other studio heads, was invited along—Warner liked to show off to his competitors that he could attract such splendid company.

As Jack liked to say: 'Everyone was there—who's who and who's through.'

He wasn't suggesting that Sam was one of those who was through. In fact, he asked him to propose the toast to the guest of honour.

Warner's son-in-law Bill Orr, who was later to be head of production at the family studio, was there. 'We'd heard that Sam had been saying all evening how pleased he was at the thought of meeting Marshall Field' (Marshall Field was a big department store). 'We'd all been joking about it,' Orr told me.

'Then sure enough, when it came to propose the toast, Sam got up and paid tribute to "Marshall Field". Well, we all collapsed.' Jack Warner, in fact, said: 'You mean Marshall Ward'. (That was another department store.)

Orr had had pleasant memories of Goldwyn for a long time. Sam was in Jack Warner's office on the day that Orr met his boss for the first time.

'Goldwyn was sitting outside the office, humphing and phumphing that he had been waiting twenty minutes and I was being shown straight in.'

Warner's secretary assured him it wouldn't be for long. 'The boy's just meeting Mr Warner,' she told the rival mogul.

'Well,' said Sam, 'he'd better meet him fast.'

His relationship with Warner was a great deal better than with Harry Cohn.

His old friend and former business associate David Rose, who was making a couple of pictures as a producer at Columbia, had a call from Sam saying he wanted to see one of the films when it was ready. Rose invited him to Columbia to see it. When Cohn heard about this, it was as though the producer had opened the safe for Goldwyn. His expletives flew in a dozen directions at once.

From that moment on Cohn wouldn't speak to Sam. They met, accidentally, at Las Vegas airport. Sam and Frances and David Rose and his wife had gone to the town to see Noel Coward in cabaret.

'I went up to Harry,' Rose told me, 'and asked him to say "hello" to Sam. He refused. "I'll talk to Frances," he said. He wouldn't do more.'

Hollywood writer Mel Frank's ex-wife was once Sam's secretary—at just the moment he was beginning to worry about the amount of space being taken up by files and other documents that had long since lost their importance or value. She suggested ditching them. 'A good idea,' said Sam 'only be sure to make a copy of everything before getting rid of it.'

It was long before the days of photo-copying and microfilm, in particular.

The poor girl stuttered—particularly with the initial 'G'. Being unable to say anything but 'Mr G-g-g-oldwyn' her former husband told me, 'drove Sam absolutely out of his mind.'

Frank and his partner Norman Panama went to work for Sam several years afterwards. He liked what they did. 'Boys,' he said, 'that new picture is sweeping the country like wildflower.'

Norman Panama recalled: 'But he was a shrewd son of a bitch.'

His rows with exhibitors continued. There was one in particular about the price he got for one of his movies. Nicholas Schenck was brought in to arbitrate. Finally, the man agreed to give Sam all the profits the picture made. Schenck came to Goldwyn with the good news—but Sam still wasn't content.

'If he had been showing any picture other than mine,' said Sam, 'he would have *lost* money.'

Sam himself wasn't doing much in the losing of money department. In October 1947 it was announced he had *overpaid* his 1945 taxes by $383,407.

But he still wasn't letting anyone get away with what he considered to be financial murder. In 1948, he sued the Cagney organization—James and his brother William—for $21,000 in the Los Angeles Superior Court, money he said was owed him for use of the Goldwyn studios.

He was continuing his battles against the distributors as well. When the Government's anti-trust legislation was handed by the Supreme Court to the Statute Court, Sam hailed it as a 'distinct victory toward restoring free enterprise in the motion-picture industry. The court clearly recognized the monopoly exercised by the major companies in their control for the first run field.'

Saying that sort of thing was highly predictable. But not everything Sam did was. Quite suddenly, for instance, in December 1948 he announced that he was releasing Teresa Wright from her contract.

Now this was a time when stars everywhere were trying to get out of the 'bondage' of long-term contracts. Bette Davis, Olivia de Havilland and Joan Leslie had all had celebrated rows with Warner Bros. and had been released with varying degrees of acrimony. But Goldwyn had never really seemed to be that kind of employer—no matter what David Niven had been saying—and Teresa Wright was a Goldwyn discovery who appeared to have done very well out of him.

According to Goldwyn spokesmen, Teresa was having her agreement terminated because 'she had refused to perform services required'.

As they explained: 'Instructed to go to New York in connection with pre-opening publicity for the Goldwyn production *Enchantment*, in which she appears, Miss Wright refused the assignment.'

It was the old story—and repeating what had happened with Niven and Colman—of the studio publicity department turning nasty at Sam's behest. As for Goldwyn himself, he declared: 'I think the time has arrived when studios must assert their rights more than they have in the past. No one has a greater appreciation of artists and no one wants to treat them more fairly than I have in my career.'

Teresa herself said that she hated those promotion trips and did several of them, feeling extremely uncomfortable. David Niven, on the other hand, revelled in them. He made tremendously amusing speeches—the verbal preludes to his fantastically successful books, *The Moon Is A Balloon* and *Bring On the Empty Horses*.

Niven wanted to get out of his contract, too—and went on suspension for refusing to star in *The Elusive Pimpernel*, to be filmed in England for Alexander Korda. But he gave in when he realized the amount of money he would be losing.

He admired Teresa Wright for sticking to her guns.

She was declaring: 'I accept Mr Goldwyn's termination of my contract without protest—in fact, with relief. The types of contracts standardized in the motion picture industry between players and producers are archaic in form and absurd in concept. I am determined never to set my name to another one.'

Archaic was the word. Before very long, the full contract between studio and stars would be a thing of the past.

Teresa was not going to see Goldwyn to discuss hers.

It was over. 'I have worked for Mr Goldwyn seven years because I consider him a great producer and he has paid me well, but in the future I shall gladly work for less if by doing so I can retain my hold upon the common decencies without which the most humble can be carried off with dignity. I think the time has come for professional people to reject contracts like the one of which Mr Goldwyn has so kindly relieved me.'

Sam himself, meanwhile, was severing one of his own links. He was quitting—not for the first time—the Motion Picture Association of America and the Association of Motion Picture Producers, which supposedly looked after the West and East Coast production offices of the business. He was, instead, going to ally himself with other independent producers.

Said Sam: 'I find myself unable to agree consicienciously with many of the policies formulated by the associations and feel that they do not represent the interests of the independent producers.'

Eric Johnston rejoindered by saying that Goldwyn had 'a singular flair for saying one thing and doing exactly the opposite'.

That made Sam see scarlet. 'It is indeed unfortunate', he said in what *The New York Times* said was the strongest and bitterest Press release in the history of Hollywood, 'for the motion picture industry that Mr Eric Johnston's manners are as bad as his judgement. I had hoped to withdraw from the . . . association without comenting on Mr Johnston's leadership, but this latest effusion [it was that ghost-writer again] from his word factory impels me to state a few matters for the record.

'During the period that Mr Johnston has been president . . . the public relations of the industry have declined alarmingly. Mr Johnston's contribution to building fine relations between the public and our business has consisted mainly of turning the offices of the MPAA into a personal Press bureau for Eric Johnston. The motion-picture industry has survived many misfortunes and I am confident that it will survive Eric Johnston.'

Meanwhile Sam announced another deal. He was going to link up with Roberto Rossellini to produce films in Europe—with Rossellini's wife Ingrid

Bergman. It was another brave move. Bergman was being ostracized by the rest of Hollywood for giving birth to twins sired by Rossellini out of wedlock.

Before long the scheme foundered and Rossellini did a deal with RKO instead. Bergman told Sam that every time he visited them in Italy he would find himself gagged and with his hands tied.

In 1949 Sam made *My Foolish Heart*, often described as the archetype woman's picture starring Susan Hayward and Dana Andrews. It was about a woman who deceives her husband into thinking her expected child is his. It was written by Julius and Philip Epstein, for long stalwarts of the Warner studios where they had written a whole string of outstanding movies, including *Yankee Doodle Dandy* and *Casablanca*.

They didn't always get on with Jack Warner. Sam Goldwyn they loved.

'Warner spoke better English,' Julius Epstein told me. 'Goldwyn represented class to the industry. It was rather a pleasant experience. We worked at home—which meant that we didn't have any day-to-day tumult with the studio boss and so I loved working with him. He was one of the very few people I ever worked with who thought first of all of the quality of what we were doing. He was the only mogul who gave us a fair shake. There was never any fighting with him—and I can't say that about anyone else in the business. If there was trouble with a director, for instance, he called people in to arbitrate.'

That was not always the way people like Alex Korda and David Niven found him.

Sam was in partnership with Korda in making *The Elusive Pimpernel*, but they ended up suing each other again.

Michael Korda says that Sam worried about that. He still liked Alex. Once in the course of one suit or another, he phoned Korda from his suite at Claridges, inviting him for dinner. Then he added: 'Alex, I hope you know I'm still suing you.' Korda, his Hungarian charm oozing from every pore, replied: 'And so am I you, but my dear Sam, not during dinner.' The suit was soon off, as it always would be.

Niven so much hated his role in what is generally regarded as a disaster that he vowed never to work for Goldwyn again—no matter what it cost.

He agreed to be lent for a Shirley Temple film called *A Kiss For Corliss* and then said it was all over. Goldwyn did not object.

He wasn't going to worry about it. Other people found him easier to get on with.

19
The Hurricane

Like the rest of Hollywood, Sam was worried by television. But, unlike the rest of Hollywood—and particularly Warners who played ostrich and refused to even allow a set on one of their pictures to contain a TV—he admitted it was there and said it presented a challenge to the industry. He had forecast as much a generation before.

In a far-seeing article ghosted in his name in *The New York Times* magazine, Sam pointed out that motion pictures were on the threshold of the television age, their third major era after silents and the coming of sound.

'The future of motion pictures, conditioned as it will be by the competition of television, is going to have no room for the dead wood of the present or the faded glories of the past. Once again it will be true as it was in the early days of motion-picture history, that it will take brains instead of just money to make pictures. This will be hard on a great many people who have been enjoying a free ride on the Hollywood carousel, but it will be a fine thing for motion pictures as a whole.'

He said that the stance the industry had to take was if you can't lick 'em, join 'em. And, he pointed out, no film mogul was going to be able to lick TV, although nobody was calling it that. People would continue to go out to the movies because they were naturally gregarious. 'But before the movie-goer of the future arranges for a baby-sitter, hurries through dinner, drives several miles and has to find a place to park, just for the pleasure of stepping up to the box-office to buy a pair of tickets, he will want to be certain that what he pays for is worth that much more than what he could be seeing at home without any inconvenience at all.'

He thought that films made for television would have strong story lines and would require a 'lustier' form of acting.

But the most important point was that the studios had to consider making TV films.

'The people best fitted to make pictures for television will be those who combine a thorough knowledge of picture-making techniques with a real sense of true entertainment values and the imagination to adapt their abilities to a new medium. The weak sisters in our ranks will fall by the wayside.'

True to his word, he was to be the first of the moguls to sell their films to television—originally in Britain to Lew Grade.

'That really put Grade in business,' David Rose, who arranged the deal told me. 'Sam was really courageous in that because the British industry insisted they were going to blackball Sam and not show his pictures. But he went on to do it. He knew it had to come. And he took the first step.'

At the same time he made a deal to sell the features to CBS.

Even in 1950 he was saying, 'Hollywood must face the facts squarely. Television, which in the beginning was little more than a gimmick used by tavern-keepers to induce persons to linger over another drink is today a lusty billion-dollar baby and growing like Paul Bunyan.'

The film industry was then as frightened of television as the legitimate theatre had been of the 'flickers' when he first went into the business. It gave him a heaven-sent opportunity to mount another Goldwyn hobby-horse.

It was more important to deal with the small screen and feed it with products than to make 'B' pictures. As he said, '"B" pictures must eventually disappear almost completely from the Hollywood production scene. "B" entertainment is available on television free.'

As always, he was in the prediction business and doing well out of it. 'Even the number of Hollywood "A" pictures will be drastically reduced. With production focussed on "A" pictures, I believe that coming films will be far superior in quality to the average films of today.'

Not that he was allowing the television people to have it all their own way.

At a meeting at New York's Waldorf Astoria Hotel he offered a challenge to the people in television. Other speakers had included the head of RCA, David Sarnoff, ex-Mayor William O'Dwyer, financier Bernard Baruch, all of them extolling the virtues of the small screen. Sam was called last.

He looked at the television sets in the room. 'All these machines are very beautiful. In fact, I have one in my own home. But there is only one thing that is really important—what comes out of those screens. That is visual entertainment—and we in Hollywood know how! I'll be seeing all you television people in Hollywood soon.'

That saying, he said he was going to give Hollywood an additional name—Television City. He would be proved right in that regard, too. As he would in his attitude to theatre owners who he said were still trying to take business away from him.

He was still charging exhibitors with operating trusts that locked out independent producers. He was right. It *was* still happening. He claimed damages amounting to more than $6 million against the owners of 445 theatres. The matter was settled, but with every case, every claim, he was hammering that nail still deeper. That was the persistence that kept him in business and it was an example the studio heads were still comfortably trying to ignore.

Sam had his problems. One of them was when Sam Junior was recalled into the Army. He didn't want any preferential treatment for his son, but he thought it was a waste of time and talent—he had told 'Sammy' that the film business was to be enjoyed. 'Never stop enjoying it,' he cautioned—but he said neither he nor his son could see any reason to be called back, even if it was the time of the Korean war.

Sam said he had been very proud of his son's ambitions in the film business and now he was being taken away just as his career was taking off.

Both father and son were distraught and sat up all night discussing it. Since they were both called Samuel Goldwyn, they turned their discussion into a film—which became *I Want You*, about the problems caused by just such a situation. It wasn't any great movie, but it showed how almost everything could be turned to advantage.

Meanwhile Sam himself was fighting what the *Los Angeles Times* called a 'crusade' against film censorship and was still suing Mary Pickford for control of his studio premises.

It was the hottest gossip in the film community—particularly when it seemed that Miss Pickford would try to physically evict Sam, lock, stock and writers.

The court said he should sell up and go and Sam stayed put, awaiting yet another legal injunction. There were sixteen acres of property involved and Sam was making a film called *Edge of Doom*, the title of which could be seen to be prophetic. Now it could not be completed in time. Sam, though, carried on as though there were no edge of doom anywhere near him.

Mary wanted more money before Sam could renew his lease. Sam refused. He then withdrew all his equipment to studios over the road occupied by the Eagle Lion firm. On the other hand, he stayed in his own office. That was the property of Samuel Goldwyn Productions, Inc., and that firm couldn't be moved by the order. It was very complicated and Sam appeared to be enjoying every second of it.

Finally, a solution was found: Sam had to sue himself. Judge Paul Norse was asked to untangle twenty year of complex leasing arrangements with regard to the studio. Mary owned 48 per cent of the lot.

The real problem was that both Pickford and Sam had offices and other buildings on each other's territory.

Sam sued for 'partition of the lot' in the form of the Formosa Corporation and Samuel Goldwyn Inc. The defendant was what remained of the United Artists company—owned jointly by Sam and Pickford. In other words he was both defendant and plaintiff.

If anyone thought that was confusing they were advised by Sam and his lawyers to try to work out how the judge felt.

It was not a fight that Sam seemed to be winning. He was still making films, still had valuable lighting, sound and picture equipment on parts of the lot. Mary wasn't making films, only owned real estate. On 22 December 1949 Mary Pickford would acquire a share in all Sam's equipment still left on her part of the lot if it were not all removed.

Finally, Judge Norse decided the only thing to do was to put the studio up for sale. None of Sam's friends dared to offer him the slightest bit of competition and in the end, his bid (neither side knew what the other one was offering) of $1,920,000 was the bigger—by $20,000, although it would take about six years before the matter was finally settled.

Pickford got her share of that $1,920,000—48 per cent—and Sam had the rest; he was paying himself 52 per cent, plus the entire studio.

With that settled, he was free to go on making his films—although there were now going to be fewer of them, and of these only two or three more were to have any great effect on the imagination of either audiences then or motion-picture historians afterwards.

For a long time he continued to regard himself as the expert witness for the industry whenever it was being put on trial by one group or another. To some he was what today would be called a guru.

Daily Variety in 1950 voted him the best movie producer in America. The right-wing journal *The Saturday Review* described him as Hollywood's 'loyal opposition'. The *Review* had called for greater censorship of Hollywood films by choosing which pictures were suitable for export and which were not.

It opened an old sore and Sam let people see the wound in all its festering nastiness. Governments had no more right to dictate which films people saw than what newspapers they read or which programmes they listened to on short-wave radios. (No one told him to offer that piece of advice to the Voice of America.) He said:

'A distorted picture of American life might well be any one aspect of it taken alone. Our way of life can be as dishonestly portrayed if one shows only sweetness and light, as if one would present America only as a haven for gangsters. This is America! We have all types here!'

America needed the money its films made. But it also, he said, needed to show the complete American way of life. 'Why was one of Hitler's first acts on assuming power the barring of American films from Germany?'

How many American films were shown behind the Iron Curtain? But if Hollywood was not given a chance to get to the rest of Europe, then the Communists might have it all their own way. It was a simplistic argument, but was worth saying.

Later, on his return from an eleven-week trip to Europe, he said he was worried that America was losing the propaganda war with Russia. It needed to spend 'a billion dollars a year' to get over its case.

On one trip to Europe he met Lillian Hellman who told him that America's ambassador to Italy Clare Boothe Luce had been taken ill as a result of poisons coming from the ceiling in her room. For a moment, Sam was transported to the New York garment industry. He asked her: 'What's a poi-son (person) doing on the ceiling of her room?'

People were still listening to him, still honouring him—he was made a life member of the British Film Academy—still saying that he was setting examples to everyone else.

His film *Edge of Doom* had created a few problems—it appeared to criticize the Roman Catholic Church—and he got Ben Hecht, that nice Jewish boy, to write a prologue and an epilogue to reduce some of the barbed effect.

It worked well enough for Sam to be received by Pope Pius XII, not usually considered the most tolerant of pontiffs. He and Frances were granted an audience with Mr and Mrs Robert Sherwood and Mervyn LeRoy and his wife.

'Sam was marvellous, quite gracious,' LeRoy told me.

The problem came before he and the other Hollywood people were shown into the papal presence. 'Say,' piped Sam to LeRoy as they prepared to leave their Rome hotel. 'Tell me something. When we get to the Vatican where do I find him?'

He and the other moguls were still rivals, even now when the studio chief seemed at risk of being an endangered species.

They even competed with each other in charity. At one United Jewish Appeal dinner, after hearing a rousing speech from Abba Eban, before long to be Israel's Foreign Minister, Sam started the bidding with a donation of $50,000. Jack Warner said: 'I'll give $75,000.' Louis B. Mayer topped them all with $100,000. When Sam heard that he came in: '$150,000.' It was an auction.

The charities did very well when those men were together. 'But,' said producer Milton Sperling. 'Go to these guys and say "my wife is sick and I need a $10 raise" and they'd fire you. That was different. That's business.'

In *Colliers* magazine in 1951 he asked pointedly 'Is Hollywood Through?' He sounded confident. More people than ever would be going to the movies, if they were good. But television was going to be even more important—and particularly in cable. (Nobody else was going to take cable TV seriously for another twenty years.)

'Television is the newest, most vigorous and exciting contender for Hollywood's place as the leader of the entertainment parade. It has shaken us out of living in the past and has made us look to the future.'

That said, he was concentrating on making films that would enchant audiences and get them young. That was why he was doing a new film with Danny Kaye and why he was glad he had listened to his son. This time it would be called *Hans Christian Andersen*.

20
Hans Christian Andersen

It was going to be a fairy story—about the man who told fairy stories. Fortunately for Sam and for Danny Kaye that announcement was made fairly early on and was also stated very boldly indeed in the opening moments of the picture—before the local schoolmaster was seen to ring his bell and virtually drag his pupils away from the spot where Hans Andersen was regaling them with yet another crazy tale.

Hans Andersen, note. Until the movie came out, nobody dreamed of calling him Hans *Christian* Andersen. And nobody, but nobody called him *Harns* or the Danish capital Copenh*ar*gen. Least of all, nobody outside certain parts of America. The fact that everyone seemed to be doing so for ever after—and certainly for the next thirty-five years—says something for a movie which was never the most exciting that Hollywood produced. It was not the most thrilling Danny Kaye film ever. It definitely wasn't the best film Samuel Goldwyn made. But hundreds of thousands of adults look back on it now as either the first movie they ever saw, or the first of which they have definite memories. And they all appear to love it.

That, too, is fortunate. For this looked like the closest America has been to war with Denmark since the Declaration of Independence.

The Danes took the picture very seriously indeed—which is what Sam would have wanted them to do. But, as he might or might not have said, matters got from hand to mouth, if not more so.

It was, of course, great publicity for the picture before it was seen by a single person outside the studio. But the depth of feeling even seemed to worry Sam, who was forced to initiate an apology or two.

As he constantly pointed out, it wasn't the true Hans Andersen story. Incidentally, it only became the Hans *Christian* Andersen story because the writer of the music and lyrics, Frank Loesser, needed an extra word to fit in with his score. Thus, in effect, he gave the writer a new name and one with which he would for ever after be associated.

Sam had had an Andersen manscript for fourteen years and, as we've seen, he had more than once tried to unload it. On one occasion Pat Duggan, story department editor, reported a particularly good offer.

Sam had put a copy of the original Andersen script in his desk drawer the moment it was bought. At least five subsequent tries had joined it, but until now he hadn't had one he liked enough to make. But he knew it was worth making—at least that was the story he was telling, ignoring that row with Sam Junior.

Eventually, Moss Hart submitted a story that Sam liked. Charles Vidor was brought in as director. Rodgers and Hammerstein were originally asked to produce a score, but they were too busy even to organize a meeting with Sam. So Frank Loesser, newly delivered of *Guys and Dolls*, was approached and most people at Goldwyns were pleased that he was.

Solving the problem of the Danes' sensitivities was going to be more complicated. Danny Kaye went on a tour of the places associated with his new subject—the first time he had ever played a real person (even one who made up fairy tales).

The trouble was he was seen to have the effrontery to try out Andersen's bed. To the Danes that was like putting on his shoes—and he did that, too.

Sam's aim with the film was established—or so he prayed—with that opening notice: 'Once upon a time, there lived in Denmark a great storyteller named Hans Christian Andersen. This is not the story of his life, but a fairy tale about this great spinner of fairy tales.'

Of course, what he really aimed for was to make a great deal of money. Since the film cost him all of $4 million in the first place—a huge amount for 1952—there could be no guarantee of achieving that. But the publicity generated by the ire (if not the ore, the local currency which looked like being withheld) of the Danes was keeping Sam's latest project very much in the public eye.

The money wouldn't just come from the picture itself. Loesser's score would be produced by the Goldwyn publishing company and would contain a score of numbers (almost literally in both senses of that term) that became Danny Kaye standards, songs for which he is now totally associated, like *The Ugly Duckling, The King's New Clothes, Thumbelina* and, of course, *Wonderful, Wonderful Copenhagen*.

Nobody ever suggested subsequently that Hans Andersen—or even Hans Christian Andersen—ever sang that song or that anybody in Denmark pronounced the country's capital Copen*har*gen. But it did more good for that city than a million picture postcards showing a mermaid sitting on a rock, and immediately afterwards the number of tourists going there was increased tenfold.

Frank Loesser's score was plainly as full of standards as a convoy of ships, but for this Goldwyn needed something more.

The story, as supplied by Moss Hart—a name as legendary in show business as Andersen's in his—revolved around the cobbler-storyteller's romance with a ballerina.

Sam thought that would be a good way of ensuring a Danish content and so hired Erik Bruhn of the Royal Danish Ballet. His principal ballerina would be the Scottish-born Moira Shearer, who had so recently delighted a whole generation of little girls—and their mothers—with a pair of *Red Shoes*.

But, for a ballet, he had to have ballet music and that was not in Frank Loesser's music bag at all. That was how Walter Scharf, the musical director, made his impact and principally earned his Oscar nomination.

He called the musician—one of the most respected names in the California music scene—in for consultation. 'How long is the longest ballet ever seen in a film?' he asked him.

Scharf did some research and came up with the answer. It was in *An American In Paris* and lasted fourteen minutes. 'This one's got to be longer,' said Sam without for a minute doubting the wisdom of his demand. Then he went on to specify exactly what he needed. 'This one's got to be eighteen minutes,' he said, determined not to leave the matter in any doubt.

It was like a man having a house built and demanding of the developer, 'four yards of books', but to Sam it was another one of his missions in life. He kept an eye on what he regarded as much his own creation as Scharf's like a nurseryman tending a prize orchid.

The musician had an office on the ground floor of the Formosa Avenue studio. Every day as he came into work, Sam would poke his head through Walter's window. 'Scharf,' he'd scream in that near-falsetto voice, 'Scharf, you dere?' Schar was always 'dere' and produced the music required.

(The experience was not as unnerving as that told to me by another prominent figure in the Hollywood music scene, Sammy Cahn. 'I went to see Sam Goldwyn in his office, and he was sitting behind his desk, his wife at his side. As he spoke to me, he suddenly disappeared from view, sank beneath his desk. Why I'll never know. He came up for air, looked at me again as I was talking and then ducked below again. I've never found out why.')

There were innumerable problems with a ballet that long, so long, in fact, that it spread over two reels and the join of the two is never a good spot for a musical number. Scharf turned it all into a complicated arrangement of several pieces of music by Liszt. It was called *The Mermaid Ballet*, which turned out to be not just the longest in films to date, but certainly the most expensive. As usual, Sam didn't quibble about mere cost.

There was a twenty-eight member corps-de-ballet, who accounted for most—but by no means all—the 100,000 man-hours (or perhaps it should be *person* hours) work that went into it. The dancers earned $55,000, which was precisely what was spent on their costumes, too.

The mermaid at the centre of the ballet (to be played by Miss Shearer as the object of Han's affections) was unhappy. Hence, she had to have tears. The designers came up with rhinestones for this purpose—at a cost of—$472.

The most expensive incidental of all was written into the ledgers as 'flying the kite.' The picture opened and closed with a shot of a kite flying off into the bright blue yonder. The trouble was that the cloudless, windless skies of

California weren't right. In the end, after waiting from January to April to do the filming, Sam sent off a camera team to Arizona to do the shot. It took eight men two weeks to complete the task.

These matters sorted out, everything looked clear to start work, or rather complete work. Miss Shearer had been at the bar, practising, when she confided to Walter Scharf a little problem she had—she was ever so slightly pregnant.

'We were on the stage when I first heard about this,' Walter told me. 'I had already noticed she was bulging slightly, but I didn't think very much of it. She was standing up against the bar where ballerinas practised.' It wasn't the little bulge he noticed in November 1951 that made Scharf concerned. He knew that Sam would be much more concerned—and mainly about the much bigger bulge that would be obvious in the middle of 1952 when the work would be principally completed, and there were at least six months of that still to go.

Miss Shearer was too embarrassed—and not a little scared—to tell Sam about her problem. Since Scharf always had a fatherly look about him, even then when he was barely in his forties, she asked him for his help. He arranged for a special 'audience' with his boss, who hadn't the slightest inkling of any trouble ahead.

Frances was told—and shuddered.

'I think we ought to let Danny tell him,' Scharf said.

Danny was less than pleased. 'I want to be in China when you tell him about this,' Kaye responded.

But go he did. 'I was so impressed with the way he handled it,' Scharf told me. '*I* was scared to death. By the time Sam heard about it he was quite calm and simply asked his casting people to try to find someone else.'

Zizi Jeanmaire was picked. She, like the film's choreographer, was a member of the Paris Ballet and was chosen partly because she happened to be in Los Angeles in the company's production of *Carmen*.

Kaye's responsibility was partly to help Mlle Jeanmaire with her practically non-existent English. 'Where you going?' he asked her.

'To the block,' she said.

'How can you go to the block. To the block! You mean round the block, you dope.'

Danny also did a lot of his own choreography—Kaye as a dancer was not a known commodity—but he organized his walks in and out of Copenhagen with as much detail as Fred Astaire used when he danced *The Continental*. It was never clearer than when he instructed the child in the *Ugly Duckling* scene how to move.

Sam watched it all anxiously. He was down on the set a great deal more now than was usual for him. As Frances later reported: 'Sometimes when he'd stand behind a piece of scenery with his head bent and his eyes closed one would wonder if he were listening or praying. Other times he'd tiptoe back and forth, back and forth, just outside the set proper till you'd want to scream.'

But there was one time when Sam himself did scream—on set and for Frances.

It turned out that Mlle Jeanmaire had decided to express her own personality—by cutting her hair. The film shot on the Friday showed her with curly hair. On Monday morning she turned up with it cut short. Sam was in despair. Even worse, the dancer had stage fright and was refusing to go on. He gave her his personal attention in her dressing-room. It was not a pleasant experience.

'What you need is a spanking,' he told her and added she ought to be ashamed of herself. 'Don't give me any of that personality talk,' he shouted. And when Sam shouted, he shouted.

She was crying. Sam called for a powder puff. Then some rouge. Then a comb and a brush. There were titters around the room and not too subdued comments about unions. He took no notice, applied the make-up, the comb and the brush himself and ordered her back to the set, where she performed her scene.

But it wasn't enough to win the picture a great deal of critical acclaim. Summing up most of the things said about it, it seemed that this was intended to be a magical film, but there just wasn't enough—magic. Bosley Crowther wrote in *The New York Times* that it was all worked out by Sam's boys who 'constructed a large fable out of a lot of smaller fables—and little more. And the mediums through which they have done this are mostly decoration, music and dance, with accuracy or even plausible definition of the central character incidental to the whole.'

Indeed, despite the protests to the contrary, whole generations grew up believing that the cobbler Hans Christian Andersen had an unrequited affair with a ballerina who pretended to be a mermaid when she danced.

As Mr Crowther went on: 'The consequence is a handsome movie—in colour, of course—in which the French dancer Jeanmaire races and twirls in graceful beauty through a couple of lovely ballets . . . .'

The *New Yorker* seemed to place most of its blame at the feet of Moss Hart who 'credits Hans Christian Andersen with a simplicity bordering on active idiocy.'

But, predictably, much worse was to come from Denmark itself. Arne Sorensen wrote in *Information*: 'It will cost America's reputation so much that it will take the United States Information Service in Denmark to make up the loss.' It didn't look like Denmark at all in the film—but 'a German principality'. Or as *The New Yorker* put it, 'a sort of community that the Shuberts used to construct when Romberg was lining out his songs. With the Shuberts of course, it was Alt Wien, but what the hell, Denmark's on the same continent.'

Danny Kaye decided he had a sort of responsibility for it all. He apologized for the disappointments of the Danes, if not for those of *The New Yorker*.

'I am playing the role as straight as I possibly can,' he declared. 'After reading the script, I couldn't see any of my particular brand of comedy. I have as much respect for Hans Christian Anderson as the Danes, and as much warmth in my heart for his writing as the millions of kids who have enjoyed his stories.'

Flying in the face of these sort of criticisms required a certain kind of courage from Sam, for they were beyond, far beyond, the snipes that could aid publicity and were being seen by some people in his organization as reflecting on his own artistic integrity.

They were not, however, the only problems he was facing. Sam was once more speaking his mind and in his own language which wasn't always the kind that the Hollywood establishment would have appreciated.

When Charles Chaplin arrived in Britain only to be told he would not be welcomed again in America, Sam jumped to his friend's (and former business partner's) defence and denied that Chaplin had ever been a Communist.

He was 'the greatest comedian and artist who has come along in my lifetime.

'I have known him for nearly forty years and I sincerely hope that what I've read will not be proven a fact. We need him in our business as we need every artist that is great.'

He realized that was sticky ground and he joked that after saying those things, he might find it difficult getting back into the States himself. It was upon that which the British Press alighted. 'They Can Include Me Out', declared the *Daily Express*. Sam said his joke had been taken out of context.

That being said, Sam said he was going to offer his endorsement to the idea of General Eisenhower becoming America's next President. It would be another shrewd decision on his part.

Eisenhower's friends no doubt extolled Sam's advice to Hollywood publicists when he spoke at their annual dinner in 1952. He said they were members of an honoured profession—he had more reason than most to honour it—provided they exercised 'honesty, integrity and decency'.

He accepted that he was in a unique situation. In fact, he said, looking at the members of the Screen Publicists Guild: 'Tonight I feel the way I imagine a college professor must feel when he attends a meeting of his old students—and finds that they have been doing very well ever since they left the peace and quiet of the campus to shift for themselves. I am sure all of you—particularly those who have worked with me—will agree that this is a very apt comparison, for what words could better describe the day-by-day relations at Goldwyn College between my publicists and myself than "peace" and "quiet".'

They laughed—and like that for there wasn't a man among them who didn't appreciate the irony.

And there were not a few who remembered some of the things they did at his behest, the not so true love affairs of Vilma Banky, the street signs, the letters sent in his name but which he had never written . . . . Now he was disclaiming it all.

'As far as I am concerned,' he declared with all the self assurance of a convicted murderer speaking against violence to a church assembly, (there) 'is no excuse for the mass of phony publicity that goes out about Hollywood every day of the year from non-existent love affairs to shattered romances that never began, through announcements of pictures that will never be made and grosses that will never be reached.'

Then he said he hoped the people who had been there had enjoyed his address. Now he hoped to see them at his other address, 11,041 North Formosa Avenue. 'I'd love to see you there!' That was perhaps an invitation that was not intended too seriously.

Later that year the city of Beverly Hills decided it was time to honour Sam himself. They declared, now that he was by their reckoning seventy years old and in business as a producer for forty years, it was time to make it Samuel Goldwyn Day. A special ceremony was held in the city council chamber where old friends joined civic leaders and film personalities to pay him homage. Sam's reply was to remind his listeners that it took more than one man to make a movie. 'And as for my charitable works, I believe it's the least a man can do for the privilege of living in Beverly Hills.'

The American Newspaper Women's Club gave a luncheon in his honour and said he was 'a great producer of motion pictures, a pioneer in the field of entertainment and a great American'. The dinner was held in Washington DC at the Mayfair Hotel.

It gratified him more than did a communication from twenty-three film-workers. This alleged that Sam was one of a group of film people who were blacklisting some of their fellow-workers for refusing to answer questions from the Un-American Activities Committee. They were demanding a total of $51,750,000—which was hard on Sam considering all he had been saying over the past couple of years.

But Sam was nothing but persistent. Sometimes he was even consistent. His battle with the Johnston office for instance continued.

At the end of 1953 he was demanding a change in the rules of the production code which had been unchanged since the Revd Daniel A. Lord and the film trade publisher Martin Quigley had devised it in 1929—couples were still prohibited from having lengthy kisses and men and women could only be seen in bed if one foot of the man was on the ground. He did not specify what he wanted changed, but he said 'Unless the code is brought reasonably up to date, the tendency to bypass it, which has already begun, will increase. This can lead to excesses which will do our industry a great deal of harm.'

Other independent producers backed him, but the studios said they were sticking to the code they had grown to love. Even Sam Goldwyn couldn't envisage how standards would change within the next two decades, let alone thirty years. Meanwhile Mr Johnston—never Sam's friend—was denying he had agreed to call a producers' meeting to discuss the matter.

Sam believed he knew the business and everyone in it. He thought he could read the minds of them all. He thought he knew the way people ticked as well as he knew his employees. He did. Once, he looked out of the window and called out at one of his workers: 'Look at this lousy haircut you gave me.'

The man looked at him incredulously. Certainly, he was an employee. Certainly he knew Sam intimately—very intimately. He was Doc, the studio first-aid man who for twenty-five years had been giving Sam vitamin shots in the buttocks, twice a week.

Sam, meanwhile, had something more interesting in mind. He was going to do another Frank Loesser project—*Guys and Dolls*.

21
Guys And Dolls

As usual, Sam was steeped in controversy. He bought *Guys and Dolls*, the hit Broadway show based on Damon Runyon's favourite characters. Names like Harry the Horse, Liver Lips Louis, Big Julie, Nicely Nicely Johnson and Nathan Detroit would soon be echoing from wide screens all over the world.

But Runyon himself—who had died in 1946—couldn't possibly have imagined the troubles that would be involved in making the show into a picture. Never, as he sat eating cheese cake in Lindy's (or Mindy's as it became in his books and the consequent show) could he imagine the effects of the production which was to worry certain citizens of Hollywood and Broadway more than somewhat.

Both MGM and Twentieth Century-Fox had put in rival bids, but Sam was going to do it big—possibly by bringing in a new process like Todd-AO which had been introduced in *Oklahoma!* When the deal was finalized in one of the most commercial arrangements yet seen in Hollywood, the picture was shot in Cinemascope.

But the trouble was over Abe Burrows who with Jo Swerling had adapted the Runyon stories—particularly his *Idyll of Miss Sarah Brown* about a Salvation Army girl who becomes the subject of a bet between Nathan Detroit and Sky Masterson—and turned them into *Guys and Dolls*.

Every man was called a guy and every girl a doll on Runyon's Broadway. But neither name was what some people were calling Mr Burrows. The Motion Picture Alliance declared him to be a Red. By association, Sam—who paid $1 million for the rights plus a guarantee of ten per cent to Mr Burrows after the picture had grossed $10 million world-wide—was a Communist too.

The Alliance also attacked the RKO and its boss Howard Hughes for agreeing to distribute the movie. (They would later back out, although not for political reasons.)

Sam was worried but was no more bending now than he ever had before. 'We have been assured time and again that Mr Burrows has been cleared by the House Committee,' Sam declared. 'Everyone who bid on the show knew he had been cleared and if anybody doubts my loyalty as an American let him come forward and say so.'

Burrows himself said 'I'll swear to my loyalty . . . I never took the Fifth Amendment.'

Sam meanwhile was among the signatories to a resolution condemning Senator Joe McCarthy for 'abusing' his position.

The show's ownership was so complicated, some twenty-two documents had been signed before the film finally became a Goldwyn property, which was now to be distributed by MGM.

The story was changed hardly at all. But even though this was a tale that was as New York as a Brooklyn cab driver, a number of references to the city's environs were changed to make it more palatable to people in other parts of the country, to say nothing of overseas.

The race track at Saratoga, for instance, became Niagara. Scarsdale, a New York suburb, became 'small town' and so on. Strangely no one had considered altering the place names when the show went on tour.

There were the usual casting problems. Sam wasn't so sure that his director Joseph L. Mankiewicz was totally sane in having Marlon Brando as Sky Masterson but he accepted his judgement. He thoroughly approved of Jean Simmons—a brave move, this since she was English—as the Salvation Army 'doll' and loved Vivian Blaine who was recreating her Broadway role as Everlasting Adelaide. But who to play Nathan Detroit, the owner of the oldest established permanent floating crap game in New York?

Danny Kaye was suggested. Norman Panama and Mel Frank sat in a hotel room for two days with him trying to persuade Kaye to take the role. They walked down Broadway with him, sat with him in Lindy's and tried to convince Danny that he would be good for the role of Detroit. He was almost persuaded—except that Sam was exhibiting one of his old (and certainly one of Hollywood's oldest) prejudices. He didn't want the part played by a Jew.

Detroit was undoubtedly Jewish. He even shrugged his shoulders and said 'noo?' But Sam didn't like Jews to play Jews, which was precisely why he didn't want the man who created the part, Sam Levine—a player of a hundred gangsters on film previously—in it now.

It was part of a long, long, story. For twenty years or more, rabbis in stories had been turned into priests, synagogues became churches and Jews turned into Italians or even Irishmen. The Jewish moguls were still sensitive about being thought to make Jewish films.

Finally, Frank Sinatra was brought in as Detroit. He didn't look Jewish, though he also shrugged his shoulders and said 'noo?' (He was also given more songs to sing than the stage Nathan.)

None of this should give any indication that Sam didn't consider himself a Jew.

Michael Kidd, the (Jewish) choreographer of the movie, told me of being in New York during the planning stage of the film when both of them were trying to soak up the atmosphere of Broadway. Kidd was living on 58th Street. Goldwyn stayed nearby at the Sherry-Netherland Hotel. He chose

Kidd because he had staged the numbers in the show.

Sam asked him if he liked Jewish food.

'Yes,' said Kidd, 'I like Jewish food.' It was difficult for a man born on the Lower East Side where gefilte fish seemed to swim from one kitchen to another—if you could accept the idea of minced fish balls swimming—not to like Jewish food.

'You like Lindy's?' he asked, warming to the theme, the saliva virtually cascading down his mouth. 'You like kreplach and kneidlach and that chicken soup?'

'Yes,' said Kidd. He liked all that.

'Let's go down there. Let's have a little walk.'

They walked as only Sam could walk. All the way down Broadway, they walked and talked. With each footstep Sam rejoiced in the Jewish dishes he loved best. The gdempte meat balls, the kishke, the gefilte fish, the lockshen kugel . . . .

Finally, they got to Lindy's. The Maître d', introduced by Kidd, was suitable impressed and showed Mr Samuel Goldwyn to a centre table which miraculously was conjured seemingly from nowhere (though doubtless by displacing someone else).

'They have lovely Jewish food here,' Sam told Kidd, the saliva now almost dripping from his chin. 'I love it all. At heart, I'm a good Jew,' he said.

At which point the Maître d' returned.

'Jewish food,' Sam repeated and Kidd waited expectantly. 'I love it all. What's the speciality today?'

'Irish stew,' replied the waiter.

'Good,' said Sam, 'That's what I'll have.'

Food wasn't his only mental block. As we have seen, he had trouble with names.

He had a name problem with Michael Kidd.

He was convinced he was actually Mike Todd. The previous day in his Sherry-Netherland suite he had asked Frances to get Mike Todd on the phone. She told him she couldn't reach him. 'Mike Todd is in Arizona,' she said. 'He's making *Oklahoma!* in Todd-AO.'

'Nonsense,' said Sam, 'I saw him in New York this morning. He's staging the numbers for *Guys and Dolls*.'

'No Frances informed him. 'That's Michael Kidd.'

'Yes,' said Sam, 'that's right. Michael Todd. Get him to come over here.'

In his office he would call him 'Todd' all the time.

'It happened again in Lindy's,' Kidd recalled for me. 'We were having lunch and I spot, several tables away, Michael Todd. He was coming towards us, stopping at a whole load of other tables on the way.

'He gets to our table and Sam gets up all excited. "Say Mike," he says, "It's good to see you. How are you? I'd like to have you meet . . ." At that point, he was totally nonplussed. His mouth remained open. He did not know what to say. Words failed him. Finally, his voice dropped and he said. "You know it's a funny thing, I was just about to call you Mike Todd".'

A few weeks later, Sam was in New York again. Once more, he rang the choreographer's home from the Sherry-Netherland.

'Say Mike,' he said 'what do you think about that number *Bushel and a Peck*?'

Kidd told him he liked it.

'You think it ought to be in the picture?'

Kidd replied: 'All I can tell you is that the Lucky Strike Hit Parade had had that as its number-one song for twelve weeks. It's the song that became the number-one hit from *Guys and Dolls*.'

'They had it for the last twelve weeks, eh?'

Kidd confirmed it.

On his next three visits, he went through the same routine. What did he think of the song? It's still on the the hit parade?

Always the same answers. It was a big, big hit.

'I think,' Kidd told him eventually, 'you ought to keep it in the picture because it is the most popular song.'

He pondered. Then he said, 'What does it mean—"I love you, a bushel and a peck"?'

Kidd told him that in this instance it was about girls on a farm using farm terminology. 'I told him a bushel was a big basket and a peck was a smaller basket.'

'So what does this mean?' Sam rejoined, 'I love you a big basket and I love you a small basket?'

'He was dead serious; desperately trying to find out what made that song a success. He had this ability and burning desire to do things of quality and before he made quality he had to know what it was all about. That was why he goaded people to do their best work.'

Making *Guys and Dolls* Sam fought with Joe Mankiewicz as only he could fight with a director—although, since he was also the writer, the battle was doubly hard.

It was one of those times when he was trying his hardest to be on equal terms with an intellectual, a man skilled in the use of words Sam had never even heard of.

But he wasn't embarrassed. He knew he had the power to exercise and was determined to do just that.

The first scene—in which the Broadway gamblers assure each other that they have 'The Horse Right Here', the *Fugue for Tin Horns*—was shot in a hotel room.

'Goldwyn didn't like it in a hotel room,' Kidd who staged the musical numbers, told me. 'He suggested they sang the song at a news-stand.'

Mankiewicz said that although it was done that way on stage that was because there was no other convenient place to do it. But he said, in real life they would pitch their racing prowess in the confines of a hotel room.

'I don't like it in a hotel room and you'll do it by the news-stand,' Sam insisted. Finally, he got really angry and started shouting and pounding his foot. 'Look,' he said, 'it's my two million dollars. When it's your two million dollars, you shoot it in a hotel room.'

In the end, the film would cost nearer five million.

As Kidd told me: 'He wouldn't submit to arguments of logic by intelligent people. He wasn't embarrassed.'

On the set he was running around like a scalded cat, quite as anxiously as he had been doing during the making of *Andersen*.

And always Frances—who still kept her private office, still went in there on days when Sam was away to 'answer the phone or deal with the mail'—was within earshot.

She saw that he had his daily nap, that he ate the food which she thought did him most good. It seemed that this concern was infectious. When Louella Parsons was taken ill, Sam went to see her. 'How are you fixed up with money?' he asked—and offered her $5,000 or more. 'When you get well you can pay me' he said. And then, with the kind of honesty that got him where he was, added: 'And if you don't, no one will know about it.'

'I'd be lost without Frances,' he confided as this time. 'She's the only real close partner I've ever had.' The completion of the picture would coincide with their thirtieth wedding anniversary—and be his sixty-eighth picture as an independent producer.

There were meetings galore about the film, between the producer, the director, the choreographer, the musical director. 'Look,' he told them, 'I want this to be different from the show. I don't want it to be a *cardboard* copy of the stage show.'

Kidd insists that Goldwyn really didn't understand the film at all. 'It was an idiom that was totally strange to him. The people in it he didn't know at all.'

He asked whether the *Take Back Your Mink* number should be retained. Kidd told him that not just on Broadway itself, but in other cities, in Kansas City, in Chicago, in St Louis, it had been the number that stopped the show.

'They liked the song, eh?' he asked.

'They loved it,' said Kidd, strongly.

'Wherever it played?' replied Goldwyn. 'In all those cities, they liked it eh?'

'Yes, they liked that number.'

'So tell me,' Sam wanted to know. 'What was there about it they liked?'

There were no Oscars for *Guys and Dolls*, although on the whole the Press was favourable. *The New York Times* commented:

'Sam Goldwyn was playing an odds-on favourite when he plunked down to make a film of *Guys and Dolls* . . . the gamble this time has paid off richly. *Guys and Dolls* romped across the finish line it its premiere . . . well in front where it belongs.'

It once again had something to say about Sam's dedication to that word 'quality'. A year later, he was declaring that the 'amazing' improvement in Hollywood's fortunes had been due almost entirely to that factor. 'The only miracle to me is that Hollywood did not realize earlier that the only way to recapture the public was by giving it quality instead of quantity in entertainment.' Once more, it seemed that a Goldwyn dictate had been vindicated.

Sam gave both Sinatra and Brando white Thunderbirds, ostensibly in gratitude, but in reality to try to persuade them to publicize the film on television. Brando did so—until he finally decided he had done enough for his car—Sinatra didn't. But the film was as successful as the show.

Thirty years later, it is surely one of the most entertaining Goldwyn films of all.

This was a happy time for Sam, professionally and at home. He and Sam Junior were apparently the best of friends and were named by the National Fathers Day Committee as Father and Son of the Year. That was a tribute indeed, they might have thought.

It seemed like success all the way—and not just in the film itself. He was still banging the drum in other spheres, mainly concerned with the industry and the way, as he saw it, he was being cheated by the exhibitors. He sued a group of theatres for more than six-and-a-half million dollars and persuaded a judge to order the company to open the books for his inspection.

Goldwyn was sure he was still King. And even at wooing the ladies. He still chased them around the table in his office. One now super-star reacted with typical bluntness. 'Do you want to screw me?'

'Yes,' he said.

'Well', she replied, 'why don't you come out with it?'

Was he losing that Goldwyn Touch?

22
Porgy And Bess

It seemed only right that *Guys and Dolls* should be so successful. Even if he was now in his seventies, Sam was entitled to receive nothing but plaudits. (He thought he was entitled to receive money, too, but that was another matter with which no one found himself in dispute.)

With his sixty-eighth film under his belt, he was aiming for his seventieth and in his own middle-seventies, at that.

To all appearances he looked as vibrant as ever. He certainly didn't seem his age. He still did a lot of walking, and when he did, people would come up to him and say, 'Aren't you Mr Goldwyn?'

Sam was glad he could still answer that yes, he was.

He only smoked two cigarettes a day and before dinner he had one drink. 'I find it relaxes me,' he would say. The drink was always Scotch. Twenty-five years earlier he had brought back a case of the whisky from Britain and he still hadn't gone through it all.

He never drank at the office and the only time he smoked there was 'out of boredom—when someone tells me a dull story'.

It was soon after *Guys and Dolls* was finally sealed in the cans that a writer came to him with a story idea. Sam fell asleep while the man was in mid-flow. 'But you weren't listening,' the young man chided. 'Don't you know', said Goldwyn, 'that falling asleep is also a comment.'

Meanwhile, some of the old Goldwyn-type rows were continuing as though Sam had recently moved into North Formosa Avenue and was fresh for an invigorating new challenge.

Once more Mary Pickford was challenging for control of her old studio—even though the building's fate had supposedly been sealed by the court order and subsequent action.

'I never start a fight,' she declared in March 1955. 'But I always finish one.'

There were still parts of the studio that they owned in common and the following month the courts would finally judge on the auction. The matter was somewhat complicated now since Charles Chaplin had decided to sell his 25 per cent stock interest in United Artists. Pickford said that the company was still very much part of her and she had no intention to rid herself of her own holding.

If she could persuade the courts to give her control after all, she would change the name of the operation from the Samuel Goldwyn Studios to the Mary Pickford Studios.

She would want to film her own life-story there. How about Sam as producer? She was asked. 'Fine,' she said. 'He's a very good producer. It would be all right, so long as we had a referee.'

She also claimed that Sam owed her $500,000. That was summarily rejected although the court did award her $15,000 for maintenance income incurred while Sam was her tenant, but not co-owner. Sam's counter claim to half-a-million dollars was disallowed. He had claimed operating expenses for his property. But the judge did give him $819 for utilities charged on Pickford's offices at the studio. It was all very, very, complicated.

Eventually, Sam was delared the winner. His bid of $1,920,000 for the studio was at last final.

Mary said afterwards that she was delighted he had won and that the studio had not gone to an outsider. Such are the vagaries of the cut and thrust of the film industry. (Two years later, she gave evidence on his behalf against Twentieth Century-Fox when Sam complained about the 'legal monopoly' organized by the company to fix the charges paid to Goldwyn for showing his films.)

He was disassociating himself from the independent producers organization now—he said he saw no need for a group who were so narrow-minded. At the same time he was continuing to give money to what he judged to be good causes—like the $75,000 he gave to house a building for the Permanant Motion Picture Charity in 1956. The building was named after him, since he had founded the charity. He opposed the idea of the naming, but was induced to do so as an encouragement to others.

It seemed only right that a man of his calibre should by now be treated with a great deal of deference. When President Eisenhower invited him to the White House in September 1956, it was no more than anyone might have expected—even if one reporter spotting him talking to Pressmen actually had the innocent audacity to butt in: 'Excuse me, I didn't get your name.'

'It's Sam Goldwyn,' he replied more than a little disdainfully.

People wanted to know about his plans for the future. Being over seventy was no excuse not to look ahead. He wasn't interested in *My Fair Lady*, he said, because it had at least another five years to run on Broadway. But he *was* interested in Lerner and Loewe, who had created it and had asked them to look at the possibility of turning *The Bishop's Wife* into a musical.

It wouldn't happen—and neither would the people of Holland be seeing *Guys and Dolls*. In January 1957 they declared that the movie and its people in the Save-a-Soul mission insulted the Salvation Army.

There were those who still put it down to Sam's love of publicity. 'People say', he declared, 'that whenever I have a picture coming out I always start a controversy about something that gets into the papers. Well, in all sincerity, I want to assure you that, as a general proposition there's not a single word of untruth in that.'

But now he was walking into a bigger row than ever with still bigger fish to fry—in a place called Catfish Row. Sam was going to make *Porgy and Bess*.

Ira Gershwin, who wrote all the lyrics for his brother's songs in the show, said at the time that he had been approached at least ninety times for the film rights and had always turned them down. 'We felt that a movie might not have all the qualities of the live performance, it might lack the three-dimensional quality.'

So how did Sam succeed where all the others had failed? 'Mr Goldwyn,' he said, 'is a very persuasive man.' That he was. And a big fan of the show.

He had loved the *Porgy and Bess* story ever since he had been among the first to see it twenty years before. When the show first opened few of the critics had been really sure what it was—a musical or an opera. George Gershwin, who had collaborated with DuBose Heyward—he wrote the original straight play (about a crippled Black in Charleston, South Carolina) called *Porgy*—always described it as a 'folk opera'. Songs like *Summertime* and *It Ain't Necessarily So* were generally regarded as among the best Gershwin ever wrote, but the show itself was not to everyone's taste.

It was ahead of its time. In 1952 *Porgy and Bess* had a stupendously successful revival on both sides of the Atlantic.

Two other studios had bid $1 million for the rights. Sam offered $650,000. But, he said, that was only a down payment. He was also promising 10 per cent of the film's gross—which meant a certainty of a lot more to come in, even if the movie failed.

The making of this film would turn out to be perhaps the hardest in Sam's career. He might have forecast that. He wouldn't know that it would also be his last.

First of all there was the question of casting. There weren't many Negro—the term in polite use at the time—actors; but those at the top were very good indeed.

Three years earlier, Otto Preminger had produced and directed an all-black and updated version of Bizet's *Carmen* called *Carmen Jones*, with lyrics by Oscar Hammerstein, II. It starred Harry Belafonte—by then an American pop idol singing folk and folk-type songs like *Jamaica Farewell* and *Mary's Boy Child*, but who for reasons no one has ever adequately explained had his voice dubbed on screen—and Dorothy Dandridge, with Pearl Bailey in a supporting role.

Sam obviously had *Carmen Jones* in mind when he went to cast *Porgy and Bess*. He, too, planned to dub the voices and he also asked Harry Belafonte, Dorothy Dandridge and Pearl Bailey to take part.

All the people he approached rejected his offers. They didn't think that

Goldwyn could produce a film that would show their people in a good light. But then Rouben Mamoulian was brought in as director and Dorothy Dandridge and Pearl Bailey said yes. Sammy Davis Junior agreed to play Sporting Life, the neighbourhood 'wide boy' who sang *It Ain't Necessarily So*. But Belafonte said a loud and much-quoted 'No'. As he explained, he had no intention of spending an entire film on his knees. *Porgy and Bess* was an Uncle Tom story and he wasn't in the mood to play anyone's Uncle Tom himself.

Before long, Sidney Poitier, a close friend of Belafonte and a superb actor in his own right, said 'Yes'.

The vociferous sections of the Black community were in ferment. The picture, they declared, would be everything Belafonte had said it would be, demeaning of their race and their stature as human beings.

They felt so strongly about it that the Council for the Improvement of Negro Theatre Arts took a double page advertisement in the trade press and the *Los Angeles Tribune*—in those days not just a figment in the imagination of the writers of the *Lou Grant* TV series.

The writer Almena Lomax charged: 'Dorothy and DuBose Heyward used the race situation in the South to write a lot of allegories in which Negroes were violent or gentle, humble or conniving and given to erupting all sorts of goings-on after their day's work in the white folk's kitchen or the white folk's yard was over, like sniffing happy dust, careless love, crapshooting, drinking, topping it all off with knife play.'

The reason for this outburst was one of two other equally serious explosions during the making of the movie. The first was in early July 1958. Soundstage eight of the Goldwyn studio was destroyed by fire. It was the one containing the Catfish Row set. Damage was estimated at more than $2 million and not a stick was saved.

It was Frances who broke the news. Later, she described how she did so when the phone call came to the house at Laurel Lane:

'I looked at the clock. It was not yet six. I decided Sam might as well get his rest. There was nothing he could do. I knew it was going to be a brute of a day for him. I had my breakfast. At the first sign of his stirring, I brought up his orange juice.' That was when he saw the look on Frances's face. 'What happened?' he asked. She told him 'something dreadful'.

'Anybody hurt?' he demanded. Then he went to his office and called a meeting of his closest aides.

Wasn't he going to see the fire and what it had done? 'Hell no,' he said. For him it would be like looking on the face of a newly dead much-loved relative. He wanted to remember it as it was—and as it would be again. It was one of those occasions when he was glad he ran the studio on his own. No one around to try to persuade him to cut his losses and end production there and then. As he so often said: 'I don't have a board of directors. It takes too long to explain things to them.'

There would be for ever after talk of sabotage by pro-Black interests, but that notion remains locked in the files of the Los Angeles Fire Department. No explanation has ever been given. What it did was to add a considerable amount of money to the film's budget—even after the settlement of insurance claims—and delay production by three months. The film was due to have started on that stage three weeks later.

It was only a little more troublesome than the explosion which had come with the appointment of the director a few months earlier and was not now damping down either.

Sam had invited Rouben Mamoulain to take on the job which would have been the first time he had worked for him since *We Live Again* in 1934. But the invitation came in a typical Goldwyn way, allowing his quarry to be chased until it caught him.

He had imagined his invitation would be accepted. Mamoulain, then 61-years-old, had directed the original opera and even more significantly, the original stage version of the play *Porgy*.

'I had wanted to do a film of *Porgy and Bess* for years, but nobody would touch it,' he told me. 'My agent Charlie Feldman insisted that nobody would touch it because they didn't think that a film with a Black cast would get anywhere. Three years earlier I could have got the rights for $25,000. Now Goldwyn was paying $650,000.'

It would not be a happy story. But for the moment, as so often happened with Goldwyn stories, it was funny. Sam was refusing to reveal his hand—having asked Mamoulian down to his office for a convivial meeting, in the first place. 'By then,' Mamoulian insists, 'Sam was suffering from the first signs of senility and incredible vanity.'

He heard that Sam wanted him to take the job, but the vanity of directors is quite the equal of that of producers. Mamoulian wanted to wait for Goldwyn's call before displaying more than his already well-known interest in the idea. The call came. The director went to his office.

'How are you?' Goldwyn asked.

'I'm fine, Sam,' he replied. 'How are you?' The niceties, the discussion about the weather, about each other's wives over, the two men got down to business.

'Is there anything you would like to talk to me about?' Sam asked him, playing the coy young lady once more, reprising his conversation with Darryl Zanuck a decade earlier.

'No', said Mamoulian, '*you* asked me to come to see you.'

'What are you interested in these days?' Sam asked, still skirting the real issue at hand. 'He wanted me to *ask* for *Porgy and Bess* and I wouldn't do it.'

After the dance of courtship, the director smiled, leaned over Sam's desk to shake his hand and said he would be leaving.

'No,' Sam ordered. 'Don't go. How about *Porgy and Bess?*'

It was the talk of Hollywood that Sam was going to make the film and everyone knew that he was going to ask Mamoulian to direct. But the Armenian-born director was not going to play his hand. So the question was repeated.

'What about *Porgy and Bess?*' Sam danced on.

'Well,' replied Mamoulian, 'what about it?'

'Mmm . . .' said Sam, 'would you like to direct it?'

Mamoulian answered, 'Yes, providing you accept a stylized version.'

You mean cheap sets? asked Sam.

'Well,' Mamoulian replied, 'the way I have in mind happens to be cheap, but I'm suggesting it because it would be right for *Porgy and Bess*.

'Wonderful,' said Sam. 'Let's do it.'

What Mamoulian—who had directed five previous all-Black shows—had in mind, he told me, was 'something that didn't just reflect life. You can do that in a mirror. It has to *reveal* life, see something that you didn't immediately notice. It was going to be a specifically Negro contribution to American music and acting. It would be stylized in acting and gestures. It is more revealing and expressive than a realistic gesture.'

For eight months Mamoulian worked on the preliminaries, the designing and building of the sets, the casting, the musical adaptations, the problems connect with the fire. As he told me:

'*Porgy and Bess* was so tied up with my name that every writer connected me with it. Sam didn't like that.'

In fact, Goldwyn told him that when he was in Washington two weeks before, President Eisenhower talked about the film and Sam's contribution to it, too.

It wasn't the only thing he told him about the President. 'He talked to me like a carpenter,' Sam said. 'He talked to me like I was the boss. He listened to me, he knew about me—because I *am* the boss. I'm the strong man in Hollywood.'

Mamoulian asked him to come to the point. 'I know who you are, you are Goldwyn and I'm Mamoulian,' he said impatiently, breaking off Sam's meanderings.

'Well,' said Sam, 'the point is all this publicity.'

What he objected to most of all were the statements that Mamoulian had been making about films going to television. The director was mounting a campaign against it. The essence of good films was the audience response to them—a response that could not be echoed in the living-room, he insisted in interview after interview.

Sam was livid. 'Here am I trying to sell my films to TV and you are saying that. From now on, you don't give interviews,' he ordered.

It was the first serious bust-up they had. Mamoulian refused to be censored in that or any other way.

Frances came on to the set where Mamoulian was recording the music for the picture. She apologized on her husband's behalf. 'He is sorry he's upset you. Why don't you come to dinner next Sunday evening?' she invited.

The invitation was accepted and Mamoulian and his wife rang the bell at the door at Laurel Lane. Promptly on the dot of eight o'clock.

The Goldwyns, Sam and Frances, were the perfect hosts, as always. Sam toasted the picture and its director, both of which he said were wonderful.

'I said to myself, "Well, the son of a bitch has some sense of decency",' Mamoulian recalled for me.

The following morning the director arrived at his office to find the place in turmoil—with his secretary not knowing what had hit her. 'There are all these messages,' she told him. 'The *Los Angeles Times* called, the *Herald Examiner* called, the *Hollywood Reporter* . . . .'

She didn't know what they wanted. Mamoulian didn't either, but he immediately put a call to the *Reporter*'s offices to find out. The message was simple: They had each had a letter from Goldwyn, saying that the director had been sacked.

'I have the greatest respect for Rouben Mamoulian,' said the letter, 'but he and I could not see eye to eye on various matters. Rather than go on with basic differences of opinion between us, I have relieved him.'

Sam had appointed Otto Preminger in his place.

'Is that what he says?' Mamoulian asked incredulously. 'Last night he gave me a banquet.' And he added: 'There has not been one iota of dissension concerning the film between Mr Goldwyn and myself.' The reporter told him there had been allegations of dissent concerning 'personal and professional life'.

Mamoulian issued his own statement:

'Mr Goldwyn's bland statement hides a story of deceit and calumny. It will be necessary at long last to expose his publicity greed, his professional hypocracy and selfishness.'

He said that Sam threatened to ruin him professionally and economically.

He also alleged that Goldwyn was 'a liar, an intriguer and a hypocrite'.

Jack Cummings, the producer, was in Mamoulian's office at the time and begged him not to issue the statement, but issue it he did.

Mamoulian said he would sue.

George Gershwin would doubtless have done the same had he been alive. Preminger abandoned Mamoulian's ideas of stylizing the story and promptly ruined it—even though he was full of praise for Goldwyn and said he loved the play and its music.

Meanwhile, the fight went on. The Screen Directors Guild threatened to boycott Goldwyn and said they accepted Mamoulian's statement. They also said that Preminger was breaking the guild's regulations. Even so, he went on with the film with the results too many people still remember. (There were Oscars, but not for the picture or the director. André Previn and Ken Darby shared theirs for the music and Leon Shamroy, the director of photography, got a nomination.) But what is most memorable now is not the film but the rows it caused.

And it was that which sparked off the biting advertisement in the trade press and the piece in the *Los Angeles Tribune*. It stated:

> Not even Mr Mamoulian, who is supposed to have done something truly phenomenal in transmitting the original novel to the stage could direct it so that it would be anything except a smear, a stereotype, a disgrace and an embarrassment to Negroes. We have taken account of Mamoulian's statement detailing his spat with Goldwyn and we aren't surprised. The whole atmosphere at the Goldwyn studio is calculated to impress you that you are in the presence of a 'Great I Am', the High Lama of Celluloid . . . The place is dotted with the private preserves of Mr Goldwyn. Mr Goldwyn parks here . . . Mr Goldwyn drinks here . . . Mr Goldwyn goes to the potty here . . . .

Never in his entire career had Sam been subject to that sort of tirade in public and it was a great pity it had to happen in the midst of his sixty-ninth film.

The piece alleged that Sidney Poitier was brainwashed to make the film and that the Chairman of Legal Redress for the National Association for the Advancement of Coloured People, Loren Miller, was an inadequate representative for his people. Miller had given his support to the movie.

They chaffed at his statement that he had 'complete confidence that Mr Goldwyn's production will be done in the best of taste with the utmost regard for the dignity of the negro people'.

As Almena Lomax commented: 'That lower case "n", which was the mistake of the secretary out at the Goldwyn Studios, is about as symbolic as what Mr Goldwyn thinks of the Negro people's dignity and of what Mr Miller, with his chippying around with it on many fronts, has made of it.'

Sam would have liked to have made a memorial for himself with that picture. Instead, he had all but created a tombstone.

23
Edge Of Doom

There's no doubt whatever that he would have loved to have produced a seventieth movie. But at the end of the fifties he was busy looking for new projects that somehow didn't make new films. The man who so often had taken on the studio system single-handed was now one of its principal victims.

For a time he was selling *Porgy* as enthusiastically as he had made it, and as he had sold his films over the years. It was his decision to put off the London opening. There was only one cinema equipped to show Todd-AO films—the Dominion—and this was taken up with *South Pacific*. Rather than authorize a British premiere in some other system—as would have to happen with distribution elsewhere—he decided to wait until *South Pacific* finished its quite incredible five-year run. He predicted that film would last a long time—if only it had been his.

As it was, so many of the things he had predicted had come to pass. Stars were no longer under long contracts. Film companies started making far fewer pictures—and were selling those they did make to television. Studios were ordered to separate themselves from their theatres. The censorship regulations of the Johnston Office came crumbling down.

And since there were fewer films to be made, Goldwyn somehow stopped making them, too—which was not one of the things he predicted.

Without a picture to make, Sam was like Stradivari suddenly deprived of a block of wood and his instruments, Michelangelo without a paint-brush or a chisel, Horatio Nelson without a ship.

He went on walking, talking to groups, alternately astonishing and embarrassing aides with his Goldwynisms. He kept up his campaign for decency as well as quality in movies—he didn't want the age of pornography to dawn while he was still alive. Despite the occasional stray towards temptation, he continued being a loving husband blessed with an equally loving—and some would say equally clever and efficient—wife.

'I guess I'm not an angel,' he confessed. 'I'm not always too sweet. I admit I have a temper. I can get angry sometimes. But I know what I want and I fight for it.' Indeed he did. 'I'm in love,' he declared soon after *Porgy and Bess* had received the judgement of its audience, 'in love with . . . the work.'

The Directors Guild reversed their order boycotting Sam's studio and he breathed a sigh of relief. 'I'm exhausted from not talking,' he declared—and those who knew him understood precisely what he meant. But it would not be enough to find a new film project for him.

He kept an eye on what the opposition were producing. In 1960 they were shooting *West Side Story* on the Goldwyn lot. Sam bumped into the producer Robert Wise. 'I loved your picture,' said Sam after seeing it in the studio projection theatre. 'Lovely film that *West Side Avenue*.'

Sam could have had the rights to *West Side Story* himself—for $450,000. Instead, he paid the $650,000 for *Porgy and Bess*—which cost him $8 million and took far less than that, even considering the $1 million he got for a 'two-shot' television deal.

'He had had big losses before,' recalled his friend David Rose, 'and he took this like any other big gambler took a big loss. Right until the end, he thought he was on top and knew what he was doing. He had smart business men and tax people helping him.'

Meanwhile, there were the awards—seemingly every day a new one. The Los Angeles Chamber of Commerce presented him with an achievement award for 'forty-six years of contributions to the general well-being of our community and the stability of its business climate.'

Cecil B. DeMille testified on Sam's behalf in his suit against another theatre chain and declared that Goldwyn was and always had been 'the tops'. (Sam was awarded $300,000 damages against the distributors.)

The Screen Producers Guild—not to be confused with Mr Johnston's organization—gave him their Milestone Award for his 'historic contribution to the American motion picture'.

The Japanese presented him with the Order of the Rising Sun—Third Class—for his work building friendship between Japan and the United States with his movies.

Israel made a similar award 'in gratitude of his two decades of service to world Jewry'.

And so they went on. Awards. Dinners. Medals. Citations. In 1959, he even presented his own prize—the Samuel Goldwyn International Film Award for the best non-American picture.

The only dissent still came in the wake of *Porgy and Bess*. Rouben Mamoulian demanded a screen credit, but the Directors Guild decided not to back him on that one.

Meanwhile Robert Breen, the Broadway producer who had organized the Broadway revival of *Porgy*, sued for $5 million. He claimed he had been promised the status of co-producer and would receive a share in the profits. That, too, would be settled before it could get to court.

As for his own health, it seemed good enough for a man approaching seventy-eight. In October 1959 he was operated on for a damaged cartilage in his right knee—he had injured it in a croquet game. But it wasn't anything serious.

In 1962 Sam celebrated his eightieth birthday.

'Isn't it rather late to celebrate your barmitzvah?' Bob Hope asked at the gala dinner held at the Beverly Hilton Hotel. He liked that as much as his friends, stars, directors—with the notable exception of Rouben Mamoulian—and business associates who were there for the occasion.

'In the eyes of those who have known him, worked with him over the years and had opportunity to measure his strength,' said *The New York Times*, 'Samuel Goldwyn represents wisdom as well as wit . . . He has, in fact, been a remarkable figure in the culture of films and American life.'

Ed Sullivan said he was 'witty and literate'. Yes, he conceded, these weren't terms automatically associated with Samuel Goldwyn, but he thought he was both those things.

At the Beverly Hilton dinner, they toasted not only his eightieth birthday, but also his fiftieth anniversary in the business. They ribbed and they roasted Sam.

Joey Bishop persisted in calling him 'Mr Goldman'. It was poetic justice for a man who could never get anyone's name right. Loretta Young—the one he always called Laurette Taylor—gave him a big kiss. But then that was what everyone was doing that night. Even if they couldn't get near him. Frank Sinatra and Eddie Fisher sang specially for Sam.

Former President Eisenhower sent a message of support and admiration and Richard Nixon, then Republican candidate for Governor of California, said that Sam was 'one of those who began with nothing but his own ability and achieved greatness on just that'. Herbert Hoover, President of the United States before Franklin D. Roosevelt, paid tribute too.

Danny Kaye wrote a letter:

> Dear Sam,
>
> 'You know from all the years we worked together, and from all the years that we have been friends, that you are a very special person to me. As a matter of fact, you are one of those rare people who have given a unique lustre to anything you've touched—certainly to the art of motion pictures—and to me at an important time in my life. So with deep pride, Sylvia joins me in saluting you on your fiftieth anniversary in the film industry you helped to create, and we send our most loving wishes for a happy birthday.
>
> With deep affection,
> Danny

Goldwyn was obviously moved. But it was an occasion for business, too.

He said it was time to give actors a share of the profits. There were those who guffawed slightly into their dinner-jacket sleeves. 'It is the only way this industry is going to be saved.' Within the next decade top stars would do more than that. Like Samuel Goldwyn they would become independent producers.

And he wasn't beyond fighting, himself. He attacked the action of the British Cinematograph Exhibitors Association who decided to boycott his films in England when he licensed the fifty features to be shown by Associated Television in Britain. In a letter to Sir Alec Douglas-Home, the Prime Minister, he vented his spleen at this 'economic blackmail'.

But once again he was in the forefront of what every other producer would do before long—and indeed would establish for himself his most important market.

This Week magazine asked Sam to take what they headed 'Words To Live By' and proclain his philosophy in a whole page featurette. Sam chose: 'You always meet people a second time.' As he said: 'Never forget that. Never act toward someone as though you were never going to come across him again in life. Remember that the long pull in life is much more important than any monetary gain . . .' He still had his ghost-writers.

The sentiment was fine. But did Sam always think like that? There are those who would testify otherwise.

Sometimes he didn't want everything he said to go down for posterity. He frequently used to ban reporters coming to talk to him with a tape recorder in their hands. 'I'm making only miscellaneous remarks,' he said on one occasion. 'I don't think they'll be of any interest.' The fascinating thing about the aged Sam Goldwyn was that, even now, they were always of interest.

Having started *selling* his films to television, Sam now said he was going to actually *make* them for the small screen. It didn't happen, but it showed that he was still thinking of new worlds to conquer.

There were persistent rumours that he was selling his back lot—the one that he had cherished for all those years. A story appeared in the trade papers that he was seeking $20 million.

A man called Rube Kaufman read this and asked movie producer Milton Sperling (he was the son-in-law of Harry Warner) if he could affect an introduction. 'He said', Sperling told me, 'that he was coming out here with $20 million to buy the lot.'

Sperling, who had sold his own real estate to Kaufman, told him not to bother. 'I said that Sam had no intention of selling it. "Don't waste your time," I said.' Nevertheless, at his friend's request, Sperling called Goldwyn. The message he got, in that still piping voice, was 'I'd be glad to see him'.

'I came over with Kaufman. On the way to the studio I told him, "Rube, I want to caution you about Goldwyn. He's a very strange man. He may say or do something that'll throw you off your stride. He's surprising and rude."

'Kaufman replied: "Don't worry about that. He's just another Jew. I can take care of that." So we got to the office and the secretary buzzed us in.'

As they went in, Goldwyn rose from his chair and pointed a finger at Sperling.

'You, I know,' said Sam. 'But who's that thief you've brought with you to steal my life's work from me?'

That was not an opening calculated to ensure either a satisfactory business meeting or an amicable social occasion.

From that time on, said Sperling, 'Goldwyn insulted and assaulted this man. He kept saying, "You and your $20 million! Do you know what it cost me in blood to make these pictures? Who are you, some sort of *shloch* merchant to take away my pictures?"

'He then shouted: "Get out! Get out with your lousy money!"'

Not even that could take away the other side of Sam.

As Sperling said: 'Goldwyn was a highly visible character about town. but he was an artist, a bespoke film-maker. Compared to him, Jack Warner was a mass-market-maker. It was the same business, but they ran it as different businesses. Sam was ruthless, brutal.'

The voice stayed the same. His eyes pierced beneath his bullet-shaped bald head. But nothing was going to take away his 'life's work', even when he had no more pictures to make. Yet his office began to look a bit shabby. The English-made mahogany desk was showing its signs of wear, but as he looked at the shelf behind his desk, with the family pictures, the photographs of celebrities, the Oscar for *The Best Years of Our Lives*, he felt as though he were still in charge.

When he walked up the external Spanish-style staircase leading to his office, it was still the procession of a Roman emperor.

There were also the theatre owners to contend with. In 1966 he won a $1,242,500 award against Twentieth Century-Fox and a group of theatre chains alleging 'monopolistic practises from 1937 to 1950'.

It would be the last of his film battles. In March 1969 it was announced he had a 'circulation ailment'. In fact, it was a stroke. It impaired his movement, partly paralysed him and—worst of all meant the end of almost all the Goldwynisms.

David Rose told me: 'You couldn't tell whether he knew what was going on or not. You couldn't tell.'

He had to be fed, washed and helped into occasional moments of lucidity. In one of these brief interludes, Darryl Zanuck came to see him. 'How come,' he asked the Twentieth Century-Fox studio chief, 'your making a pornographic film?'

Zanuck couldn't understand what he meant. Sam said he had heard he was filming a recent best seller that dealt with sex and drugs. 'No,' said Zanuck, 'I've just made *Hello Dolly*.' 'That's right,' said Sam, '*The Valley of the Hello Dollies*.' But it was a rare moment for laughter.

In another break of lucidity—sometimes things were so bad, Sam would fall out of bed or from his wheelchair—he saw a picture of Charles Chaplin in a newspaper. Sam could barely pick his head up from the pillows. 'Is that Charlie?' he asked Frances. 'He looks terrible!'

Eventually, Sam was sent away to a geriatric hospital at Pasadena. No one outside his immediate family and circle of friends ever knew. David Rose saw him there. It was one of those brief moment of lucidity.

'For God's sake', said Sam, 'get me out of this place.'

Rose told Frances and Sam was brought home.

Until now, that story has never been told.

In November 1969 Frances officially took over the studios and the administration of his personal estate—valued at some $19.7 million.

In March 1971 President Nixon awarded Sam the Medal of Freedom—the highest civilian decoration after the Congressional Medal of Honour. The President, still in his honeymoon period and before he might even have heard the name Watergate, journeyed from the Western White House at San Clemente, California, to Laurel Lane to present the award in person. Sam, looking immaculate but distant, a pair of carpet slippers on his feet, sat in his wheelchair.

Frances had taken a call from the White House the previous day saying that Mr Nixon and his security staff would be calling. She, of course, was thrilled. But she didn't tell Sam, simply made sure he was dressed in his finest clothes, had his hair cut and was properly shaved.

Later, she told him who was coming and was to say he told her: 'The President is coming? I'll be glad to see him.' It may just have been a nice story.

No one could really be sure that, when the President arrived on the dot of 11, Sam understood what was going on. He was then eighty-eight years old. Nixon said he had made films that 'weren't square, but exciting entertainment, great box-office. . . .'

In August 1972 Sam celebrated his ninetieth birthday—if not knowing it was his birthday or very much else which could be called celebrating.

The year before there had been a party. But there wouldn't be one this time. The previous event was, Frances declared, 'a fiasco'.

It all struck her as just too much. 'I don't lie any more,' she said in a moment of unexpected frankness. 'He has the heart and blood pressure of a young man. But nothing else seems to work. Except his appetite.'

People still sued on his behalf and people still sued him—including his former deputy James A. Mulvey, who got $1,044,000 owed to him as his share in the money Sam received from sales from TV. But, of course, it was a business transaction and Sam knew nothing of it.

Almost unexpectedly, early the following January, Sam was taken to St John's Hospital, Santa Monica. He was undergoing treatment for a kidney ailment, said a statement.

On 3 January 1974, at home, Samuel Goldwyn died. He was ninety-one years old and at last, he had his way—and Frances had hers. The words may not have come, but in his mind he had doubtless for long been saying them as he contemplated what was no more than an existence: 'Include me Out.'

24
Splendor

The funeral service was private—just for family.

Sam Junior said it had been his father's expressed wish. 'He had attended enough Hollywood funerals to know that he didn't want one. It wasn't his style.'

He might also have been afraid of some of the comments allegedly made after the deaths of Louis B. Mayer and Harry Cohn. Like 'They only came to see if he was really dead' or even more cruelly: 'Give 'em what they want and they'll come.'

They wouldn't have said that about Sam. The tributes came and everyone heard about them.

Jack Warner, with Adolph Zukor, one of the only two surviving moguls, said of him: 'Sam Goldwyn was one of the most capable and accomplished men in the film business. He had great talent and taste, which were displayed in the very, very important films he made over the years.'

From Bob Hope came this succinct and so true statement: 'Sam was one of the classiest film-makers this town has seen.'

The funeral was at Forest Lawn, with its ornate statues and mausoleums, frequently joked about as the Hollywood Way of Death. It was not a Jewish cemetery, but Rabbi Max Nussbaum, the head of Temple Israel on Hollywood Boulevard, a Reform congregation, said in his tribute: 'He was a real man. His story of family devotion and dedication to an industry is without parallel. In this he lived in the ideals of Judaism. With his contributions to the Jewish causes, he identified with his religion.'

Perhaps the biggest tribute of all came from the other Hollywood studios. At the time of the funeral, at 3 pm. on 1 February, they all observed a two-minute silence.

The New York Times paid its tribute and took up that 'include me out' allusion—but added, 'In the annals of great movie producers, indisputably Goldwyn is in.' *Variety* for once was lost for words and said he was simply one of the 'great' producers. They added that he was the only one of the founding fathers of Hollywood who finished his life still in undisputed charge of his own studio (a little licence here, since it was Frances who was in charge).

Charles Champlin wrote in the *Los Angeles Times*: 'A unique and colourful career rather than an era died with Goldwyn. The era in which he flourished had essentially ceased to be with the dawn of television, although the final passages of both the man and his time were slow and touched with sadness. He leaves a dozen pictures at least which have to be counted in any reckoning of Hollywood's best. He leaves as well a tradition of quality and craftsmanship and of a continuing excitement in the possibilities of the movies.'

Garson Kanin wrote of him: 'In some ways he was an American primitive, but he had taste. Great taste. The feeling, the absolute instinct were always there.'

Sam remembered his loved ones—some of them as expected, some surprisingly. Sam Junior received a $1 million trust fund plus all his father's jewellery and personal items. His four grandchildren got $100,000 in trust and each of his servants was given $3,000.

The surprise was that his daughter Ruth, now Mrs Ruth Caps, received a $250,000 trust fund. He had remembered her—at last.

And it seemed, the Goldwyn influence was always there—always maintained by Frances and by Sam Junior, who was to open his own production company a decade later.

Soon, Frances herself was to be bedridden after a heart attack and she then died in July 1976.

In April 1980 Warner Bros. bought the Goldwyn studios for $35 million. Not even Mary Pickford was around any more to put in a counter bid.

In fact, almost nobody was around any more. By then, all the moguls had gone. An era had gone. An industry had gone. Or at least changed.

And yet the mark they left was so indelible, so vital that nobody could underestimate the effect they had on the lives of people who aspired to do nothing more than to find a few cents or pence for a seat at a cinema.

Perhaps—as is so often the case in such situations—the best tribute came from himself. A few years before he died, Sam said: 'I've never made a bad picture. Sometimes the public doesn't agree with me.' But history tried its best.

As Gilbert Soldes said in that *Esquire* piece: 'He (was) living proof that you don't have to cater for the intelligence of the moron. He is not only the proof, but he is a conspicuous one.'

Hal Wallis, a contemporary of Sam's who once helped to run Warner Bros. and then, like Goldwyn, became an independent producer, told me: 'He was a quality producer, as his pictures show. I admired him for his ideals. It was strange that coming from his background, he was able to do that. But he was *never* satisfied with what he did unless it was the best.'

That influence will go on for as long as there are people who enjoy seeing motion pictures, whether in a theatre on a programme beamed by a television organization, a cable company or on a cassette.

It's been a long story, one that is almost as long as the century, but then

Samuel Goldwyn always knew he was doing something very Important. In Warsaw he knew he was an important man. Vilma Banky thought so. So did Ronald Colman and Gary Cooper, Merle Oberon and Bette Davis, Eddie Cantor and Danny Kaye, Frank Sinatra and Sidney Poitier.

A few dozen other stars knew it, too. But, of course, we've all passed a lot of water since then.

INDEX

Other than in the main entry under his name, Samuel Goldwyn is referred to throughout this index as 'SG'